Exercising Hum:

MW01101166

"In this excellent book, Robin Redhead explores some very big questions with a commendable, thoughtful subtlety and methodological rigour. Her discussion of why human rights are not universally empowering—the ubiquitous question for human rights advocates—is particularly useful and makes a significant contribution to the field of human rights studies." — *Damien Short, University of London, UK*

Exercising Human Rights investigates why human rights are not universally empowering and why this damages people attempting to exercise rights. It takes a new approach in looking at humans as the subject of human rights rather than the object and exposes the gendered and ethnocentric aspects of violence and human subjectivity in the context of human rights.

Using an innovative visual methodology, Redhead shines a new critical light on human rights campaigns in practice. She examines two cases in-depth. First, she shows how Amnesty International depicts women negatively in their 2004 *Stop Violence against Women* campaign, revealing the political implications of how images deny women their agency because violence is gendered. She also analyses the Oka conflict between indigenous people and the Canadian state. She explains how the Canadian state defined the Mohawk people in such a way as to deny their human subjectivity. By looking at how the Mohawk used visual media to communicate their plight beyond state boundaries, she delves into the disjuncture between state sovereignty and human rights.

This book is useful for anyone with an interest in human rights campaigns and in the study of political images.

Robin Redhead is Senior Lecturer in Politics and Applied Global Ethics at Leeds Metropolitan University, UK.

Routledge Advances in International Relations and Global Politics

For a full list of titles in this series, please visit www.routledge.com

Exercising Human Rights
Gender, Agency, and Practice

Robin Redhead

Routledge
Taylor & Francis Group

NEW YORK AND LONDON

First published 2015
by Routledge
711 Third Avenue, New York, NY 10017, USA

and by Routledge
2 Park Square, Milton Park, Abingdon, Oxfordshire OX14 4RN

First issued in paperback 2016

*Routledge is an imprint of the Taylor & Francis Group,
an informa business*

Library of Congress Cataloging-in-Publication Data
Redhead, Robin.
    Exercising human rights : gender, agency and practice / Robin Redhead.
        pages cm — (Routledge advances in international relations and global
politics)
    Includes bibliographical references and index.
    1. Women's rights. 2. Feminism. 3. Human rights. I. Title.
HQ1236.R42   2014
323.082—dc23
2014017362

Typeset in Sabon
by Apex CoVantage, LLC

ISBN 13: 978-1-138-28623-8 (pbk)
ISBN 13: 978-0-415-83301-1 (hbk)

In memory of Sharon

Contents

Figures

Acknowledgments

The process of writing this book was made easier by the encouragement and support of many people. Most importantly, Nick Turnbull, for your generosity, compassion and confidence in me. You never stop surprising me. A special mention to Violet Redhead, who brought me plastic monkeys for breakfast when I needed sustenance in the latter, difficult stages of writing. For their unwavering kindness, friendship and support over the long term, I wish to thank Hazel Burns, Guro Buchanan, Donovan Ingram, Kate Colgrave, Stacey Heslop, Sarah Humby, Pam Lavery, Jonathan and Melissa Redhead. To Robert Redhead, for his belief in me. Mille mercis to Yaëlle Ingram for her solidarity and sisterhood.

For their helpful guidance in the early stages of my research I thank Simona Rentea, Véronique Pin-Fat, Marysia Zalewski, Cristina Masters, Ursula Vogel, Paul Cammack, Angelia Wilson, Andrew Russell, Rorden Wilkinson, Juanita Elias and Gillian Youngs. Access to primary research materials was kindly provided by staff at Amnesty International's International Secretariat in London, the United Kingdom, and the Canadian Broadcasting Corporation Video Archive in Toronto, Canada. Hilary Pooley, University of Manchester Faculty of Humanities IT Officer, was most helpful in helping me transform my raw video footage to still images. Thanks to The Canadian Press, AP/PA Images, Panos Pictures, Contact Press Images, The Hamilton Spectator, CBC Licensing Division and Amnesty International for giving me permission to use the images in the book. Thanks to my editors, Natalja Mortensen, Darcy Bullock and Colleen Roache, for all their help in taking me through the process.

Many people engaged in discussions with me in thinking through the conceptual aspects of the book, including Stephen Bowen, Hannah Miller, Damien Short, Amandine Scherrer, Emmanuel-Pierre Guittet, Karen Clarke, Paul Dixon, Philip Spencer, Jonathan Gilmore, Robin Pettitt, Anita Howarth, Ilaria Favretto and Atsuko Ichijo. Thanks also to my colleagues in Politics and Applied Global Ethics at Leeds Metropolitan University. I am especially grateful to Asli Birik for all her research assistance.

Thanks to my students for their curiosity and desire to change the world.

Abbreviations

AI	Amnesty International
CBC	Canadian Broadcasting Corporation
CEDAW	Convention on the Elimination of all forms of Discrimination Against Women
PoC	Prisoners of Conscience
SQ	Sûreté Québec
UDHR	Universal Declaration of Human Rights
UN	United Nations

Part I
Gender, Agency and Practice

1 Overview

Why do some people struggle to exercise their human rights? This is a political question, not a legal one. Yes, the law and institutional mechanisms are essential tools to further the protection of human rights. I am not suggesting otherwise. However, what interests me is how people are left out of the legal framework; they slip through the cracks and are overlooked. Recognition is essential in human rights if respect and dignity, the tenets of the Universal Declaration of Human Rights, are to be achieved. Legal frameworks provide a structure in which people can seek recognition. Moreover, they define what aspects of humanity are to be respected and what constitutes a dignified life. But international human rights law is often an abstract umbrella under which people live often oblivious of the protection it can and does provide. What matters to people are how their daily lives are affected by events that deny them recognition, respect and dignity. In order for the legal framework to do its job, people experiencing a denial of human rights need to know (a) that they have rights and (b) how to use the law to get protection. This process is political. The ways in which people learn about their human rights and use legal mechanisms to address abuses are political practices. The majority of this political practice takes place through campaigns. Campaigning, which includes those who organize them, has become so prominent in the field of human rights that we can now speak of a human rights culture.[1] Some even go so far as to suggest human rights is a global social movement: the human rights movement.[2] This culture of human rights is organized around international law but has become more than that now. The human rights culture provides ways of recognizing disparate concerns as human rights issues. It draws strength from the international recognition of human rights as legal and moral frameworks, meaning that making something a human rights issue carries weight. The human rights culture draws attention to the issue and makes it global. This means that what may have seemed to be a local and specific issue is now acknowledged as something affecting all of humanity in one way or another. The culture of human rights has developed around international law because when law is vague, as it often must be, culture becomes more important, because it is then the source of meaning, the source of recognition, respect and dignity.

This phenomenon is academically interesting because it differs from political theory and institutional approaches. When we look at recognition from a people (real-world) point of view, we see that actions and language matter. What academics can contribute is knowledge, knowledge of how to make actions and language (campaigns) stronger and more effective. Knowledge is the key to nurturing respect and dignity. When I teach my students, I am aware that they will be the next generation of campaigners, so it is paramount that they be informed not only about the legal and moral frameworks but also about the political aspects of human rights and about how they as practitioners are part of that culture and will shape and transform it as they engage in their own practice.

This book starts from the position that human rights are political. It is a book about political campaigns in practice. I am interested in human rights as a cultural phenomenon made up of campaigns and the activists making the campaigns. I do not deny the role of law, international courts, police forces, states and institutions; rather, I seek to integrate campaigning and culture in a complementary way. Taking this approach and exploring it through empirical case studies allow for a focus on agency and practice.

Agency matters. How events are reported in the media, are documented in campaign materials and are discussed via social media all contribute to building the context of the event. The context frames what interpretations are possible, which in turn has an impact on how those involved in the event will be represented. Often in human rights these stories are polarized between victims of abuse and the perpetrators of the violations. With regard to civil and political rights, in many cases the perpetrators are agents of the state carrying out offenses on their citizens. Perpetrators of violations against economic, social and cultural rights tend to also include individuals acting without state authority. In both circumstances, the violated are interpreted as victims. There is an inherent tension in representations of human rights between the victim, who is seen to be without agency, and the perpetrator, whose agency is called into question because of the acts he or she performed. The political dilemma for practitioners and activists is how to empower victims in a structure that needs victims in order to recognize a violation has taken place. This predicament is often overlooked by campaigners and yet informs the very nature of their work. Those whose rights have been violated must first become victims before they can use the language of rights to extricate themselves from their disempowered position. The international human rights framework is designed to provide legal tools that offer agency to those who have lost it. The language of rights is intended to empower victims of abuse and now provides international arenas, which may otherwise not be available, to try perpetrators. The legal framework is powerful and does enable the protection, defense and promotion of human rights. However, as I show in this book, often claimants are recognized as little more than victims. This means that their perpetrators may be brought to justice, ending their immediate suffering, but little is done to remove the stigma of being a victim. This is why we must look at practice, because it shows us the unintended consequences of human rights law. Victims need agency to overcome the fixed interpretations, and cultural consequences of those interpretations, of being a victim of human rights abuse. It is the role of activists to provide this support for victims by reminding the public that there are human lives at stake.

What practitioners and activist *do* really counts because how they use language and what actions they take shapes who can be protected and how that protection can be sought. The politics of human rights relies on political activism. A significant part of that activism involves educating the public and gathering support for particular issues. How practitioners and activists interpret their practice as human rights is significant because it structures what is seen as a victory. Visual images play a crucial role in this process because they are very powerful cultural artifacts. When we look at images as a set of symbols that frame human rights questions, we can see how images also set the terms of the debate. Images are emotive and appeal, on an emotional level, to the public asking them to see their own humanity in the plight of others. Images are powerful because they speak across different languages and can be used to shock their viewers, provoking lasting responses, such that some images become iconic of particular events. In this way, the power of images supersedes words because they fix particular interpretations of events within history. This makes images very powerful as a tool to raise peoples' consciousness, but this comes with its own particular politics. There is a visual discourse, a set of visual symbols that influences how human rights issues come to be represented. These visual symbols imprint themselves on the audience and create human rights stories. We view these stories as true representations of the actual events taking place and from this gain knowledge of what human rights mean. The power to produce meaning is vital to the success of human rights campaigns. Being the one who dictates the parameters of the debate enables organizations to capture their audience and advocate for the protection of human rights. These political moments are fleeting, as we can see from the growing number of human rights campaigns, so it remains imperative that campaigns have the most impact, but often this comes at the expense of those seeking protection. In this book I look at two cases of how visual images are used to attract support from the viewer. With the aim of understanding the nuances of such practices, I look at the discursive elements of visual representation, such that the political representation of agency is exposed.

Discourse analysis is a method of inquiry that reveals the logic of symbols within a specific context. Through an examination of language, it exposes the power relations between terms, between identities and between agents. For it matters how "women" and "Indian" (two marginalized groups) are understood in a particular context, because this meaning determines what women and indigenous people can and cannot do within said interpretations. This book shows how normalizing practices happen and how devastating they can be to the successful representation of agency. As a political tool, discourse analysis provides the researcher with an understanding of the dominant symbols and of how they operate within the discourse. In other words, discursive analyses are ways of looking at the production of meaning within a context. These analyses are only ever partial in that they only tell us something about symbols; however, they yield interesting insights into the power of images and their use in human rights advocacy.

In particular, I am interested in how feminist discourse analysis uncovers gender inequalities within language. Feminists argue that language is political and that discursive meaning can be harmful. In the context of human rights, feminists articulate this harm as a dehumanising phenomenon, leading them to ask, "Are women human?"[3] Attempts to empower women discursively require first, a change in discursive meaning, such that women are no longer subordinate to men. Historically, women have been understood in opposition to men and, as a result, have been rendered inferior. Discourse feminism turns this problem on its head and suggests that if we can change our understanding of women from a biological to a sociological one, "women" will not only refer to female; it can mean a whole host of other things. A "woman" subjectivity would then perform differently in the discourse and represent a more fluid existence. This is why discourse feminists speak of gender, because it liberates women from fixed biological interpretations, thus addressing inequalities by making everyone a gender being.

In the conclusion I reflect on a discursive approach and take a critical view. It seems to me that understanding symbolic power is important and does provide a philosophical basis for identifying why certain people (subjectivities) are at risk. At a philosophical level the idea works, but it makes no reference to material reality. Language is only part of life; it does not tell the whole story, so to look at the politics of human rights we need to take into consideration the sociological frameworks that look at the role of language and practice within culture.[4]

There are two case studies in this book. The first looks at Amnesty International's 2004 campaign *Stop Violence against Women*. This was a groundbreaking campaign for Amnesty because it was its first thematic campaign. Previously, Amnesty had focused on Prisoners of Conscience or specific types of human rights violations, such as torture. Historically, Amnesty International has concentrated on civil and political rights, whose perpetrators are agents of the state. However, the *Stop Violence against Women* campaign required a consideration of economic, social and cultural rights, as well as taking individuals in account as perpetrators. This was difficult for Amnesty International on many levels. First, it needed expertise in how to mount large-scale campaigns, so it sought advice and assistance from others within the field. Further, there was tension within the organization regarding a focus on "women" and, by extension, gender. With Amnesty International being a Christian-based organization, the topic of violence against women opened the question of sexual rights. This challenged the ethos of the organization because some members felt uncomfortable with the new direction Amnesty would need to take in order to mount this campaign. Divisions within the organization posed problems for the execution of the campaign. There were concerns that this issue was not a priority in all regions and that mounting this campaign took away from necessary work more relevant to individual regions.

When I went for my first interview with Amnesty International's campaign coordinator, tensions within the organization, and the refurbishments taking place in the building, meant that my interview was held outside in the rain under an umbrella. The campaign coordinator was candid but reluctant to let me in the building. In stark contrast, my next set of interviews with the section and audio/visual researchers took place in their own offices, and they gave me a tour of the building. They were also very candid, willing to explain how they chose the images for the campaign and how Amnesty International wished to represent women's agency. Through discussion with my interviewees, I was able to conduct an analysis of the images used to represent women's agency and get a sense of how Amnesty wanted to convey women and gender. The case study that follows in Chapter 5 is a discourse analysis of the campaign document *It's in our Hands: Stop Violence against Women.*[5] This document states the aim and focus of the campaign and clearly sets out Amnesty International's position on how to stop violence against women, through enforcement of international human rights law. Because Amnesty International is a major player in the human rights field, and has been globally recognized for its human rights work, what it says and how it pitches its campaign matters. Once Amnesty International takes on a particular issue, it then becomes a human rights issue. This changes the contours of the debate and instantly moves the issue into a global framework. Making violence against women a human rights issue affects how other organizations can carry out their campaigns, and not always in a constructive way. What is important about this case study is that it shows how language matters, and that simply changing the discourse is not a solution in itself. How Amnesty International portrays women who have experienced violence encodes this interpretation in human rights culture and thus affects how the issue comes to be understood and, consequently, the strategies taken to protect those women in the future.

One of the central questions for Amnesty in the campaign was how to empower women who have been victims of violence. Victimhood is a singular and isolating experience. Therefore, Amnesty's strategy was to show that these women can overcome their experiences of violence by joining voices and fighting to bring their assailants to justice. The tool Amnesty uses is international human rights law. Its position is that if international human rights law is upheld, then women will no longer be the victims of violence. In pursuit of this goal, Amnesty encourages victims of violence to join forces and hold their aggressors accountable by exposing them as perpetrators. Violence against women is often perpetrated by individuals in the women's homes and communities. Encouraging women to confront their attackers brings the issue into the public sphere and into public debate. Once in the realm of public debate, then the issue can be brought to justice through legal mechanisms. In sum, Amnesty International's campaign strategy is to use a legal discourse to advocate on behalf of women who experience violence.

Something interesting happens when we look closely at how Amnesty International constructs its campaign platform. In order to discuss women, Amnesty International must discuss gender, because the legal language uses the term *gender-based violence* to describe the abuses women experience. Here in lies the problem. Once Amnesty International is required to look at gender, it must also consider why gender is a source of violence. Historically women have been subordinate to men, and this social phenomenon permeates the very legal mechanisms Amnesty International uses to protect women. These normative conceptions of gender are inherent in universal human rights discourse. So using this language will never fully empower women. Amnesty's portrayal of women as victims is insurmountable because they fail to understand the gendered dynamics of the violence these women have experienced.

The Oka Crisis case in Chapter 6 looks at a moment of aboriginal political protest in Canada in which the Mohawk used human rights conventions to justify their land claims. Human rights discourse was central to the politics of the dispute, because an appeal was made to the United Nations, as a way of superseding the Canadian government, to support the rights of the indigenous peoples. Canada has always been one of the most enthusiastic supporters of the international human right regime. In fact, Canadians' self-image is built around being defenders of international human rights, being committed to growing a global human rights culture. So here is a country that defines itself in terms of its support for human rights being called out as perpetrators human rights violations against their own citizens. It is no wonder, then, that the Canadian public were outraged at the images of the Oka Crisis because it caused irreparable damage to Canada's international reputation and shook the very foundations of a Canadian identity.

In 1990, the Canadian military was deployed to end a standoff between the Mohawk Warriors and Quebec provincial police. The event became known as the Oka Crisis and changed the shape of the indigenous rights debate within Canada. No formal activists mounted a campaign; rather, this event unfolded daily on Canadian television and in newspapers. Aboriginal activists used the media presence strategically to air their historic grievances and tell the country, and the world, about the treatment they receive as wards of the Canadian state. The event took place in the small town of Oka, Quebec, where local officials had approved the expansion of a golf course onto land already used as a burial site by the local Mohawk community. Tensions rose as Mohawks protesting at the gates of the golf course became embroiled in a skirmish with the Quebec provincial police force, at the height of which a police officer was shot. To this day it remains unknown which side is responsible for the police officers death. Mohawk protesters, fearing prosecution, then dug in, and a standoff ensued. The death of the police officer drew media attention to the otherwise unreported event. The standoff lasted an entire summer, disrupting the lives of aboriginal and non-aboriginal people living in the area. UN observers were called in, and the Canadian government was forced into talks with Mohawks, an outcome they hoped to avoid. What makes this case so interesting is that it is a perfect example of the conflict between state sovereignty and human rights. The Mohawk sought sovereignty over their land and culture that had been promised and denied them through processes of colonization. The expression of Mohawk sovereignty required the Canadian state to assert its own sovereignty because the nation now occupying that land. The historical consequences of colonization was brought into twentieth-century politics and played out in new contexts. Canada was forced to culturally defend the legitimacy of its statehood not only to the Mohawk but also to Canadian citizens, who were at odds with images of tanks being used against people on Canadian soil.

The Mohawk communities have reservations in both Canada and the United States, further complicating the issue of sovereignty and indigenous rights. Indigenous rights pose a mortal challenge to Canadian sovereignty and Canadian concepts of Canada. The Oka Crisis remains a lasting challenge that is difficult to suppress because the Mohawk continue to employ tactics developed at Oka to protest for further rights to land. I undertake a discourse analysis of the visual images aired on Canadian Broadcasting Corporation (CBC)–televised news reports covering the crisis to show the political power of images. I interviewed CBC video librarians who explained how images were chosen and the narratives the journalist sought to build about the crisis. For instance, images of Mohawk Warriors face-to-face with a Canadian soldier act as a visual metaphor for the politics of human rights versus state sovereignty. The image captured the historic relationship between indigenous communities and the Canadian state and became iconic. A battle for control over visual representation ensued, and there were victories on both sides. Journalists trapped behind the barricades on Mohawk territory enabled the Mohawk to tell their side of the story and to counteract attempts the Canadian government made to change the debate by publicly vilifying the Warriors. The images and events of Oka are essential now to indigenous rights claims in Canada because Canada is forced to uphold its state sovereignty rather than to uphold human rights. What would have previously just been a protest action is now a human rights issue. Using human rights conventions turns the dispute into something that redefines cultural politics itself. It is more than a social movement; it becomes a human rights question, which makes it global. Canada's support for human rights globally is then tested on its own soil. The Mohawk use Canada's international success in advocating for the protection of human rights against itself to expose, as the Mohawk see it, Canada's disingenuous commitment to human rights at home. Something that might not have been a human rights incident has now become one. The crisis internationalized the issue and gave agency to the quest for indigenous rights.

Analytically, I use feminist discourse analysis to demonstrate how within the human rights discourse sex and gender are conflated such that agency is lost, rendering "human" the object of human rights, instead of its subject. Discursive practices are concerned with exposing the production of meaning by considering phenomena in context. Hence, discursive analyses are concerned with how language constitutes, rather than represents reality. I show that discursive analyses allow for more than binary concepts of gender, which provides a space in international human rights for the possibility of recognition, respect and dignity. I examine how the conflation of the terms *sex* and *gender* limits understandings of gender in the field of international politics broadly and human rights specifically. The tension created by this conflation impacts directly on questions of agency. Asking questions about the relationship between gender and agency helps understand how the concept of "human" is socially constructed throughout international politics. Orthodox interpretations of human rights are founded on a liberal, Western conception of universal human rights, which takes moral agency as a given. Alternatively, I demonstrate how feminist scholars have opened debates on human rights through critiques of the universality of human rights, arguing that orthodox analyses interpret "human" as gender neutral. However, I claim that given attempts to problematize "human" in human rights, little is done on agency. Looking at agency blurs the distinction between theories and practices of human rights such that "human" becomes the subject rather than the object of such rights. The book argues that exclusion from "human" in human rights has punitive consequences for expressions of particular genders in contexts that seek to fix meanings of gender to specific sexualized bodies. I explore this desire for embodiment as an attempt to represent "human" in human rights discourse.

The main focus of this book is to look at intersections of interpretations and the practitioners making those interpretations. I draw substantially on a discursive framework but use a sociological framework as a counterweight because sociological approaches value the agency of practitioners and campaigns. These frameworks are at epistemological odds with one another, but I use them in a complementary sense to support a critical analysis of agency and practice. My goal is to provide an understanding of how practice contributes to the development of human rights culture. A discursive approach tells us that language is constitutive, in that what counts as reality is constructed through language. Discourse offers a logic of interpretations whereas sociological approaches look at the production of cultural power. A sociological view sees discourse as too narrow because it only focuses on the symbolic. What matters in a sociological sense is that practitioners do things in unreflective ways; they change things, which discourse does not account for. Therefore, when looking at agency and practice it is vital that we consider not only how meaning is produced through language but also how that language informs and is used by practitioners to enable individuals to exercise their human rights.

NOTES

1. Kate Nash, *The Cultural Politics of Human Rights: Comparing the US and UK* (Cambridge: Cambridge University Press, 2009).
2. See, for example, Fiona Robinson, "Human Rights and the Global Politics of Resistance: Feminist Perspectives," *Review of International Studies* 29 (2003): 161–80; Kiyoteru Tsutsui and Christine Min Wotipka, "Global Civil Society and the International Human Rights Movement: Citizen Participation in Human Rights International Nongovernmental Organisations," *Social Forces* 83, no. 2 (2004): 587–620; Emilie A. Hatner-Burton and Tsutsui Kiyoteru, "Human Rights in a Globalising World: The Paradox of Empty Promises," *American Journal of Sociology* 110, no. 5 (2005): 1373–411; Michael A. Elliott, "Human Rights and the Triumph of the Individual in World Culture," *Cultural Sociology* 1, no. 3 (2007): 343–63; Jeong-Woo Koo and Francisco O. Ramirez, "National Incorporation of Global Human Rights: Worldwide Expansion of National Human Rights Institutions," *Social Forces* 87, no. 3 (2009): 1321–353; and Neil Stammers, *Human Rights and Social Movements* (London: Pluto Press, 2009).
3. Catherine, A. MacKinnon, *Are Women Human: And Other International Dialogues* (London: The Belknap Press of Harvard University Press, 2006).
4. See, for example, Michael Freeman, *Human Rights: An Interdisciplinary Perspective* (Cambridge, UK: Polity Press, 2002); L. Hajjar, "Toward a Sociology of Human Rights: Critical Globalisation Studies, International Law, and the Future of War," in *Critical Globalization Studies*, ed. R.P. Appelbaum and W.I. Robinson (New York: Routledge, 2005): 207–16; A. Woodiwiss, *Human Rights* (London: Routledge, 2005); Damien Short, "The Social Construction of Indigenous 'Native Title' Land Rights in Australia," *Current Sociology* 55, no. 6 (2007): 857–76; R. Morgan and B.S. Turner, eds., *Interpreting Human Rights: Social Science Perspectives* (London: Routledge, 2009); P. Hynes, M. Lamb, D. Short, and M. Waites, "Sociology and Human Rights: Confrontations, Evasions, and New Engagements," *International Journal of Human Rights* 14, no. 6 (2010): 810–30; Hannah Miller, "From 'Rights-Based' to 'Rights-Framed' Approaches: A Social Constructionist View of Human Rights Practice," *International Journal of Human Rights* 14, no. 6 (2010): 915–31; and Darren O'Byrne, "On the Sociology of Human Rights: Theorising the Language-Structure of Rights," *Sociology* 46, no. 5 (2012): 829–43.
5. Amnesty International, *It's in our Hands: Stop Violence against Women* (London: Amnesty International Publications, 2004).

2 The Fallacy of Gender-Neutrality

Human rights discourse is an attempt to introduce into law a universal morality, to be practiced globally. Its main tenets are the notion of a common humanity and that all human beings in all countries should be treated with respect and dignity regardless of nationality. At its origins, human rights discourse assumes a universal human subject on whom is bestowed inalienable rights. This unquestioned assertion of a universal rights-bearer is born out of eighteenth-century attempts to enshrine liberty and freedom for all in the declarations and constitutions of the times.

In this chapter, I set out to problematize the dominant liberal, Western conception of universal "human" that serves as the foundation of human rights. To begin, I explore what the liberal, Western conception of "human" is that is being posited as universal. I then move on to examine the important feminist challenges to this. Claims of universality must refer to a referent object—an object common to all.[1] This object is articulated as the subject of human rights, and as I show, when interpreted in a universal human rights context, "human," as the subject of human rights, is assumed to be gender-neutral.

HUMAN RIGHTS: A UNIVERSAL DISCOURSE?

In the liberal, Western conception of universal human rights, "human" is conceived of as the subject of rights attributed on the basis of an innate humanity.[2] This ontological position is rooted in the idea of natural rights, which claims individuals have certain basic rights because they share an essential human nature.[3] The concept of an essential human nature appeals not to physical but moral nature, and it is in this vein that human rights come to be considered *inalienable*, meaning no "human" is without them.[4] A popular claim in universal human rights discourse is that liberal political philosophers, such as Thomas Hobbes, John Locke and Thomas Jefferson, who advanced the notion of natural rights, conceived the individual "human" subject to be a sovereign entity, meaning every human being has a natural and equal right to everything necessary for the preservation of life and a right to the free pursuit of individual interests and ends.[5] These individual rights precede any form of social life—thus, they are acquired at birth—and involve the individual "human" subject to submit freely to participation in a social contract set out in the laws and institutions that will protect their natural rights. It is a widely held view that Kant's social contract offered a moral grounding for universal human rights because he defined rational autonomy (what is referred to earlier as an individual's sovereignty) as the capacity for free self-determination—paired with his notion of a universal capacity for goodwill—which established the necessity of respect for every rational being as a potential member of a community of rational beings.[6] The natural rights positions put forward by liberal, Western thinkers served the ideological function of legitimizing the construction of "human" as a self-interested, rational person whose social ties originate in a contract. This philosophical mechanism, encapsulated in respect for the individual (who was to be protected from unwanted state intrusion) and claims to universality (humans qua humans were born with certain rights), provided a foundation upon which the "human" person could resist various forms of social and political oppression.[7]

However, this construction of "human" was an inadequate description of "the complexity of the human person who is born into a network of relations to other human beings and who develops over time within a context of social and political institutions."[8] Yeatman confirms that "the subject of human rights is the *individual* human being" (my emphasis).[9] She argues that it is a universal individuality that is constituted in human rights discourse because it is assumed that all human individuals to an equal degree—and regardless of differences between them—become the bearers of human rights. Yeatman attributes universal human rights discourse as historically responsible for constituting individuality as such. She invokes Durkheim to make the point that "law, as an index of social solidarity allows us to understand how society morally constitutes the subject" and that it is this "juridical constitution of the individual as the irreducible unit of humanity" that is the foundation for all thirty articles of the Universal Declaration of Human Rights (UDHR).[10]

The central premise of a universal "human" as the subject of human rights rests on a specific normative conception of humanness that is projected onto the general category of human being as inherently *natural*.[11] The combined processes of decolonization and the world's horrified reaction to the Nazi holocaust provoked an awareness of the denial of the status of "human" for those who are discriminated against, sparking the formalization of the principles of natural rights into international human rights law.[12] Therefore, a liberal, natural rights thinking underpins the development of the international legal regime on human rights.[13] Moreover, it sees the creation of the universal "human" subject as a mechanism to prevent further disregard for "human" life. For evidence of this we need look no further than the United Nations Charter (1945) that aims to "reaffirm faith in fundamental human rights"[14] or the preamble to the UDHR (1948), which states that the "recognition of the inherent dignity and of the equal and inalienable rights of all members of the human family is the foundation of freedom, justice and peace in the world."[15]

For some, it is not of particular concern what origins of human moral behavior are given (be it nature, God, reason, etc.), the point is that actual social practices suggest a common humanity. The foundation for this common humanity is derived from nothing more than common biology as a species.[16] Human rights are a response to the "universal social facts" that it is wrong to torture, starve, humiliate and hurt others.[17] These "universal social facts" are derived from the animal nature in human beings to need food and shelter and from the social character of human beings to live within communities.[18] It can be argued that human rights are generated as a humanizing principle rather than simple attributes bestowed to humans because we are humans.[19] In other words, were we to recognize our common humanity, we—"humans"—would not abuse each other. Respect for a universal "humanness" is what is needed to stop human rights abuse. Human rights are, in this view, validated because of the almost universal acceptance of the discourse of universal human wrongs.

A universalist approach to finding ways to stop human wrongs emphasizes human rights as part of "human" moral evolution, demonstrating how the concept of human rights emerged as a specific historical response to the challenges of modernity, the root of liberal, Western thinking.[20] Presenting a historical account of "human" as the subject of universal human rights, this view credits repressive political and economic structures of the early part of the twentieth century with the birth of Western human rights as a way to overcome these threats.[21] The subject "human" is assumed to mean the biological phenomenon *Homo sapiens*, of which all human beings are to be considered members.[22] Furthermore, it is this special feature of "humanity" as an exclusive category that makes it possible for human rights not only to be universal in their application to this homogenous group but also inalienable: "one cannot stop being human, no matter how badly one behaves nor how barbarously one is treated."[23] The most important aspect in this approach is the "remarkable international normative consensus on the list of rights" found in the UDHR, the 1966 Covenants and 1993 Vienna Declaration.[24] This argument is substantiated in the appeal to cross-cultural consensus on basic rights as the right to life, liberty and security of the person; the guarantee of legal personality; protection against slavery; arbitrary arrest, detention or exile; and inhuman or degrading treatment.[25] The phenomenon of an international consensus on this can be understood in the daily rounds of diplomacy as state leaders justify their human rights policies in terms of these standards.[26] In this way, universalists claim that the human rights discourse sets the limits and requirements of social action. For them, when "human rights claims bring legal and political practice into line with their demands," they create the type of person posited in that moral vision.[27]

The moral vision articulated here is the liberal, Western notion of a basic moral commitment to the idea that all human beings, simply because they are human, have the equal and inalienable individual rights recognized in the UDHR.[28]

This liberal concept of a *common humanity*, which has particular rights based on a shared existence, was codified into international law in 1948 with the UDHR. The preamble to the UDHR reaffirms that "faith in fundamental human rights, in the dignity and worth of the human person and in the equal rights of men and women."[29] These human rights are both inalienable and should be protected by the rule of law.[30] Article 1 of the UN Charter clearly encapsulates the liberal, Western perspective on human rights—"All human beings are born free and equal in dignity and rights"—and demonstrates the underpinnings of liberal, Western thinking that have been codified in the development of the international legal regime on human rights.[31] These liberal formulations of human rights shape the ideological context, in which "human" is understood in a context of human rights. The UDHR

> not only gave meaning to the phrase "human rights and fundamental freedoms" used in the Charter; over time, it also came to be accepted as a normative instrument in its own right, which, together with the Charter, spelled out the human rights obligations incumbent upon all UN member states.[32]

In other words, the UDHR provides a starting point from which "human" could be understood in international politics. For many practitioners of human rights the problem is not what constitutes "human"; instead, "the problem is how to ensure the observance of human rights in practice."[33] Therefore, "for the most part, the theory and practice of human rights is conducted in the language of legal and philosophical reason; the former focusing on international law and methods of implementation and the latter on the meaning, source and justification for rights claims."[34] The language of human rights has become the acceptable voice of morality in global affairs, and with it, human rights have become the source for understanding "human" in international politics.

International law has significantly shaped how "human" is understood in human rights discourse because it was lawyers who turned the philosophical concepts of human rights into rules of law. Within international law, "the development of the rights-bearing subject was not a legal process, but a social one which is reflected in law."[35] As such, through the social construction of international legal mechanisms, encompassing assumed homogeneity, subjectivity is attributed to "human" in international politics. The emergence of "the language of human rights out of the political culture of liberalism meant that the discourse from the beginning would be inhibited by premonitions of universalist grandeur."[36] The adherence to universalist conceptions of human rights, which have become codified in international law,[37] demonstrate a preoccupation with the notion of *rights* instead of "human" as the subject of universal human rights.[38] The *language* of human rights seeks ways to implement and enforce these inalienable, universal rights without problematizing the individual to which these rights apply.

The following quote from Perry illustrates the ambiguity inherent in liberal, Western notions of universal "human,"

> Every human being, simply as a human being, is sacred (is inviolable, has inherent dignity, is an end in himself, or the like); therefore, certain choices should be made and certain other choices rejected; in particular, certain things ought not to be done to any human being and certain other things ought to be done for every human being.[39]

Teitel reiterates that "whether referring to 'humankind' collectively, or to an attribute of 'being' human, the norm is ambiguous."[40] This ambiguity, which is intentionally written into international law, results in the exclusion rather than the inclusion of women. Those critical of universalizing rights discourse have begun to challenge not just the assumptions of universality and inalienability inherent in orthodox doctrine, but have also taken issue with the assumption of homogeneity in the articulation "human" within the language of human rights.

FEMINIST CHALLENGES

Feminist human rights scholarship is critical of liberal, Western understandings of "human" as universal because such conceptions express a gender-neutral subject. The question, "Are women human?" is surprisingly not unfamiliar to feminist analyses of international human rights.[41] In showing how language is a central dimension in analyzing the construction of subjects (humans), feminists examine the constitution and meaning of the category "human" in relation to the binary codification of "men" and "women."[42] This binary coding of masculine/feminine and privileging of that which is masculine is shown to be embedded in language itself; thus, the subject is implicitly a man, and women will find themselves subtly excluded.[43] Feminists take aim at a universalist defense of a universal "human" that rests on biological essentialism because the male/masculine will always be privileged over the female/feminine in such biologically reductionist dichotomous articulations. The concern is that this reduction, implicit in liberal, Western structures of universal "human," defines certain people as "less human, as not deserving of human rights or full participation in society" and "becomes the basis upon which violence against them is tolerated and sometimes even supported."[44] It is for this reason that feminists argue that the construction of "human" as the subject of rights is gendered.[45]

In seeking to expose the universalist "human" as gender neutral, feminist theorists and activists have challenged the androcentrism of the liberal, Western view of moral philosophy. These challenges reveal the theoretical foundations for universal "human" to be a masculinist ontology in which elite, white men impose their understanding of human nature as generic.[46] The presumed gender-neutrality of universal "human" in theory and in practice of human rights disguises a "trenchant masculine bias in the selective promotion and protection of human rights," which in turn established a hierarchy between men and women, dictating their legal capacities and their approved behaviors.[47] Activism in the women's human rights movement charts attempts to dispel this male-oriented view in the buildup to the 1993 Vienna Declaration. The feminist objective of having women understood as "human," thus guaranteeing the protection of women's human rights, was paramount.[48] Without such objectives, "the gendered nature of the human rights system" itself cannot be recognized and transformed; thus, no real progress for women can be achieved.[49]

This argument is substantiated by tracing the exclusionary roots of the public/private distinction in international human rights law.[50] Historically, the division of men and women followed a division between public life and private life. Men were associated with the public sphere, and women were associated with the private sphere. In political, legal and moral terms, this meant that those associated with the public sphere were citizens of a state, were legal subjects and were rational actors.[51] This offered acceptance as fully functioning "humans" to those in the public sphere, while those relegated to the private sphere became absent from public life, thus seen as not being fully functioning human beings. Sullivan draws attention to the legitimizing function of international law and outlines human rights as a powerful tool for affecting political processes at national and international levels.[52] Most practices of international law have yet to focus on gender-specific abuses because, traditionally, violations have been committed directly by the state against individuals.[53] The problem with including women as members of the universal "human" is that many abuses enacted on women take place in the private sphere by private individuals, rather than by agents of the state. This conundrum is explored in detail in Chapter 5, where I look at Amnesty International's *Stop Violence against Women* campaign.

Three main features of international law prohibit women's inclusion. First, international law is state centered and remains focused on the behavior of states and not individuals.[54] Second, civil and political rights dominate human rights discourse, neglecting the institution of the family, where most women are located. Third, placing emphasis on civil and political rights, as opposed to economic and social rights, neglects gender-specific abuses suffered by women in private life (such as rape and domestic violence). Hence, the male-oriented and state-focused nature of international human rights law developed out of liberal, Western, white, elite male fears of violations of their civil and political rights, resulting in their neglect (and often negation) of the fears and violations experienced in the private sphere because they were masters of that territory.[55]

Much contemporary feminist work on human rights in some way focuses on public/private divisions because women are seen as the other, as less powerful or as absent.[56] Feminists criticize the definition of both rights and "human" as being male oriented and seek ways of shaping international law from a feminist perspective.[57] When applied to women's human rights, the public/private argument in feminist international politics tends to locate the source of division within concepts of state construction and citizenship. Traditionally, members of a state are citizens and, as such, are constructed as rights-bearing individuals. However, given the public/private divide human rights are in fact men's rights and those citizens who enjoy human rights are understood implicitly as male/masculine.[58] Therefore, what is argued is that it is only men's bodies, experiences and perspectives that are reflected as the subject of human rights law. Existing models of citizenship rest on gendered constructions of the public/private division, in which only the public sphere is associated with politics and privileged masculinity.

The claims that women are not "human" serve as an analytical platforms for feminists critiquing international human rights mechanisms. Catherine MacKinnon[59] takes specific issue with this when she observes that women are recognized as inhuman in the eyes of international law and as such remain unprotected by it. She argues that the present exclusionary state of international law must be corrected to include women in the interim, while feminist scholars work to find new ways of imagining human rights. The exclusion of women is not only conceptual but empirical as well. The universal definition of "human" that renders men as humans and women as others precludes women's experience being included in how human rights are conceptualized—and hence practiced.[60] Legally, one is less than human when one's violations do not violate the human rights that are recognized.[61] This particular predicament is shown empirically to be the case in Chapter 5. As MacKinnon points out, "becoming human in both the legal and lived senses is a social, legal, and political process."[62] In other words, to guarantee a fully human existence, international law must uphold its standards and delivery of the protection it is designed to provide. However, MacKinnon claims that in order for international law to provide for women, women must first be seen as "human," which traps human rights practitioners in a "circular epistemic fashion, seeing what subordinated groups are distinctively deprived of, subjected to, and delegitimated by, requires . . . that they first be seen as human."[63]

The problem MacKinnon identifies here can be clarified in terms of sex equality. In the mainstream interpretation of international politics, gender is conflated with sex. This means that by being defined as female, women are accorded second-class status in international law. Furthermore, "if equality of the sexes is recognized to be a fact, equalizing socially unequal groups is merely a problem to be solved."[64] However, "if sex equality is seen as a value, it can be accepted or rejected as one side in a normative discussion."[65] The relevance of this distinction is that in human rights policy, a fact can be rejected or distorted whereas a value can be endlessly debated. Wherein sex equality is understood as a value, and women are defined by sex in the exclusionary language of international human rights law, the ability for women to claim protection of human rights is distorted through the creation of women as "other" instead of "human." When "women are abused, human rights are violated; anything less, implicitly assumes women are not human."[66] Chapters 5 and 6 look more closely at how the legal language of international human rights law is gendered.

The feminist literature shows that in liberal, Western notions of universal human rights, women are not assumed to be "human." But even more than the gender dimension, it is the assumption of *self-evidence* of human rights that needs to be questioned. Self-evidence is not only the normative basis of human rights, but it is also what produces an exclusionary relation. This unquestioned assertion of a universal rights-bearer is born out of eighteenth-century attempts to enshrine liberty and freedom for all in the declarations and constitutions of the times. In 1776, Thomas Jefferson wrote, "We hold these truths to be self-evident, that all men are created equal, that they are endowed by their Creator with certain inalienable rights."[67] He proclaims that, without question, men know within themselves they are created equal and that this brings with it inalienable rights. The idea of something being self-evident is crucial here, because it is the root of philosophical understanding of human rights insofar as it becomes the basis for concepts of universality. When something is self-evident, it is assumed to be understood without question. So Jefferson's statement speaks to the unquestioned equality amongst men and their possession of rights, based on their common humanity. Jefferson's assertion directly influenced Article 1 of the Declaration of the Rights of Man and Citizen, which proclaims that "[m]en are born and remain free in equal rights." This universalizing sentence, with a meaningful modification in language, became "All human beings are born free and equal in dignity and rights," Article 1 of the Universal Declaration of Human Rights.[68] The term *whereas* replaces *self-evident* in the UDHR: "Whereas recognition of the inherent dignity and of all the equal and inalienable rights of all members of the human family is the foundation of freedom, justice and peace in the world."[69] But the meaning is intended to be same, for "whereas" is "simply a legalistic way of asserting a given, something self-evident."[70]

It is this assertion of self-evidence that leads to the assumption of gender-neutrality. Universal means applicable to all people, which removes the need for that person, that bearer of inalienable rights to be described in any specific detail. It is self-evident. This internalized sense of equality and the fundamental ability to recognize the humanity of others are the philosophical basis on which human rights works. Individuals become part of a political community, one in which their inalienable rights are to be protected, based on their common humanity. However, in the eighteenth century, because moral autonomy (ascribed by Jefferson only to men) was the key to becoming a bearer of inalienable rights, those deemed lacking in such moral autonomy were denied access. Women and children were among the most prominent morally deficient groups, but children, because they would mature into adults, were seen to one day regain this capacity, something women would not.[71] This meant that "the proponents of universal, equal and natural human rights automatically excluded some categories of people from exercising those rights."[72] Because human rights are not rights of humans in a state of nature but rather rights of humans in society, then "human rights only become meaningful when they gain political content."[73] Jefferson's assertion politicized the concept of self-evident, when it was written into the American Declaration of Independence. The influence his words have had on subsequent legislation, including the UDHR, further politicizes the concept and renders self-evident to be universal as Article 1 of the UDHR stated earlier demonstrates. This universal self-evident concept of inalienable rights has as its subject, or its bearer, a gender-neutral individual. When human rights are politicized, then that assumption of gender-neutrality enters into practice, as people act on the assumption, and laws and legal mechanisms are written with this assumption. However, it is not just legal documents that enshrine the assumption of gender-neutrality. They also "rest on a disposition towards other people, a set of convictions about what people are like and how they know right and wrong in the secular world."[74] Without this the concept of self-evident human rights would not occur because there would be no empathy with others. Rights cannot be defined once and for all because of the ever-changing emotional grounds of rights, which change in reaction to declarations: rights are open questions as to what they are and who has them, such that "the human rights revolution is by definition ongoing."[75]

While the self-evidence of equality as humans underpins the common norm to all individuals, feminist critics point out that such norms are, in fact, embodied. In fact, "autonomy and empathy are cultural practices, not just ideas, and they are therefore quite literally embodied, that is, they have physical as well as emotional dimensions."[76] This quest for embodiment is how feminists have sought to locate women within international politics generally and within human rights specifically. If women were part of the landscape, then it would become easier to conceptualize their contributions. However, feminist discourse analysis challenged the *naturalness* of women and moved toward socially constructed concepts because they were looking to present women as embodied creatures who had rights. But this idea of embodiment was not tied to any eighteenth-century concept of humanity but rather to one that empowered women as actors in their own lives. An unfortunate feature of society is that people still fail to recognize their own humanity in others, which is the source of all the inequalities of rights throughout history.[77] A main component of Hunt's writing is about how women were defined as being the "opposite sex" and "weaker sex" such that their individuality in terms of rights was undermined. This happens after the rise of universalizing ideas in the eighteenth century, in the move toward nationalism, which required distinguishing between people. These distinctions happened based primarily on sex and race, rather than on culture. This provides a more complete explanation of why feminists now are looking to language to empower women, whose bodies have been their curse.

The idea of human rights is to provide a basic level of respect and dignity to the treatment of human beings. Therefore, the commitment to universality presupposes gender-neutrality because the idea is that there is no difference when something applies to all. However, this is not so straightforward in practice. Human rights can be invoked legally, politically and socially.[78] The legal manifestations of human rights are the most visible. However, "the problem is that when lawmaking pen has finally met paper, the outcome has been distressingly limited."[79] In practice, Stemple points out that

So-called women's issues were virtually ignored in the early decades of the post-World War II human rights movement. In the 1980s and 1990s, when significant attention was finally paid to women's vulnerability to human rights violations—not infrequently in the form of anti-rape language—men were consequently overlooked.[80]

She explains how the conflation of sex and gender make it difficult to overcome the idea of *woman as victim*. Thus, the universality that gives human rights its strength is also found wanting because it equates costly economic, social and cultural rights in order to counteract the supporting contexts that maintain women's diminished status and power. Once again, the gendered nature of the subject and the gender divide in the public/private distinction was written into the human rights discourse:

Developing as it did in a post-World War II context of Western hegemony and the rise of postcolonial movements throughout the Third World, the dominant framework of human rights and its assumption of universal human nature largely reflected the specific experiences, needs and values of affluent white Western men . . . The nation-state's subject, whose 'rights' were to be protected, implicitly reflected the experience and subjectivity of a masculine, rational, individual, who was rooted in a significant way to community and social structure.[81]

How does this assumption work? Feminist discourse analysis exposes the fallacy of gender-neutrality by locating women and men as the subject of international politics rather than its object. A subject has the power to act, whereas an object is acted on. Distinguishing between subject and object is the cornerstone of feminist politics and vital to much feminist activism.

Locating women as subjects in international politics is an ongoing feminist pursuit. How feminist have undertaken these searches and the results they have found differ, but most important, the search has led to an insistence on gender being an essential facet of political life. To understand how an assumption of gender-neutrality works, we must follow a feminist trajectory through the study of international politics.

In the first instance, feminists sought to populate the exclusively male perception of international politics with women. Historically, feminism has always been a struggle for the proper representation of women.[82] Questions of representation involve issues of politics and power. Feminist theorizing involves showing how empowerment involves putting the politically marginalized on the cognitive map.[83] Thus, "while working to center 'woman' as a valid object of study and to validate women as 'knowers' and 'speakers' generally, feminists have understandably developed a view of men that sees them benefiting from the masculine codings of so many of the resources and activities in society in a power-hierarchy over women."[84] In seeking to expose this power-hierarchy, feminist theorizing in international politics frequently focuses on problems of exclusion, which arise when "knowledge about the world is only constructed by particular social groups who occupy a dominant position in society."[85]

For those who first introduced this concept,[86] the world of international politics appeared to be truly a man's world. In response to their own experiences and those of other women, feminists theorizing gender began by bringing women in from the margins and making their roles and concerns visible in the international arena. With women in the picture, the practice of warfare and the process behind the decision to go to war were no longer the exclusive domains of men.[87] It was shown that "women are the objects of masculinist social control not only through direct violence (murder, rape, battering, incest), but also through ideological constructs, such as 'women's work' and the cult of motherhood, that justify structural violence" such as inadequate health care, sexual harassment and sex-segregated wages.[88] Outlining the public/private debate, Enloe explained that in order to understand the politics of any given country the association of women and femininity with the private sphere must be explored.[89] She blurred the lines of the public/private dichotomy through manipulating the feminist slogan *the personal is political*. The first move was to restate the slogan as the political is personal, disrupting the masculinized political control associated with public life by suggesting that the private (personal) is also public (political).[90] Her second move was to expose the international/domestic dichotomy inherent in the public/private debate by stating that the *personal is international*. Here Enloe argues that global (international) economic, social and political forces shape individual (personal) ideas about masculinity and femininity.[91]

Accepting that the personal is international adds women to the international arena but it does not transform practices. To further challenge the heterosexist masculinist language of international politics, Enloe provides the manipulation *the international is personal*, which implies that the social roles assigned to women, such as wife, mother, or sex worker, are crucial to the maintenance of state sovereignty because these gender roles support ideas of masculinized dignity and feminized sacrifice that are needed to sustain a sense of autonomous nationhood.[92] In other words, without wives, girlfriends and mothers (and sex workers to keep them company while overseas) to protect, governments would have a harder time providing their soldiers with rationales for going to war. Conceiving the international as personal uncovered the gender-neutral language of male dominated policy-making circles. It confirmed that women were required to behave in certain ways. Even when women did enter these elite circles of men, they were made to conform in order to participate.

Entering the world of defense intellectuals, Carol Cohn describes her first-hand experiences with male dominated policy-making circles. She explains that

> if I spoke English rather than expert jargon, the men responded to me as though I were ignorant or simple-minded . . . As I learned to speak . . . I no longer stood outside the impermeable wall of techno-strategic language, and once inside . . . I began to find it difficult to get out.[93]

What Cohn and Enloe demonstrate is that simply adding women would not be enough to disrupt the *man's world*, otherwise discussed as gender-neutrality. An assumption of gender-neutrality does not mean conceiving a world of genderless individuals; rather, it describes the phenomenon of not considering gender to be an analytical aspect of sociopolitical research and policy making. Given that much of the research and policy making conducted regarding state practices in the international arena is carried out by heterosexual males, about heterosexual males, it seems quite obvious that there would be little need to reflect on their own subjectivity when large-scale questions about war and peace were at hand. However, when pioneering feminists such as Enloe and Cohen arrive at the same point to say not all actors are heterosexual males and that in fact international political practices are far more complicated than just the relation between states, it exposes the assumption of gender-neutrality for more than just overlooking gender but as a calculated strategy to control the subjects of study. The process of assuming gender-neutrality is a political move that reduces actors to heterosexual males and renders all the other people implicated in the issues as invisible and powerless. Feminists seek to populate international politics with various different people. Peopling global politics is difficult because traditionally states are its central unit, because it "makes states into international persons, most men and all women are erased from its view," revealing an "encoded masculine territory" that renders "women" homeless because "the soldier, the citizen, the political subject and the state are gendered male."[94] The problem then becomes understanding the once-simple structures of state power and security when more than men are fighting to protect women and children.

Faced with a need to demonstrate how including gender is crucial to assessments of international political practices, feminists used gender-perspectives, sometimes articulated as lens metaphors, as effective methodological and epistemological tools to define legitimate fields of inquiry. There is no single feminist methodology.[95] However, the use of gender-perspectives is frequently applied and relies on constructions and deconstructions of *frames*, understood otherwise as contested areas of international politics. To frame a debate or discourse is to limit what subjects will or can participate in a given context. Framing helps feminists legitimate women's experiences. Feminists use this tool to empower women's experiences and to politicize (sometimes repoliticize) mainstream discourses of international politics.[96] Epistemologically, gender-perspectives assert that it is possible to accurately represent women's places within the world. Thus, through gender-perspectives, the audience's gaze is focused on that which is either inside or outside the frame. Feminist critiques tend to first demonstrate what the original picture looked like and then reframe it to illustrate a different view with women included in the picture.[97]

In their book *Global Gender Issues*, Peterson and Runyan are very explicit in detailing how gender-perspectives work. Their methodology concerns itself with *gender-sensitive lenses*, which focus attention in particular ways by filtering what is looked at so one might see it "more accurately or in better relation to certain other things."[98] However, there is a risk involved with taking this approach, and that is that a focus on something particular will render other things out of focus. Nevertheless, a gender-sensitive lens, according to Peterson and Runyan, offers a more comprehensive explanation; "it enables us to 'see' how women are in fact important to the picture . . . even though women and the roles they are expected to play are obscured when we focus only on men."[99] Two aspects are of note. First, gender lenses or gender-perspectives attempt to provide explanations for gender inequalities and absences. Second, these explanations are articulated in terms of filling in the detail, or muddying pictures. Hence, gender-sensitive lenses reconstruct the dominant discourses in international politics, for instance, state sovereignty and security, by including women as actors.[100] This gender sensitivity also reorients our gaze to include marginalized identities (usually female), for example, women's diverse roles in war.[101] However, as Peterson and Runyan note, focusing our gaze on gender will "filter out" other aspects of the picture.[102] The key feature of focusing lenses on elements within a gender inclusive conception of the picture of international politics is that these methodologies all subscribe to methods of representation, in this case, representations of gender in world politics.

Those who analyze language as a means to understanding gender relationships in international politics seek to uncover how "men" and particular masculine characteristics have become the stable subject of international politics, thus rendering "women" and feminine characteristics invisible or absent from consideration.[103] Too often the assumption that all are equally oppressed and disadvantaged by gender is made, rendering the practices of domination invisible to the detriment of feminist politics.[104] Faced with these challenges, feminist analyses seek epistemological and ontological grounds for their arguments, such that biology no longer dictates how gender can be articulated.[105] For example, in her analysis of state sovereignty, Cynthia Weber observes that the state is doubly sexed and alerts us to a presumed heterosexual masculine authority inherent in the theories and practices of international politics.[106] She explains that a state can penetrate "internal (female/feminine) affairs of other states or territories" as a manner of protecting the "masculine realm of international politics (an anarchical war of every man against every man)."[107] What remains paramount for Weber is to evidence the particular historically bounded codings of sex, gender and sexuality that affect state sovereignty. The assumed heterosexuality of sovereign states needs to be challenged in order to increase those who may participate in world politics.[108] In other words, it is a requirement of feminist discourse analysis to dismantle the dichotomies female/feminine, male/masculine and domestic/international that underpin articulations of gender in international politics generally, and human rights specifically. What is stressed is the function of language and the problems associated with gender-neutrality.

THE CONFLATION OF SEX AND GENDER

The fallacy of gender-neutrality, and the assumption of universally applicable descriptions of human behavior, works through the conflation of sex and gender. The conflation of the terms *sex* and *gender* occurs when the socially constructed concepts of "woman" and "man" are understood purely as binary, biological categories of male and female. Sex does refer to the biological male or female, but gender is about how individuals exhibit both masculine and feminine characteristics. A person could be masculine without being male, such as a person could be feminine without being female. The trajectory of feminist challenges against male and masculine privilege in international politics exposes the fact that gender has always been an analytical element of the study and practice of global politics.[109] Within the context of feminist theorists there is a distinction between sex and gender, where "sex" refers to the biological difference between male and female, while "gender" refers to the practices of femininity and masculinity in social relations.[110] Feminists continue to stress that the sex/gender binary is systemic throughout the practice and study of international politics and accounts for observed inequalities between women and men in the world. For example, the hegemonic Western brand of masculinity is associated with autonomy, sovereignty, the capacity for reason, objectivity, universalism and men, whereas femininity is the lack of these characteristics. Proponents of gender analyses reject biologically constrained concepts of gender, where masculinity is an exclusively male characteristic, leaving femininity an exclusively female characteristic and preferring instead articulations of gender whereby a person can possess and exhibit both masculine and feminine characteristics regardless of their genitalia. Furthermore, gender analyses of international politics confront the domination and compulsory heterosexuality that results from reducing and or restricting concepts of gender to sex by exposing the inherent assumption that the biological assignment of sex is necessarily associated with the socially constructed gender terms *man* and *woman*.

Those feminists looking at language seek not only to populate a man's world with women, but further, to explore the relationship between femininity and masculinity in ontological terms. Perspectives, frames and pictures are attempts to problematize gender-neutrality by focusing on the position of "women" in world politics. Nonetheless, feminist epistemologies that question how we can understand women's experiences fail to ask the ontological question, What is "woman"? A feminist discourse analysis perspective argues that the failure to explore gender ontologically maintains a conflation of sex and gender, thus leaving the ontological categories of "women" and "men" unquestioned. The work of Judith Butler is often used to demonstrate the effectiveness of this approach.

GENDER PERFORMANCE

Butler sets out to problematize women as the subject of feminism.[111] She explores the gender category "women" and finds that within feminist theory, "there is very little agreement after all on what it is that constitutes, or ought to constitute the category women."[112] Her aim is to demonstrate that the category "women" is "produced and restrained by the very structures of power through which emancipation is sought."[113] She identifies a conflation of sex and gender and offers an alternative in her concept of *performance*. She suggests that the mapping of socially constructed terms onto corporeal realities has produced the assumption that "women" are female-bodied and that "men" are male-bodied.[114] For Butler, gender requires repeated performance and this repetition is simultaneously a reenactment and reexperiencing of already socially established meanings. Therefore, performance cannot be understood outside of a process of repetition. This repetition "is not performed *by* a subject; this repetition is what enables a subject."[115] Hence, performance is not a singular act or event, but a ritualized production reiterated under and through constraint—where constraint is not necessarily that which limits performance, but rather impels and sustains it.[116] Butler believes that beings are socially constructed and that they are produced discursively through certain kinds of repetition. Legitimacy for these repetitions lies within their mundane and ritualized enactments. Therefore, for Butler, there is a tension between a tacit collective agreement to perform gender and the normalizing processes insistent on polarized gender identities.[117] Further, gender norms are impossible to embody, meaning that the repetitive performance of a particular identity normalizes that identity within a specific time and space. However, there will be certain identities whose performance challenges the norm in the way that it is unable to be normalized. This challenge occurs because performance destabilizes the assumed subjectivity, hence resisting the desire to limit particular performed subjectivities. In the end, for Butler, what is most at stake is one's ability to restrict and resist "frames of masculinist domination and compulsory heterosexuality."[118]

Feminist scholars argue that the dichotomy of masculine/feminine is a "structural feature of social life, rendering gender an analytical category with systemic implications for advancing our understandings of social relations."[119] In this respect, gender "humanizes" individuals within contemporary culture and thus, as a strategy of survival within compulsory systems, one's gender has clearly punitive consequences.[120] The implications for this in the study and practice of international politics, including human rights, are considerable. Looking at the humanizing affect of gender allows gender theorists to ask "questions about the construction and ascription of identity and the effects that these everyday processes have on the ways alliances are sustained, the ways wars are waged, the ways foreign investment is attracted."[121] Accounting for gender changes "what we think of 'us' and thereby changes what we perceive as threats to 'us.'"[122]

THE ASSUMPTION OF GENDER-NEUTRALITY

In international politics the concept of "human" is assumed to be gender-neutral so that it be universally inclusive. However, when we look closely at the dynamics of the legal and political language used to construct a gender-neutral concept of "human," we realize that in fact what appears to be neutrality, expressed as objectivity, is actually an inherent preference for male and masculine characteristics. Policies that assume gender-neutral actors in international politics have an impact directly on one's ability to exercise one's human rights. Questioning this assumption illuminates how long-standing expressions of human behavior are mired in language that fails to reflect the lives people lead. Understanding these limitations motivates the need to see human behavior, in the context of international human rights, as subjective rather than as objective. Effective practices of exercising one's human rights rely on political discourses that account for gendered subjectivity to fully express the potential for agency within the field of human rights. It is through practices of gendered human subjectivity that one exercises one's human rights.

What are the implications of this assumption? Many people are invisible in law; therefore, they cannot exercise their rights. The discourse of human rights makes a difference in practice:

> Hierarchical binary thinking in human rights discourse is widely institutionalized and its effects are very real; everyday denials of human rights are explicitly or implicitly condoned and concealed by privileging the "public" over the "private" sphere, "civil and political rights" over "economic and social rights," and North over South.[123]

Thus, binary mechanisms encoded in discourse have limited the emancipatory potential of human rights. Therefore, we have an incomplete estimation of the success or possibilities human rights can provide. However, this assumption has been successfully challenged in practice. The 1990s Global Campaign for Women's Human Rights is an important example of praxis that effectively confronted the failure of the international human rights community to recognize the gravity of abuses such as sexual or domestic violence and address them meaningfully in global human rights agendas.[124] Reilly argues that a paradigmatic shift has resulted from the successful contestation of such private abuses as human rights violations. These shifts can only be attained through emancipatory human rights praxis. Such a praxis

> means making visible previously invisible violations and sustaining pressure for changes in the ways that human rights are conceptualized, institutionalized and implemented [and] demands the participation of broad-based movements (grounded in bottom-up, democratic values), which play a pivotal role in the dialectical relationship between political and legal theorizing, human rights law and practice, and institutional and policy change.[125]

She concludes that human rights discourse is still marked by the conflict between classical liberalism and the expansive aims of Kantian ethics. What human rights is considered to be, and who is held responsible for violations will, in part, be a result of how this debate is negotiated.[126] Reilly articulates well the dilemma concerning the advancement of women's human rights: on one hand, the goal is incompatible with cultural relativism, while at the same time, feminists must critique universalist, top-down approaches. In sum, both approaches are necessary: a bottom-up, dialogic process in which meaning is freely negotiated and a top-down, universalist system of human rights.[127]

The benefits and the problems of employing both approaches are evident in the campaigning practices of Amnesty International (AI). AI has been highly influential in creating the meaning of human rights issues for the public. The organization is known for challenging state violations of rights, including attacks on political rights, such as repressing expressions of public dissent or shutting down political mobilization and arbitrarily detaining activists. However, through the early 1990s, this came to be the dominant view of what the international community regarded as the locus of human rights concerns.[128] Other issues then became marginalized as this became the dominant framing of human rights. When activism translates into the universalist, top-down view, it can undermine other efforts at activism in defense of human rights. Both perspectives are necessary; however, this can produce unforeseen consequences when considered for its effects on generating dominant discursive frames and marginalized discourses.

Now, we move from the general critique of exclusionary discourse to how specific institutional contexts have marginalized female voices. Historically, this stems from the patriarchal features of state building and citizenship, where citizenship and legal rights were restricted to particular groups of elite white men. Feminists have long since argued that women have been excluded from formal and mainstream interpretations of political and legal life. The implications for assuming human rights to be gender-neutral are plentiful. Feminists have outlined the impact on security, sovereignty and identity as well as on modes of empowerment. Divisions such as public/private have implications for how power is understood in often unproblematic ways. To empower people through human rights mechanisms and international law, one must understand subjectivity and how people are created as subjects or are denied subjectivity in international politics. The key for discourse feminists has been to look at the limits of language and situate gendered beings within that context.

For feminists, the concept of *patriarchy* provides scholars with a means of articulating how particular traits associated with masculinity are perpetually imbued with power, rendering all other constructions "less than masculine" and as such less powerful.[129] These dynamics of "dominant masculinities produce characteristic representations of maleness vis-à-vis women."[130] Dominant masculinities are constructed such that "men" are seen to be in roles of protectors, while "women" are seen to be in roles of needing protection. Despite the many feminist analyses of patriarchal power, structures that see maleness in a dichotomous relationship with femaleness remain problematic because they tend to see "women" and "men" as universal categories.[131] Universal categories are only useful if they are truly applicable to all they describe.

In sum, gender-neutrality is the assumption that "human" in human rights is a universal category. This conceptual phenomenon has its roots in the liberal, Western philosophical ideas that underpin international human rights law. Gender-neutrality is intrinsic to the idea of universal human because it is meant to provide an inclusive term to refer to all of humanity. However, when discussions of universality take place, as I have shown, they are in fact exclusive because the language used to express universal "human" assumes a male-oriented subject and precludes women and others as subjects through a binary logic.

The rest of the book operates on the premise that universal human rights is an *exclusionary discourse* because it assumes gender-neutrality as a strategy for inclusion. Gender-neutrality leaves out certain subjects because it adheres to biological distinctions rather than sociological conceptions of gender. Discursive feminist challenges to the patriarchal nature of human rights present activists with an interesting predicament. If the only tools available to women to protect their universal rights are international legal mechanisms, then the likelihood of success is minimal because as stated above, this is an exclusionary discourse, which by very definition cannot include women as subjects.

The goal of human rights activists is to seek protection for the violated and promote human rights. Feminist discourse analysis is effective in demonstrating how the language of universal human rights was not originally written with women in mind. However, they claim that in the growing human rights culture, some success has been made, for instance, the Convention on the Elimination of All Forms of Discrimination Against Women (CEDAW). So a dilemma exists between the moral values enshrined in the idea of universal human rights and the way it is interpreted in practice. This comes down to agency. If one is empowered to exercise their human rights, then one can see human rights as a useful tool. But when one is not empowered to exercise their rights, this tool loses its allure. This is not to suggest that human rights be discarded but rather that a consideration of the affects of discourse on the practice of using human rights to empower people must be taken into account. I suggest this is most effective when looked at through the concept of agency.

NOTES

1. Véronique Pin-Fat, "(Im)possible Universalism: Reading Human Rights in World Politics," *Review of International Studies* 26 (2000): 663–74.
2. Tim Dunne and Nicholas Wheeler, "Introduction: Human Rights and the Fifty Years' Crisis," in *Human Rights in Global Politics*, ed. T. Dunne and N. Wheeler (Cambridge: Cambridge University Press, 2001), 4.
3. Henry Shue, *Basic Rights: Subsistence, Affluence, and US Foreign Policy* (Princeton, NJ: Princeton University Press, 1980), 18–22.
4. R.J. Vincent, *Human Rights and International Relations* (Cambridge: Cambridge University Press, 1986), 14.
5. See Michael J. Perry, "Are Human Rights Universal? The Relativist Challenge and Related Matters," *Human Rights Quarterly* 19, no. 3 (1997): 461–509; Thomas M. Franck, "Are Human Rights Universal?" *Foreign Affairs* 80, no. 1 (2001): 191–204; Michael Goodhart, "Origins of Universality in the Human Rights Debates: Cultural Essentialism and the Challenge of Globalization," *Human Rights Quarterly* 25, no. 4 (2003): 935–64; and Anthony Padgen, "Human Rights, Natural Rights, and Europe's Imperial Legacy," *Political Theory* 31, no. 2 (2003): 171–99.
6. Immanuel Kant, "Perpetual Peace: A Philosophical Sketch," in *Kant: Political Writings*, ed. H. Reiss (Cambridge: Cambridge University Press, 1970), 98; Ken Booth, "Human wrongs and international relations," *International Affairs* 71, no. 1 (1995): 103–26; Tony Evans, "Introduction: Power,

Hegemony and the Universalization of Human Rights," in *Human Rights Fifty Years On: A Reappraisal*, ed. T. Evans (Manchester: Manchester University Press, 1998): 2–23; and Anna Yeatman, "Who Is the Subject of Human Rights?" *The American Behavioral Scientist* 43, no. 9 (2000): 1498–513.
7. Belden A. Fields and Wolf-Dieter Narr, "Human Rights as a Holistic Concept," *Human Rights Quarterly* 14 (1992): 2.
8. Cheryl L. Hughes, "Reconstructing the Subject of Human Rights," *Philosophy and Social Criticism* 25, no. 2 (1999): 49.
9. Yeatman, "Subject of Human Rights," 1498.
10. Durkheim, 1963, in Yeatman, "Subject of Human Rights," 1499–1501.
11. Anna Yeatman, "Right, the State and the Conception of the Person," *Citizenship Studies* 8, no. 4 (2004): 405.
12. See Michael Freeman, *Human Rights*, 2nd ed. (Cambridge: Polity Press, 2011); Fuyuki Kurasawa, *The Work of Global Justice: Human Rights as Practice* (Cambridge: Cambridge University Press, 2007); John Charvet and Elisa Kaczynska-Nay, *The Liberal Project and Human Rights: The Theory and Practice of a New World Order* (Cambridge: Cambridge University Press, 2008); and Micheline R. Ishay, *The History of Human Rights: From Ancient Times to the Global Era*, 2nd ed. (Berkeley: University of California Press, 2008).
13. Charvet and Kaczynska-Nay, *Liberal Project and Human Rights*; and Dunne and Wheeler, "Introduction: Human Rights."
14. United Nations, *Charter of the United Nations: Preamble*, 1945, accessed March 23, 2014, www.un.org/en/documents/charter/preamble.shtml.
15. United Nations, *The Universal Declaration of Human Rights*, 1948, accessed March 23, 2014, www.un.org/en/documents/udhr/.
16. Ken Booth, "Human Wrongs," 52.
17. Ken Booth, "Three Tyrannies," in *Human Rights in Global Politics*, ed. T. Dunne and N. Wheeler (Cambridge: Cambridge University Press, 2001), 64.
18. Ibid., 52.
19. Ibid., 51–52.
20. Jack Donnelly, "The Social Construction of International Human Rights," in *Human Rights in Global Politics*, ed. T. Dunne and N. Wheeler (Cambridge: Cambridge University Press, 2001), 72.
21. See Charvet and Kaczynska-Nay, *Liberal Project and Human Rights*; Michael Freeman, *Human Rights*; Kurasawa, *Work of Global Justice*; Ishay, *History of Human Rights*.
22. Jack Donnelly, *Universal Human Rights in Theory and Practice*, 2nd ed. (London: Cornell University Press, 2003), 10.
23. Ibid.
24. Jack Donnelly, *Universal Human Rights in Theory and Practice* (Ithaca, NY: Cornell University Press, 1989), 23.
25. Ibid., 122.
26. Donnelly, "Social Construction of Rights", 99; and Kate Nash, *The Cultural Politics of Human Rights: Comparing the US and UK* (Cambridge: Cambridge University Press, 2009).
27. Donnelly, *Universal Human Rights*, 2nd ed., 14.
28. Donnelly, "Social Construction of Rights," 99–100.
29. United Nations, *UDHR*, 71.
30. Ibid.
31. Dunne and Wheeler, "Introduction: Human Rights," 5.
32. Thomas Buergenthal, "The Normative and Institutional Evolution of International Human Rights," *Human Rights Quarterly* 19, no. 4 (1997): 707.

33. John P. Humphrey, "Why Human Rights?" in *Human Rights Issues and Trends*, ed. A. Lodhi and R. McNeilly (Toronto: Canadian Scholar's Press Inc., 1993), 5.

34. Evans, "Introduction," 3.

35. Norman Lewis, "Human Rights, Law and Democracy in an Unfree World," in *Human Rights Fifty Years On: A Reappraisal*, ed. T. Evans (Manchester: Manchester University Press, 1998), 98.

36. Anthony J. Langlois, "Human Rights: The Globalisation and Fragmentation of Moral Discourse," *Review of International Studies* 28, no. 3 (2002): 480.

37. That is, United Nations, UDHR; 1966 Covenants, 1993 Vienna Declaration.

38. Randall Peerenboom, "Human Rights and Asian Values: The Limits of Universalism," *China Review International* 7, no. 2 (2000): 295–320; Thomas M. Franck, "Are Human Rights Universal?"; Chris Brown, *Sovereignty, Rights and Justice: International Political Theory Today* (Cambridge: Polity Press, 2002); Michael Goodhart, "Origins of Universality"; and Padgen, "Human Rights, Natural Rights."

39. Michael J. Perry, *The Idea of Human Rights* (Oxford: Oxford University Press, 1998), 43.

40. Ruti G. Teitel, "For Humanity," *Journal of Human Rights* 3, no. 2 (2004): 225.

41. See Charlotte Bunch, "Transforming Human Rights from a Feminist Perspective," in *Women's Rights, Human Rights: International Feminist Perspectives*, ed. J. Peters and A. Wolper (London: Routledge, 1995), 11–17; Arvonne S. Fraser, "Becoming Human: The Origins and Development of Women's Human Rights," *Human Rights Quarterly* 21 (1999): 853–906; Christine Ainetter Brautigam, "International Human Rights Law: The Relevance of Gender," in *The Human Rights of Women: International Instruments and African Experiences*, ed. Wolfgang Benedek, Ester M. Kisaakye, and Gerd Oberleitner (London: Zed Books, 2002), 3–29; Catherine A. MacKinnon, *Are Women Human? And Other International Dialogues* (London: The Belknap Press of Harvard University Press, 2006); and Moya Lloyd, "Women's Rights: Paradoxes and Possibilities," *Review of International Studies* 33, no. 1 (2007): 91–103.

42. Margherita Rendal, *Whose Human Rights* (London: Trentham Books Limited, 1997); Hilary Charlesworth and Christine Chinkin, *The Boundaries of International Law: A Feminist Analysis* (Manchester, UK: Manchester University Press, 2000); and Stephanie Farrior, "Human Rights Advocacy on Gender Issues: Challenges and Opportunities," *Journal of Human Rights Practice* 1, no. 1 (2009): 83–100.

43. Nicola Lacey, "Feminist Legal Theory and the Rights of Women," in *Gender and Human Rights*, ed. K. Knop (New York: Oxford University Press, 2004), 27.

44. Bunch, "Transforming Human Rights," 12.

45. See V. Spike Peterson, "Whose Rights? A Critique of the 'Givens' in Human Rights Discourse," *Alternatives* 15 (1990): 303–44; Marysia Zalewski, "Well, What Is the Feminist Perspective on Bosnia?" *International Affairs* 71, no. 2 (1995): 339–356; Rendal, *Whose Human Rights*; Patricia Richards, "The Politics of Gender, Human Rights and Being Indigenous in Chile," *Gender and Society*, 19, no. 2 (2005): 199–220; and Farrior, "Human Rights Advocacy."

46. Peterson, "Whose Rights?," 306.

47. Georgina Ashworth, "The Silencing of Women," in *Human Rights in Global Politics*, ed. T. Dunne and N. Wheeler (Cambridge: Cambridge University Press, 2001), 259.

48. Dana Collins, Sylvanna Falcón, Sharmila Lodhia, and Molly Talcott, "New Directions in Feminism and Human Rights," *International Feminist Journal of Politics* 12 (2010): 298–318.

49. Donna Sullivan, "The Public/Private Distinction in International Human Rights Law," in *Women's Rights Human Rights: International Feminist Perspectives*, ed. J. Peters and A. Wolper (New York: Routledge, 1995), 103.
50. Stephen Baskerville, "Sex and the Problem of Human Rights," *The Independent Review* 16, no. 3 (2011): 351–79; and Sullivan, "The Public/Private Distinction."
51. Charlesworth and Chinkin, *Boundaries of International Law*; and Fraser, "Becoming Human."
52. Sullivan, "The Public/Private Distinction," 126.
53. Ibid.
54. Ibid., 127.
55. Bunch, "Transforming Human Rights," 13; and Charlesworth and Chinkin, *Boundaries of International Law*.
56. See Rhonda Copelon, "Intimate Terror: Understanding Domestic Violence as Torture," in *Human Rights of Women: National and International Perspectives*, ed. R. Cook (Philadelphia: University of Pennsylvania Press, 1994), 116–152; Julie Dorf and Gloria Careaga Pérez, "Discrimination and the Tolerance of Difference: International Lesbian Human Rights," in *Women's Rights Human Rights: International Feminist Perspectives*, ed. J. Peters and A. Wolper (New York: Routledge, 1995), 324–34; Siobhan Dowd, "Women and the World: The Silencing of the Feminine," in *Women's Rights Human Rights: International Feminist Perspectives*, ed. J. Peters and A. Wolper (New York: Routledge, 1995), 317–23; Pamela Goldberg, "Where in the World Is There Safety for Me? Women Fleeing Gender-Based Persecution," in *Women's Rights Human Rights: International Feminist Perspectives*, ed. J. Peters and A. Wolper (New York: Routledge, 1995), 345–55; Sima Wali, "Human Rights for Refugee and Displace Women," in *Women's Rights Human Rights: International Feminist Perspectives*, ed. J. Peters and A. Wolper (New York: Routledge, 1995), 335–44; Silvie Bovarnick, "Universal Human Rights and Non-Western Normative Systems: A Comparative Analysis of Violence against Women in Mexico and Pakistan," *Review of International Studies* 33 (2007): 59–74; Juanita Elias, "Women Workers and Labour Standards: The Problem of 'Human Rights,'" *Review of International Studies* 33 (2007): 45–57; Celina Romany, "State Responsibility Goes Private: A Feminist Critique of the Public/Private Distinction in International Human Rights Law," in *Human Rights of Women: National and International Perspectives*, ed. R. Cook (Philadelphia: University of Pennsylvania Press, 1994), 85–115; Shazia Qureshi, "The Recognition of Violence against Women as a Violation of Human Rights in the United Nations System," *Research Journal of South Asian Studies*, 28, no. 1 (2013): 187–98; and Jill Steans, "Debating Women's Human Rights as a Universal Feminist Project: Defending Women's Human Rights as a Political Tool," *Review of International Studies* 33 (2007): 11–27.
57. Susanne Baer, "Citizenship in Europe and the Construction of Gender by Law in the European Charter of Fundamental Rights," in *Gender and Human Rights*, ed. K. Knop (Oxford: Oxford University Press, 2004), 83–112; Janet Halley, "Take a Break from Feminism?" in *Gender and Human Rights*, ed. K. Knop (New York: Oxford University Press, 2004), 57–82; Ruth Rubio-Marín and Martha I. Morgan, "Constitutional Domestication of International Gender Norms: Categorizations, Illustrations, and Reflections from the Nearside of the Bridge," in *Gender and Human Rights*, ed. K. Knop (New York: Oxford University Press, 2004), 113–52; and Roberta Guerrina and Marysia Zalewski, "Negotiating Difference/Negotiating Rights: The Challenges and Opportunities of Women's Human Rights," *Review of International Studies* 33 (2007): 5–10.

58. Charlesworth and Chinkin, *Boundaries of International Law*, 231.
59. MacKinnon, *Are Women Human?*
60. Charlesworth and Chinkin, *Boundaries of International Law*, 232.
61. Patricia Viseur Sellers, "Individual(s') Liability for Collective Sexual Violence," in *Gender and Human Rights*, ed. K. Knop (New York: Oxford University Press, 2004), 153–84.
62. MacKinnon, *Are Women Human?*, 23.
63. Ibid.
64. Ibid., 10.
65. Ibid.
66. Ibid., 17.
67. Declaration of Independence, in Lynn Hunt, *Inventing Human Rights: A History* (New York: W. W. Norton & Company, 2007), 15.
68. Ibid., 17.
69. United Nations, UDHR Preamble, 71.
70. Hunt, *Inventing*, 19.
71. Ibid., 28.
72. Ibid.
73. Ibid., 21.
74. Ibid., 27.
75. Ibid., 29.
76. Ibid.
77. Ibid.
78. Collins, "New Directions in Feminism," 304.
79. Laura Stemple, "Human Rights, Sex and Gender: Limits in Theory and Practice," *PACE Law Review* 31, no. 3 (2011): 824.
80. Ibid., 829.
81. Collins, "New Directions in Feminism," 304.
82. Theresa Man Ling Lee, "Feminism, Postmodernism and the Politics of Representation," *Women & Politics* 22, no. 3 (2001): 35.
83. Ibid., 39.
84. Terrell Carver, "Gender/Feminism/IR," *International Studies Review* 5(2) (2003): 289.
85. Steans, "Debating Women's Human Rights," 37.
86. Jean Bethke Elshtain, *Women and War* (Chicago: University of Chicago Press, 1987). Cynthia Enloe, *Bananas, Beaches and Bases: Making Feminist Sense of International Politics* (Berkeley: University of California, 1989); Rebecca Grant and Kathleen Newland, eds., *Gender and International Relations* (Milton Keynes, UK: Open University Press, 1991); V. Spike Peterson, "Security and Sovereign States: What is at Stake in Taking Feminism Seriously?" in *Gendered States: Feminist (Re)Visions of International Relations Theory*, ed. V. S. Peterson (Boulder, CO: Lynne Rienner, 1992), 31–64; V. Spike Peterson, ed., *Gendered States: Feminist (Re)Visions of International Relations Theory* (Boulder, CO: Lynne Rienner, 1992); V. Spike Peterson, "Reframing the Politics of Identity: Democracy, Globalization and Gender," *Political Expressions* 1, no. 1 (1995): 1–16; Ann J. Tickner, *Gender in International Relations* (New York: Columbia University Press, 1992); Jan Jindy Pettman, *Worlding Women: A Feminist International Politics* (London: Routledge, 1996); Christine Sylvester, "'Masculinity', 'Femininity' and 'International Relations': Or Who Goes to the 'Moon' with Bonaparte and the Adder?" in *The "Man" Question in International Relations*, ed. M. Zalewski and J. Parpart (Boulder, CO: Westview Press, 1998), 185–98.
87. Rebecca Grant, "The Quagmire of Gender and International Security," in *Gendered States: Feminist (Re)Visions of International Relations Theory*, ed. V. S. Peterson (Boulder, CO: Lynne Rienner, 1992), 83.

88. V. Spike Peterson, "Transgressing Boundaries: theories of knowledge, gender and International Relations," *Millennium* 21, no. 2 (1992): 46.
89. Enloe, *Bananas, Beaches and Bases.*
90. Ibid., 195.
91. Ibid., 196.
92. Ibid.
93. Carol Cohn, "'Clean Bombs' and Clean Language" in *Women, Militarism and War: Essays in History, Politics and Social Theory*, ed. J. B. Elshtain and S. Tobias (Lanham, MD: Rowman and Littlefield Publishers, 1990), 33, 46, 48.
94. Jan Jindy Pettman, *Worlding Women: A Feminist International Politics* (London: Routledge, 1996), viii.
95. Marysia Zalewski, "Distracted Reflections on the Production, Narration, and Refusal of Feminist Knowledge in International Relations," in *Feminist Methodologies for International Relations*, ed. B.A. Ackerly, M. Stern, and J. True (Cambridge: Cambridge University Press, 2006), 42–61.
96. Marianne H. Marchand and Jane L. Parpart, eds., *Feminism/Postmodernism/Development* (London: Routledge, 1995); Lois Ann Lorentzen and Jennifer Turpin, eds., "Introduction: The Gendered New World Order," in *The Gendered New World Order: Militarism, Development, and the Environment* (New York: Psychology Press, 1996), 1–12; Jenny Edkins, *Poststructuralism & international relations: bringing the political back in* (Boulder, CO: Lynne Rienner, 1999); Jacqui True, "Feminism," in *Theories of International Relations*, ed. S. Burchill et al. (Houndmills, UK: Palgrave, 2001), 231–76.
97. Enloe, *Bananas, Beaches and Bases*; V. Spike Peterson and Jacqui True, "New Times and New Conversations," in *The "Man" Question in International Relations*, ed. M. Zalewski and J. Parpart (Boulder, CO: Westview Press, 1998), 14–27; and Christine Sylvester, "'Masculinity,'" 185–98.
98. V. Spike Peterson and Anne Sisson Runyan, *Global Gender Issues* (Boulder, CO: Westview Press, 1999), 1.
99. Ibid., 8.
100. V. Spike Peterson, "Transgressing Boundaries," 183–206; Ann J. Tickner, "Re-visioning Security," in *International Relations Today*, ed. K. Booth and S. Smith (Cambridge: Polity Press, 1995), 175–97; and Cynthia Weber, "Performative States," *Millennium* 27, no. 1 (1998): 77–95.
101. Jenny Edkins and Véronique Pin-Fat, "Jean Bethke Elshtain: Traversing the Terrain in Between," in *The Future of International Relations*, ed. I.B. Neumann and O. Waever (London: Routledge, 1997), 290–315; Elshtain, *Women and War*; and Marysia Zalewski and Cynthia Enloe, "Questions about Identity in International Relations," in *International Relations Theory Today*, ed. K. Booth and S. Smith (Cambridge: Polity Press, 1995), 279–305.
102. Peterson and Runyan, *Global Gender Issues*, 1.
103. Marysia Zalewski, "The Women/'Women' Question in International Relations," *Millennium* 23, no. 2 (1994): 407–23.
104. Ibid., 409.
105. Marysia Zalewski, "Introduction: From the 'Woman' Questions to the 'Man' Question in International Relations," in *The "Man" Questions in International Relations*, ed. M. Zalewski and J. Parpart (Boulder, CO: Westview Press, 1998), 12; and Zalewski, "Distracted Reflections, 51.
106. Weber, "Performative States," 93.
107. Ibid., 94.
108. Ibid.
109. See, Enloe, *Bananas, Beaches and Bases*; Tickner, *Gender*; Peterson and True, "New Times"; and Tickner, "Re-visioning Security."

110. Myra J. Hird, "Gender's Nature: Intersexuality, Transsexualism and the Sex/ Gender Binary," *Feminist Theory* 1, no. 3 (2000): 348.
111. Judith Butler, *Bodies that Matter: On the Discursive Limits of Sex* (London: Routledge, 1993); and Judith Butler, *Gender Trouble: Feminism and the Subversion of Identity* (London: Routledge, 1999).
112. Butler, *Feminism and Subversion*, 4.
113. Butler, *Gender Trouble*, 5.
114. Ibid., 178.
115. Butler, *Bodies*, 95.
116. Ibid., 94.
117. Butler, *Gender Trouble*, 178.
118. Ibid., 180.
119. Peterson and True, "New Times," 18.
120. Butler, *Gender Trouble*, 178.
121. Zalewski and Enloe, "Questions about Identity," 281.
122. Ibid., 284.
123. Niamh Reilly, *Women's Human Rights: Seeking Gender Justice in a Globalising Age* (Cambridge: Polity Press, 2009), 22.
124. Ibid., 23.
125. Ibid.
126. Ibid., 25.
127. Ibid., 36–37.
128. Ibid., 33.
129. Enloe, in Carol Cohn and Cynthia Enloe, "A Conversation with Cynthia Enloe: Feminists Look at Masculinity and the Men Who Wage War," *Signs* 28, no. 4 (2003): 1192.
130. Terrell Carver, *Gender Is not a Synonym for Women* (London: Lynne Rienner, 1996), 8.
131. Sylvia Walby, *Gender Transformations* (London: Routledge, 1997); Peterson and True "New Times," 15; and Charlotte Hooper, "Masculinist Practices and Gender Politics: The Operation of Multiple Masculinities in International Relations," in *The "Man" Question in International Relations*, ed. M. Zalewski and J. Parpart (Boulder, CO: Westview, 1998), 28–53.

3 Agency and Practice

Liberal, Western notions of human rights assume moral agency as a given. Universal "human," considered the bearer of human rights, is taken for granted as an agent, and as Chapter 2 demonstrated, "human" in universal human rights is assumed to be gender-neutral. This chapter shows that judicial agency assumes moral agency as given, which in turn presupposes universal "human" as agent. I explore at a discursive approach to agency, which sees language as constitutive and therefore locates emancipation within specific contexts that provide the possibility of new meaning. Furthermore, I consider a sociological approach as a way of thinking about agency and practice. The discursive and sociological approaches to agency and practice intersect at the politics of language.

The beliefs people hold about the ontological status of human beings "are highly significant for the manner in which they appropriate, theorize, justify and interpret the concept of human rights."[1] In international politics, human rights is dealt with mainly in terms of the relationship between an individual (a citizen) and the sovereignty of the state.[2] In liberal, Western understandings of universal human rights, the individual (citizen) has a specific historical construction that is written into the international legal mechanisms available to rights advocates. This theoretical understanding of citizenship informs the foundation for international human rights law. Therefore, what one finds is an articulation of the citizen as a legal subject who is constructed as such through his or her relationship with a state.

TAKING MORAL AGENCY AS GIVEN

There is no generally agreed-on understanding of what moral agency means in the international community, but it is clear that the international community is presumed to possess agency.[3] State sovereignty can be defined as a particular form of inclusion and exclusion, which has dramatic consequences for the protection of human rights.[4] Liberal, Western notions of universal "human" take for granted that a bounded political entity (citizen) should have the same rights in both national and international contexts.[5]

Within the international community states police their borders and determine their own membership, which means that membership in said communities is paramount, for nonmembership can have punitive consequences. In other words, those without agency are at risk. For this reason, universalists such as Booth advocate for universal "human" emancipation, which he claims needs "clever and committed human agency."[6] According to Booth, emancipation is the "theory and practice of inventing humanity . . . it is the discourse of human self-creation and the politics of trying to bring it about."[7] In summary, the universal "human" requires agency to become human. The problem is that human rights discourse is nonspecific regarding the agency that can guarantee or implement these rights. What we find then is that "the lower the capacity of the human subject the greater the need for some form of external assistance," yet the incapacity (lack of agency) of the subject makes the delivery of external assistance entirely arbitrary and by no means guaranteed.[8] In other words, if the universal "human" is found to lack sufficient agency, support from the international community will be required. Yet because the universal "human" is conceived as both a citizen of a sovereign state and an international sovereign entity, if this external assistance is not in the interest of the sovereign state to give, there is no safeguard for protecting universal human's rights. It is in this way that judicial agency is sought as a mechanism to secure rights for the universal "human" as the legal subject of international human rights law.

The tensions between state and individual are considered inherent in a focus on agency in human rights. The state provides the individual with citizenship based on the recognition of common humanity, which then entitles that individual to human rights. The expansion of rights both internationally and domestically "is associated with a partial, but significant, shift in the mode of political engagement from democracy, or republicanism, to the principle of the individual as 'agent.' "[9] It is this concept of *individual as agent* that I wish to focus on here. According to Jacobson and Ruffer, the emergence of agency in discussions of human rights is a product of a declining nation-state. Using the issues of citizenship within the European Union (EU) as an example, they explain that international legal mechanisms create the individual as agent who is seen to stand astride national and international boundaries, which means that states are increasingly held accountable for their actions through international human rights norms and rules.[10] Agency here implies the ability of the individual to act as a *self-reliant* actor in the eyes of the law and to be "an active participant in determining his or her life, including the determination of social, political, cultural, ethnic, religious, and economic ends."[11] Moreover, "international human rights law has relocated the individual, as opposed to states, as the object of the law," thus attributing sovereignty to the "human" as the legal subject as opposed to states.[12] The problem for human rights practitioners is that "agency is embedded in this dense legal web, and the institutions that arbitrate this legal framework—the judiciary and other administrative mechanisms—grow in significance as a result."[13]

In other words, judicial agency functions as a somewhat self-fulfilling prophecy; legal mechanisms create the individual as agent who is capable of holding states accountable—via international law—for their actions, yet this legal framework requires the participation of states in order to function. Therefore, what is at stake in discussions of judicial agency is the presumption that the law reflects these implicit or explicit philosophical beliefs that grant the individual power to shape their own circumstances.

Making a link between moral agency and the legal subject, Norman Lewis highlights that "the foundation of the legal subject is logically prior to its expression in law."[14] By this he means that legal doctrine relies on a notion of moral agent, or rights-bearing subject, which exists in theory before being encoded in practice. However, he stipulates that the legal subject is constructed prior to its expression in law, meaning that the subject of any law is the impetus for the making of the law.[15] In human rights terms, he says, this is historically accurate. The Universal Declaration of Human Rights (UDHR) was drafted in the wake of the Nazi holocaust as a measure to ensure that such unspeakable acts were never to be permitted again. Lewis states that human rights were legally rendered value with the signing of the UDHR in 1948.[16] The inhuman acts of genocide that occurred during the Nazi holocaust motivated the need for a legal document that provided rights based on the recognition of common humanity. Thus, for Lewis, the universal "human" as rights-bearing individual became the legal subject of international human rights law. Lewis makes it clear that moral agency also preempts the writing of international law. The liberal, Western notion of the legal subject assumes moral agency. Consequently,

the central component of all modern law and its starting point is the legal subject or person. The person is assumed to be a moral agent or a self-willing actor. As a rights-bearing subject, the person of modern law is not simply coerced by a legal system that is outside of his or her influence. Rather the law is said to derive from his or her own will.[17]

It is a gross assumption that all human beings are awarded the status of moral agent and self-willing actor. Part of the problem is that this assumption of universal moral agency inherent in judicial agency stems from the exclusionary context in which the making of international human rights laws takes place. However, the more crucial aspect for this discussion is how the relationship between "human" subjectivity and agency is understood.

A DISCURSIVE APPROACH

To understand the relationship between "human" subjectivity and agency, let us consider the following: if the concept of human rights is distinct from both moral and legal rights it lends itself to what Marx termed reification, linked to the process of depersonalization and alienation, which Marx claims is induced by capitalism. For Marx, depersonalization means representing a human being as a physical thing deprived of personal qualities and alienated from vital social relationships.[18] The same criticism can be applied to human rights discourse, in which the universal "human" at the center of human rights is a being lacking subjectivity. Furthermore, whatever content human rights is attributed (universal "human," for instance), the tendency is to fix the meaning as if it corresponds to a fixed "reality." The premise of this conception is the desire to represent the *real* as a static phenomenon. Critics of the liberal, Western, universalist view of international human rights mechanisms argue that this desire to fix reality with objects frequently fails to take the reasons for human rights seriously.[19] In other words, international human rights mechanisms treat "human" as a hollow shell (a body) that is filled with a set list of moral characteristics and legal rights through the practice of international law. As an alternative to this process of filling, "agency-based reasons are the most compelling reasons for human rights" because simply making customary lists of human rights—such as international law is inclined to do—falls short of providing a concept of human rights that can protect "human" life.[20] What this means is that "a human right is clearly not an end in itself, and it is not usually a sufficient condition for the set of ends it is designed to help achieve."[21] To clarify, no list of rights can ever be comprehensive enough to accommodate all social, economic, political or civil phenomena. Instead, the importance of human rights "lies rather in its being thought a necessary condition for a set of ends, including the most abstract 'end' of living one's life in a way that is worthy of a human being."[22] Human beings are, among other things, agent-beings with the desire and capacity to act instead of merely being acted on. To be more precise, as human beings "we comprehend our experiences in terms of agency, without which our whole moral and political life as we know it, made possible by such concepts as right and wrong, responsibility, sovereignty, moral worth and guilt, resentment, indignation, and so on, would simply collapse."[23]

Agency then is a twofold concept, which consists of the attribution of power and the formation and maintenance of subjectivity.[24] What is at stake in power is subjectivity, because a self is not a given, it is formed by, and in, processes and experiences of power. It is "only through willing and acting that a self is able to emerge."[25] Hence, agency is relational between power and subjectivity in that it is through agency that the self (subject) is articulated and appreciated, while at the same time agency determines the subject's relationship to power. This is a nuanced role; agency is "not a brute fact of human existence, something we can empirically prove, but an interpretation of human experience,"[26] a practice if you will. Discussions of "human" subjectivity within universal constructions of human rights have overlooked the importance of agency because the liberal, Western notion of universal "human" takes it for granted. However, for those whose subjectivity is considered less than human, agency becomes vital to a quest for recognition, respect and dignity.

Women's Agency?

A significant proportion of feminist scholarship on women's agency in human rights attacks universal human rights discourse for consistently positioning women as victims of abuse.[27] Male dominance and power mean that men are constructed as the most active agents (perpetrators) of violence.[28] This typecasting of the heterosexual male as the perpetrator results in women being treated as the victim of such violence and, as such, reduces their agency. Women are not abstract; they are not wholly sex or gender but, instead, are marked, defined and controlled by it.[29] Reducing women (social identity) to sex (biological identity) is one of the root causes for the persistent victimization of women in human rights discourse. Abuse has been mistaken for agency, and instead of seeing the abuse women suffer as punishable, universal human rights discourse, in maintaining women as victims, serves to remind women that they are less than "human" by telling them they still have human rights.[30] In the exclusionary language of international human rights, women are assumed to be "human" because they have suffered a human rights abuse—abuse that occurs because one is "human." However, this does little more than remind women of their exclusion as legitimate subjects of "human" rights. For feminists, agency is seen as empowerment; hence, they find it a contradiction in terms to conflate abuse and agency because the very notion of a victim is to be without agency. Consequently, what makes agency problematic from a gendered interpretation is that, in practice, the fallacy of empowerment serves little more than to produce women as victims.

In the exclusionary language of universal human rights, victims are thought to be without power and without agency. Women's agency as victims is also present when feminists give the public/private divide as reasons for women's marginalization. On one level, "the classification of particular activities as public or private has been erroneous, because the classification depends on the gender of the actor rather than the nature of the activity."[31] Herein lies the key to understanding how women are reduced to victims; it is because women are gendered but the violence enacted on them is not. Agency is attributed to the perpetrator who is conceived of as a gendered actor (typically understood as masculine). The victim, made such by being abused, is also gendered. However, the activity, the act, the human rights abuse, is not gendered. What occurs then when we look for gender in discussions of agency and human rights is that we find women reduced to sexualized victims and we find gendered actors committing un-gendered violence. Agency, the vital component for securing women the status of "human," is limited for certain gendered identities based on their absence from the discourse of universal "human" in human rights. Women are not "constructed as agents/subjects/persons in their own right."[32] Instead, women are "subject to objectification and abuse."[33] The exclusionary language of international human rights law perpetuates women as less than "human" by "normalizing heterosexism," which privileges male/masculinity over female/femininity, hence making women subordinate (less than "human") to men.[34] Rendering women subordinate to men creates a victim subjectivity, which is denied power because such subjectivities are not recognized as "human" and are thus without agency in human rights. The significance of this is that it creates a common misconception among feminist challenges to the assumed moral agency of universal "human," because it assumes that "without a visible victim, there is no crime, and without a crime there is no perpetrator."[35] Actually, women as victims are highly visible in international human rights discourse, and so are the perpetrators of such abuses. What is lacking is a gendered notion of the violence (crimes) that occurs so that women can overcome this victim subjectivity, and instead begin to exercise their rights as empowered agents—as fully "human" in human rights.

Questions of gender and agency are vital to understanding how "human" is socially constructed in global politics. Discussions of living and being in the world as fully "human" can only be achieved when the exclusionary language of universal human rights is exposed and care is taken to include all people as agents. The exclusion from "human" in human rights has punitive consequences in the practice of exercising human rights. Without it, recognition is next to impossible. As feminists have demonstrated, without recognition, there is little one can do to empower oneself or others. So it matters, for practice, what language is used to express those inalienable rights bestowed on all of humanity. I will now look closely at the constitutive elements of language and at how this has an impact on the possibility of agency in a human rights context.

Another way of looking at the process of rendering particular subjects powerless within international human rights discourse is to explore how language is constitutive and thus is a source of exclusion, for instance, how the meaning of "human" is influenced by meanings of gender. This analysis looks at how exclusionary language limits, polices, maintains and reproduces particular meanings of gender and "human." Feminist critiques have revealed that the "reality" represented is only the "reality" of a select few and that the majority of people are left out of this interpretation. Attempts to represent the *real* are particular interpretations that follow an epistemological commitment to a form of knowing that holds that the question, "What is x?" (e.g., What is gender?) can be answered by referencing a fixed object that represents the *super-order* between *super-concepts*. In effect, it is the notion that the essence or essential features of an object or a subject can be apprehended such that (1) they act as a foundation of reality, (2) they can act as the bearer of meaning and, finally, (3) therefore, they can be represented as a true reflection of how reality is ordered independently of human interpretation or discursive practices.[36] Such interpretations allude to the attractiveness of a form of knowledge that requires that we dig beneath the surface of language for our answers. However, it remains impossible to accurately represent someone or something completely because the very notion of representation implies interpretation, and interpretation is a discursive act, thus overturning the likelihood of a purely objective stance. Given such distinctions then, universal discourses are inherently flawed because they adopt the view that what is being represented is a true reflection of reality. This is how discourses are constitutive; they construct, through language, what shall count as reality.

For Wittgenstein, "the meaning of a word is its use in the language."[37] Pin-Fat clarifies: "this claim summons context as the provider of meaning and not any reference to a particular object."[38] Therefore, "the meaning of a word is not the object to which it refers but rather the role the word plays in a chain of signifiers (the language game)."[39] Within the discourses of international politics and international law, for instance, "woman" refers to the object adult female body. The problem here is that these discourses, because of their search for truth through accurate representation of world politics, construct meaning in word–object formats, instead of word–word articulations. In this case, "woman" is considered to be in relation to the object "female body," hence the dissatisfaction expressed in feminist discourse analysis concerning the representation, misrepresentation and lack of representation of women seen in the previous chapter. In contrast, relating "woman" to "female body" in a word–word articulation does not fix the meaning of woman to a corporeal referent object (body) but, instead, leaves both terms open to a myriad of meanings by privileging context. To determine which meaning of a given word is being used one must explore how it is utilized—what role it plays in the language game (discourse).

It is important to distinguish between *context* and *discourse* here. Discourse refers to the rules of the language game, meaning that discourse determines the possibility and impossibility of possible meanings within a given context. Discourse is that which attempts to fix meaning, while context always remains fluid. Context cannot be predicted because context is concerned with word–word relations, not word–object relations.[40] Consequently, focusing on context requires understanding word–word relations. This is more fluid because each word is not tied to a particular object or represents "how things must be." In short, we might say that the word *context* itself must be understood as a word–word relation and not as fixed by referring to particular sets of practices in reality.

However, in exclusionary discourses, such as universal human rights, context is understood through a representational logic that assumes the word–object relation as a given. The result is a desire for an embodied subject because it is assumed to be more real. In this construction, woman can only mean "female body" as the physical object referred to by the word *woman*. Because of the representational logic, "gender" can *only* mean "sex" because sex acts as the referent object. Not only does this logic make no distinction between the two terms (because it cannot); it privileges the latter because of its status as the object to be represented as the bearer of meaning. Thus, embodiment reflects a word–object relation (woman–female body), which in turn fixes meaning in the discourse. Therefore, when the term *woman* is invoked in international law, the axiomatic process of representational logic can only produce the meaning "female body" as a referent, despite any efforts to do otherwise. What exclusionary discourses do, through a desire for embodiment, is reflect the desire for fixing meaning. However, Pin-Fat's work shows us that the possibility of fixing meaning by anchoring it to reality is only a fallacy and that representational logics are fundamentally flawed because they insist on objective explanations of the world. Hence, a more appropriate approach to understanding gender, agency and human rights is to focus on context as the discursive production of meaning (reality), while accounting for discursive attempts at fixing it.

Pin-Fat's concept of *(im)possibility* is one such approach that resists representational logic by emphasizing the importance of understanding word–word relations. As she puts it, "what counts as possible depends upon what is already tacitly accepted as impossible."[41] With regard to gender, she and Maria Stern argue that

> representations of, for example, 'masculinity' and 'femininity' can never be complete. Full representation is never possible because the inside/possible must always rely on the outside/impossible for its constitution and vice versa. This means that what 'masculinity' and 'femininity' means will always include, by exclusion, its opposite and therefore, a clear demarcation between 'masculinity' and 'femininity' cannot be successfully maintained.[42]

In this way, they are working against those discursive desires, for fixed, referential understandings of women, men and "human" in international politics. Representing the possibility of such an object ("man," "woman," "human") for particular discourses is important because it provides "an epistemological claim such that its truth or falsity is established by the existence or non-existence of the referent object."[43] In other words, the term *man* originates from the phenomenon of "male body," and as such, given the physical differences observed through the advent of the medical sciences, "female body" comes to be known (in opposition) as "woman." Furthermore, "human" also has "male body" as its original referent, because those white male intellectuals who philosophized about ontological questions concerning who we are used themselves as subjects of analysis and generalized the rest of humanity in their own image or in opposition to their own image—such as women, savages and slaves.[44] Pin-Fat claims that universalizing is in this way empty because the meaning of "human" "cannot be filled (made full) by reference to an object since the word-object relation is not the locus of meaning but word-word relations."[45] In this sense, both "woman" and "human" are empty signifiers.[46] This emptiness remains unacknowledged in exclusionary discourses because of the desire for embodiment. Consequently, the terms *woman* and *human* are both produced in reference to specific physical states of being.

Exclusionary discourses rely on representational logics that find it possible to accurately represent the subject through embodiment. In human rights discourse, gender is frequently conflated with sex. Gender is mistaken to mean *women only* and as the previous discussion has shown, the meaning of "women" is produced in relation to the object "female body." Simply put, gender comes to mean sex. Further, the human subject of both fields is assumed to be male and therefore masculine. When the term *gender* is invoked, it is done so to recall those who do not fit the narrow meaning of man (male body), those who remain left out of the initial conception, most prominently females and femininity. As a result, these "other" identities have been clawing their way in despite such processes of exclusion. Feminists claim that the "other" has always been a part of international politics but has never occupied center stage. Through various invocations, feminists have begun to transform these exclusionary landscapes to include those who have been overlooked, invisible and left out.

Embodied Agency

To recognize another's common humanity is "an act whose meaning is subject to context and therefore, differentiation."[47] Context constitutes how the meaning of "humanity" is understood. I argue this is how agency relates to context. Through recognition that the presence of what is considered impossible will always be an aspect of the possible, context creates possibilities for agency. This means that "the absence or exclusion of particularities such as gender, race, and sexuality can never be wholly successful because they play a constitutive role as the 'outside' against which one can define the 'inside.'"[48] Therefore, to recognize what constitutes "humanity" or "human" requires a more nuanced understanding than just what is "not human" or "less than human." Within language exists an infinite amount of potential meanings for any given word–word relationship. However, certain contexts are formulated with specific ontological assumptions that close down the scope of meaning by resorting to word–object formulations. In exclusionary discourses, the potential for agency is understood in word–object terms. The implication here is that the word *agency* must relate to an object, referred to as agent, who expresses agency in physical form. This adherence to word–object relations is produced from the desire for truthful representations of reality. Again we find that exclusionary discourse mobilizes representational logics to explain the phenomenon called *agency*.

When gender is reduced to sex it limits empowerment because it does not provide for a variety of actors; it comes to only mean male and female bodies, not socially constructed performances of masculinity and femininity.

Feminist discourse analysis identifies empowerment as the expression of a form of agency most sought after to improve the position of women in world politics. Rooted in the public/private debate, feminists mobilize the term *empowerment* to distinguish between public agency, associated with the state and the concept of having power over an individual, versus private agency, associated instead with the individual and the concept of an individual having the power to act in their own best interest.[49] Private agency is empowerment and recalls the feminist motto—the personal is political— in that one does not have to be incorporated in the public sphere to have agency. By way of invoking empowerment, feminist theorists sought to reveal the perception of absence as being another form of presence; "conventional analyses stop short of investigating an entire area of international politics, an area that women have pioneered in exploring: how states depend on particular constructions of the domestic and private spheres."[50] Even though historically relegated to the private sphere, women are still powerful actors within states because they do the invisible work that enables the men to function as soldiers, heads of state, and so on. Conventional analysis of international politics has discursively ignored the labor of women; however, in practice, it relies heavily on the presence of particular constructions of women to maintain the state. In this way the private agency of these particular constructions of women has an impact directly on the potential for public agency, understood as state power.

This absence of feminine gender identities shows that men are considered active agents in international politics because of their assumed presence, while women are denied agency because of their assumed absence. Historically, the public sphere was considered the place of politics and privileged men as the agents most active. Further, agency, when articulated in the public sphere, failed to acknowledge the actions of women as political. Since the 1990s, discourse feminists have rejected the public/private distinction and maintained that gender identities are made present through embodied subjectivities. Jabri explains this view in terms of discursive space, which she says continually reproduces outcomes of human action and interaction.[51] An identity articulated in this discursive space, is what she calls the *textualized self*, which is "immediately and by definition immersed within a public space," acknowledging the existence of the "other," the reader "as distinct moral, judgmental entity."[52] For Jabri,

> [t]he textualized self as self asserts agency through textual participation within a public space and comes into being, is constituted, through the existence of a reader, and the interpretive capacity of both is mutually constituted. The interaction of author and reader is mediated through the text and it is the text which confers expressional agency to both.[53]

When applied to international politics, the discursive self remains unproblematized because the historical structures of domination and exploitation perpetuated Western man as the dominant subject of modernity. Moreover, Jabri highlights the epistemological and ontological certainties that have historically excluded the voices of women and denied agency to women as the so-called other.[54] Therefore, women's agency is discursively constituted between the reader and through the presence of gendered subjectivities (textualized selves) in the language of international politics. However, because the language of international human rights assumes gender-neutrality, and the textualized self is constructed by the text, then the textualized self is constituted as an embodied gendered subjectivity. This draws attention to another dilemma: to be read as subject in the language of international politics and international human rights, one needs agency, but empowered gendered subjects are expressed as embodied in the exclusionary discourses, which removes agency by reducing "the self" from subject to object.

I show this by looking at how judicial accounts of agency remain fixed within the exclusionary discourse of international law. What is needed for gendered accounts of agency in human rights discourse is an acknowledgement of how discourses attempt to fix context, such that agency engages relationally with subjectivity and power, providing moments of social practice that disrupt exclusionary discourses, thus leaving room for an empowered "human" in human rights.

Within discursive analysis, the representational logic of exclusionary discourses reduces agency to a form of objectification because of its assumption of the word–object relation. Similarly, here I consider how concepts of judicial agency fail to escape the same representational logic, albeit for different reasons, to the detriment of an effective understanding of agency. Posing the question, "How has the proliferation of legal forms and mechanisms shifted or altered the nature and location of political engagement?" Jacobson and Ruffer claim this brings agency to the fore. They argue that legal activities are of interest because they "reveal the extent of agency as well as how the law is facilitating that agency."[55] In other words, Jacobson and Ruffer look at how international law functions as a discourse and at the impact this has on agency. Judicial agency is embedded in a dense legal web and "the institutions that arbitrate this legal framework—the judiciary and other administrative mechanisms—grow in significance as a result."[56] This growth of judicial agency, Jacobson and Ruffer observe, enables different forms of cultural expression, which the courts facilitate. Moreover, accountability is transferred to the legal realm with the individual as agent; states are held accountable for human rights through the acts of individuals.[57] Jacobson and Ruffer warn that judicial agency—when individuals invoke legal mechanisms to claim their rights—puts a strain on executive and legislative power because individuals increasingly possess the capacity to assert their rights by accessing laws outside of the national legal structure.[58] International human rights law, they claim, has relocated the individual, as opposed to states, as the object of the law.[59]

In sum, for Jacobson and Ruffer, international human rights law constitutes the individual as agent, and this agent becomes the *object* of the law. However, they accept international human rights law as an unproblematic discourse, therefore leaving unchallenged the exclusionary meaning of agent as object. Feminists have demonstrated that the legal subject in most international law is produced as meaning "man" and therefore refers to "male body." The assumption that the legal subject is male perpetuates the interpretation of "human" in human rights as also "male." Human beings comprehend their experiences in terms of agency.[60] Therefore, it seems that only "male bodies" can have judicial agency, denying "female bodies" legal mechanisms for self-expression. Moreover, in failing to challenge the exclusive construction of international human rights law, Jacobson and Ruffer force a discursive interpretation of individual agent to word–object relation, further fixing individual agent to the object "male body." Jacobson and Ruffer see agents of judicial agency as objects, not as subjects.

The loss of agency is a symptom of exclusionary discourses because the process of meaning production is restricted to word–object relations. These discourses create, maintain and reproduce assumptions that confine gender to sex, that turn subjects into objects and that lack agency. These assumptions remain hidden in the mainstream analysis of international politics and international law. As a result, only the privileged few qualify as a subject within these discourses. Agency in these discourses is lost because the meaning of "human," "woman" and "man" is fixed.

Agency as an Interface

As an alternative to the concepts of agency previously discussed, I introduce the notion of agency as fluid space between power and subjectivity in which the articulation and the appreciation for the subject occur through agency.[61] This means that the formation and the maintenance of subjectivity are understood relationally to the attributions of power through agency. In this case, subjectivity implies that "the formation and maintenance of a self and a sense of self," while power is understood as a causal efficacy and responsibility.[62] Subjectivity is formed by, and in the processes of, experiences of power; thus, it is "only through willing and acting that a self is able to emerge."[63] Hence, "agency is a twofold concept, consisting of the attribution of power and the formation and maintenance of subjectivity."[64] In summary, subjectivity and power are in constant relation to one another via agency as an interface.

Agency, understood discursively, is helpful because it allows the process of meaning production to be exposed. When the processes of meaning production are exposed, it becomes possible to reveal how the loss of agency occurs in particular contexts and thus to develop strategies that work against such limiting processes. For a subject to demonstrate power, he or she must have agency, while for power to be available to a particular subjectivity, there must be agency. This is in contrast to the previous versions of agency discussed, which seek embodied agents to enact power, because here agency is a fluid space, not a fixed state that can be definitively occupied. In this configuration, agency is always possible because meaning can never be fixed; it is constantly being negotiated between the interplay of subjectivity and power. However, it is context, and with it discourse, that determines how the relation between subjectivity, agency and power will be interpreted. Therefore, if the discourse is exclusive, then subjectivity, agency and power will relate in word–object relations, fixing meaning to single referents. Ci follows Nietzsche in arguing that agency is constructed around a word–word relation and, as such, does not require embodiment to acquire meaning: "agency is not a brute fact of human existence, something we can empirically prove, but an interpretation of human experience."[65] From this view one must be critical of discourses, such as human rights, that universalize subjectivity because "it is the powerful who are in the habit of speaking, and are able to speak, in universalistic terms, as if their condition of life were true of all humanity."[66] This disarms universalized subjectivity because it adheres to representational logic by making claims that a particular expression of conditions of life is representative of all humanity. This framework resists temptations to equate agency with the absence of direct coercion—a subject has agency if no power is being acted upon them—and instead provides agency as fluid space that acknowledges power relations as constituting subjectivity and subjectivity as constituting power relations.

This book investigates how the gendered identities "human," "woman" and "Indian" are constructed as subjects. In various contexts these identities have different potential meanings. Understanding agency as an interface is useful because for these gender identities to be meaningful, they require power, and power is acquired by activating agency. Much work has been done on subjectivity and power as separate spheres; however, little has been done on how the two relate to each other. A feminist discursive approach uses the notion of agency as an interface to analyze the impact of exclusive contexts on the subjectivity of "human." The following incorporates relational agency in discussion of embodiment and discourse by developing the claims that "human" is a gendered identity.

To explore how once the "human" in human rights is seen as a fluid, gendered identity, there is potential for agency; we need to look at the relationship between gender and agency as contextual. As shown, human rights and international law are exclusionary discourses that use embodiment to fix the meaning of gender and agency to an object. However, from a discursive approach, if the need for material embodiment is lifted by understanding language as constitutive, then the body is constituted only through language. In other words, how the body is interpreted in a given context expresses the meaning of bodily acts taking place at any given moment. These bodily acts can be understood as the act of living. The verb *living* signifies a fluid state, in that when a body is living it engages in performances of gender through nonexclusive discursive practices, which in turn empowers it as a subject. In a human rights context, being considered a living human being is a point of contention. As Chapters 5 and 6 demonstrate, for certain people, empowerment is unattainable because they remain unintelligible "humans" within human rights discourse. Exposing this loss of agency is a key aspect of feminist discourse analysis.

It follows then that because language emerges from the body, the body "carries its own signifiers, in ways that remain largely unconscious."[67] Performance (uninhibited gender practices) incorporates speech acts and bodily acts in a complicated relationship. Bodily life can never be fully represented "even as it works as the condition and activating condition of language."[68] So, from a discursive feminist approach, embodiment must also be constituted through language. Embodiment in this sense is contextual. Bodies have physical forms only when their constitutive discourse provides for it. For instance, the gender identity of the drag queen cannot be embodied as male when femininity is confined to female bodies.

Thus, a feminist discursive approach suggests the moving, talking, acting, and being of bodies is a constantly negotiated position within the language game that invents and reinvents what meanings are available to interlocutors in any given context. Performance challenges the very notions of essential sex by arguing that categories such as "woman" and "man" are "not explained through reference to an origin, but the origin is understood to be as performative as the copy."[69] Put discursively, performative gender occurs when gender is expressed in word–word relations—when gender is understood to have multiple referents, not just "female" and "male" bodies. Thus, performance equalizes dominant and nondominant gender norms. However, "some of those performative accomplishments claim the place of nature or claim the place of symbolic necessity, and they do this only by occluding the ways in which they are performatively established."[70] If gender is expressed in an exclusionary context, it will preclude gender being understood as performative. For gender performance to produce multiple meanings, context must be fluid.

The pervasiveness of exclusionary discourses is an example of what Butler considers cases in which performance claims the place of nature. Exclusionary discourses shut down creativity through an embodiment that fixes meaning. When creativity is closed off, then performative gender, and with it the potential of agency, is also lost. Contextual creativity is needed to allow gender identities to perform with, on and through bodies in meaningful ways. Therefore, performance is not simply a method of producing new experiences of gender, it is a way of finding valued expressions of gender that reflect the complexity of people's lives within a discourse, such as law, psychiatry and social and literary theory, that otherwise has sought to deny their legitimacy.[71]

When subjectivity is performative, then power, through agency, is always available to said subjectivity, because subjectivity is produced through processes of power while power is expressed through subjectivity. Gender norms are impossible to embody.[72] And, as I have demonstrated, gender norms are prolific in exclusionary discourses. Feminist discourse analysis suggests that an ontological desire for embodiment as proof of *being* is counterintuitive to a desire for agency because embodiment fixes meaning through representational logics, and thus, agency is lost.

In order to overturn gender conflation and conceive of gender as performative, one needs to resist interpretations of *being* as *knowing* and to work toward discursive interpretations that increase what becomes possible by resisting the desire to represent the real. The concept of agency at work in performative gender is

> centrally concerned with the question of survival, of how to create a world in which those who understand their gender and their desire to be nonnormative can live and thrive not only without the threat of violence from the outside but without the pervasive sense of their own reality, which can lead to suicide or a suicidal life.[73]

Agency then becomes possible through releasing the category "woman" from a fixed referent. People who live unrecognized lives because their subjectivity is not valued within their context spend their whole life searching for recognition. When recognition (or meaning) is denied, then there is a risk that such individuals will turn this rejection inward on themselves. In the worst scenarios, these individuals will take their own life. In this way, "human" is a gendered identity, and gender humanizes bodies within a given context. Fighting for recognition as "human" is as much a battle for gender recognition as it is for race, ethnicity, religion and so on. International human rights discourse is an exclusionary discourse in which the meaning of "human" is at most a "male" or a "female" body. This approach argues that a desire for embodiment is unhelpful at providing for the possibility of agency. As an alternative, it suggests that active articulations of "human" in human rights discourse become possible when context is gendered. The following section fleshes out this alternative as a progression from human being to *being human*.

The Role of Power in Subjectivity

To release "human," "woman" and "man" from the bonds of exclusionary discourse and to write them as *human, woman* and *man*, we need to consider the role of power in the construction of subjectivity. A feminist discursive approach argues that power and subjectivity relate to one another via agency. What is of most concern is the relationship between recognition as human and the promise of respect and dignity that should accompany this recognition. If recognition is a site of power, then agency enables a subject to be recognized in a given context. For a subject to be recognized, it must first be understood as present in the discourse: "To find that one is fundamentally unintelligible (indeed, that laws of culture and language find one to be an impossibility) is to find that one has not yet achieved access to human."[74] A first step toward understanding these processes of fixing is to problematize the term *human being*.

Much of the work in human rights takes its concept of "human" from the UDHR, which in turn is taken from liberal, Western philosophy. Given the context, and the effect of fixing meaning described earlier, "human being" is limited to prescribed notions of gender as sex and of agency as embodied. However, if one disrupts such contexts and interprets agency as an interface between subjectivity and power, then "human" enters into the language of human rights in a meaningful way. Performative gender provides fluid subjectivity that, through agency, can be powerful. A gendered identity with agency, it is suggested, can be delineated from the "human being" without agency through a reversal of word order to signify the importance of agency to understanding meanings of "human." For that reason, *being human* articulates "human" as an empowered gendered identity in international politics. "Human" when followed by "being" sees agency as an afterthought, as something material used to facilitate embodiment. Whereas if the context-limiting agency is disrupted, the articulation *being human* could come to mean where agency becomes the mechanism through which gendered subjectivities relate to power and provide a meaningful expression of *human* in human rights discourse specifically, and international politics generally. Then the meanings of these terms are fluid within the context and therefore are unquestioningly gendered. When these terms are gendered, they have agency and thus are powerful because they have meaning to those whose subjectivity they describe. In this case, agency becomes a crucial site of analysis in human rights because it connects meaning with power and the processes of production.

CRITICAL ALTERNATIVES TO FEMINIST DISCOURSE ANALYSIS

McNay's Critique

Lois McNay, herself a feminist, is critical of the discursive approach to agency and embodiment because, as she claims, it offers limited considerations of practice. In her book *Gender and Agency* (2000), McNay asks where the material bodies are in discourse. As a qualifier to discourse analysis, she is interested in the real world that discourse does not explain. McNay demonstrates how embodied gendered subjects can have agency by maintaining that social practices in part influence discourse, thus resisting an ontology that sees discourse as constitutive of all social practice.[75] Her book is historically driven and asks what past phenomena allowed women to be autonomous actors despite constricting social sanctions and how could this be ensured to continue in the future. McNay looks for substantive accounts of agency, which evade materialistic determinism (the notion that only physical things truly exist) but without narrowing processes of *subjectification* to purely linguistic constructions. Subjectification, as McNay uses it, is a process through which individuals are rendered governable, made subjects of particular forms of rule. In her view, different forms of power are used and different rationalities inculcated.

For McNay, substantive accounts of agency require an embodied subject, a *subjecthood*, while at the same time she does not wish to limit gender to sex by making woman the subject of feminism. In her description of gendered agency as a process of meaning production, McNay explains embodiment as a twofold concept. Embodiment is the move from object to subject—the linguistic process of subjectification—and it is the physical representation of identity—the materialistic process of subjectification. McNay achieves her substantive account of agency by generating a subject that is both linguistically and materialistically embodied: "embodiment expresses a moment of indeterminacy whereby the embodied subject is constituted through dominant norms but is not reducible to them."[76] Social practices must be accounted for, says McNay; thus, gendered identities negotiate agency through both material and linguistic transactions of embodiment. In other words, bodies exist both conceptually in language and physically in the world.

McNay would oppose the strong version of discursive analysis on the basis that she sees the position of language as constitutive too narrow. However, the impetus behind discourse, the language game, does have resonance for McNay because she also is interested in how social practices produce meaning. Nevertheless, McNay's stipulation that there be a (substantive) material reality in accounts of agency is problematic for discursive feminists. They would argue that her attempts at forging gendered agency are undermined by her adherence to a representational logic, which claims it is possible to represent a physical reality for a subject. From their perspective, this would leave in place the desire for an embodied subject that does not resist word–object relations but, instead, perpetuates them, such that gender is limited to articulations of sex and agency is lost. In sum, feminist discourse analyses would say that McNay reveals that expressions of gendered agency occurring in exclusionary discourses, such as international politics and international law, produce embodied subjects as single-referent objects. However, McNay makes a vital point about embodiment; she links it with practice. The discursive approach only takes us so far, as I explain in the following section. What is also crucial in exercising human rights is that activism produces a culture of human rights in international politics that does effect real political change.

A feminist discursive approach is valuable because discourse is what people use to exercise their human rights. We should, therefore, analyze both discourse and practice. Taking McNay's criticism seriously requires looking into a sociological approach to agency and practice. This presents another theory of embodiment, in which it is part of the habitus, which in turn influences how gender and agency are practiced in the field.

A SOCIOLOGICAL APPROACH

One way of seeing the purpose of human rights is to see it as a way of regulating behavior between human beings as members of humanity. With this comes a condition that people will be *obedient* to human rights conventions. The continued violations of human rights suggest that there is a problem with this condition of obedience. Bourdieu's oeuvre was to seek a way of understanding how behavior is regulated without being the product of "rational" obedience to rules. As we have seen in the first two chapters, universalist interpretations of human rights seem to violate the very rules they seek to protect because they leave certain people out. But this internal paradox of universalist human rights does not accurately reflect the practice of human rights. Looking to Bourdieu, we can see how practice can be understood in a way that accounts for universalist ideals as well as providing an understanding of how these ideals play out in very specific arenas. I am not advocating a return to the universalist/cultural relativist debate, because that debate polarizes the individual bearer of rights, who is seen to be autonomous from society and therefore open to mistreatment from a contextualized, culturally fixed rights-bearer, whose violations are only ever relative to his or her own situation. Instead, I am suggesting that if we consider Bourdieu's concept of social *practice*, one is enabled to recognize the place of "universal human" in societies. There are three key elements to Bourdieu's concept of *practice*: habitus, capital and field. I briefly engage with each in the following.

In the discourse of human rights *universal human* is a label that is applied to more complex socialized beings, with the hope of homogenizing certain aspects of the human character and with the aim of providing and defending the respect of fair treatment of human beings, from one to another. Individuals act in relation to one another, embedded within society, meaning that interpretations are generated between individuals, but interpretive practices can be unreflective. Sociological approaches to practice take us beyond patterns of symbolic interpretation. Here, the production of meaning is part of our embodied experience within society. The "socialized body (which one calls the individual or person) does not stand in opposition to society; it is one of its forms of existence."[77] This way of conceiving of a person does not oppose the individual and society as two separate sorts of being, one external to the other, but, instead, constructs them relationally as if they were two dimensions of the same social reality. It also indicates an important difference in the notion of embodiment than that found in discourse analysis. For Bourdieu, embodiment is expressed through *habitus*, the link between social structures and how people navigate strategically through them. Habitus is a practical rather than discursive theory of action; it is a "set of deeply internalized master dispositions that generate action" by stressing the "bodily as well as cognitive basis of action and emphasizing inventive as well as habituated forms of action."[78] Habitus results from "early socialization experiences in which external structures are internalized."[79] As a result, habitus is composed of a series of internalized, unconscious dispositions through which individuals experience the parameters of their social world, which sets what they think is possible or unlikely for their social group in a stratified society. This means that "on the one hand, habitus sets structural limits for action. On the other hand, habitus generates perceptions, aspirations, and practices that correspond to the structuring properties of earlier socialization."[80] In other words, people learn about their role in society from their experience of growing up in it. But this is embodied in their very way of being in the world, from mental structures through to bodily gestures and habits. People learn and embody all the possibilities open to them, while at the same time often being unaware of the constraints on them. People then reinforce those social structures by the way they live their lives in practice. Whereas the discursive logic outlined earlier emphasizes agency, the sociological perspective emphasizes the structuring power of habitus.

Habitus is created by social interaction and responds to it, such that societies are the result of countless interactions, each of which invokes a *relation* between individuals. This complex of relations is what Bourdieu terms a *field*. Fields are structured spaces organized around particular types of capital or combinations of capital. There are as many fields as there are forms of capital, which means that fields are arenas of struggle for legitimation. One's place in the field is established by the unequal distribution of relevant capitals rather than by the personal attributes of their occupants.[81] Thus, fields impose on actors specific forms of struggle, which are tacitly accepted as worthy of pursuit. Actors may challenge the legitimacy of the rewards given by the field, but even so, they reproduce the structure of fields in doing so.[82] These struggles are carried out over symbolic as well as material resources. Cultural resources are an example of symbolic capital. Our relation through social structures is measured through symbolic capital, which is attributed through culture. For instance, if habitus is where our human subjectivity is created or denied, then capital, in a human rights context, refers to the amount of recognizable power with regard to others one can have in any given discourse. The human rights culture is concerned with how to normalize human rights protection. This is done through cultural politics that seeks to win the hearts and minds of the global public. Nash argues that human rights are cultural and that "what links officially sanctioned state practices and public pressure from civil society is cultural politics."[83] However, it is prudent to remember that the interpretations of human rights protection are fluid, in that "human rights are defined and redefined as policies are created and administered, legal claims dealt with and so on—both inside and outside state procedures."[84] So the amount of cultural capital individuals or groups can have within the field of human rights is determined through practices including the failings of international human rights protection. Each convention that seeks to redress the general failings of the broad definitions enshrined in the UDHR—such as the Convention on the Rights of the Child, the Convention on the Elimination of All Forms of Discrimination against Women, the Convention on the Rights of Persons with Disabilities—seeks also to increase the cultural capital of those whose rights are at risk because of a particular habitus, which locates them at the margins of their social field.

The field of human rights is both international and domestic. For Bourdieu, the field is a "set of regularized social interactions in which the *value* of what is at stake is shared, and there is competition to gain status, power or material gain between actors properly designated as participants in relation to each other."[85] This means that "these actors occupy objective positions in structures of power, with varying amounts of capital whose possession enables access to the specific profits that are at stake."[86] In the field of human rights, legal mechanisms and state sovereignty are structuring forces that have an impact on the type of social interaction possible to those seeking to exercise their human rights. But what is also at stake is often the authority to decide the meaning of human rights in *practice*,[87] which carries weight in the field and is the root cause of many human rights violations. By locating social interactions in a relational field we can give equal weight to *cultural power* as to institutional forces. And, given that human rights remains a highly contested concept, culture holds an even more important role. Thus, the *practices* that make up human rights are crucial to its overall legitimacy.

The analysis of practices involves the construction of fields, where they occur and the habitus of the agents brought to those fields.[88] In the context of this book, practice is the process of exercising human rights. How certain actors gain cultural capital, and thus value, in human rights discourse, is an issue of agency. Bourdieu's concept of habitus stresses agency and the practical features of culture, rather than norms or values,[89] meaning that what motivates people's participation is not dictated primarily by institutions or morals but, rather, by the position in which they find themselves in relation to the field, of which these institutional and moral frameworks are only one aspect of its makeup. If one is considered a "member," then one has much more cultural capital than if one is on the margins. Habitus explains how activists and practitioners intuitively understand their position within the field of human rights. Therefore, the key to understanding human rights practice is not through philosophical distinctions of subjects as not being "human," as feminists have suggested, but rather about how practitioners position themselves within a human rights field, through which they campaign for the rights of others. Looking at intersections of interpretations and the practitioners making those interpretations illustrates that human rights organizations, in an unreflective way, have their own interests in running campaigns in a particular way. This is to do with their own relative position in the field. This is why a purely discursive approach is limited because it implies that discourse does the work itself. Therefore, practitioners would need only choose to use a different kind of discourse in order to resolve problems. Sociological analysis of practices of human rights enables discussions that go beyond discursive elements and allows for transformative practices. Thus, the responses of habitus that provide the mechanism by which activists reproduce structures keep particular groups subordinate, as well as the possibility of practice transforming the field by strengthening the human right culture. Looking at practice exposes these possibilities and helps scholars understand the internal paradox of universal human rights; that human rights are not applied universally.

What is crucial to this discussion is that an analysis of practice involves the construction of fields and the habitus of the agents brought to those fields. To understand how particular subjectivities remain unprotected by the universal moral discourse of human rights, we need to understand the particulars of the context in which they are trying to exercise their rights and the sociopolitical structures that operate there. Culture is produced by and produces the field, and relations in the field are marked by a power struggle. What is important in this analysis is that the field is continually remade by practices, which are in turn constructed by the field. Practitioners thereby exert an important social influence on culture and politics. In the political field, human rights has a highly contested status. The weak enforceability of international human rights conventions and their variable institution within national law means that they do not have a strong structuring role, rendering culture all the more important. There is, thus, a cultural politics within which the ideals of universal human rights may be realized in practice.

Kate Nash is the leading author on the importance of cultural politics for human rights. In her book *The Cultural Politics of Human Rights* she claims that *cultural politics* occurs as "organized struggles over symbols that frame what issues, events or processes mean to social actors who are emotionally and intellectually invested in shared understandings of the world."[90] For Nash, this concerns "public contests over how society is imagined; how social relations are, could and should be organized."[91] A social life only becomes possible through meaningful practices that resonate with those who participate in them. Nash focuses on the creation of international human rights norms as forms of global justice and illustrates how this process works through cultural politics.[92] For the human rights culture to be successful, she argues that the human rights culture must win the hearts and minds of the global public. The human rights culture "finds political and theoretical support because it marks the importance of intersubjective understandings of human rights to their realization, which are otherwise overlooked in policy debates and in academic studies."[93] For human rights to work, the consensus according to Nash is that the public must feel compelled to see beyond differences such as gender, race, ethnicity and religion such that it

> becomes unthinkable and intolerable that anyone should ever act against human rights, whether at home or abroad. Ignoring human rights ideals must become ethically and emotionally repellent if human rights ideals are to become reality. Only then is there any real possibility of establishing and maintaining institutions that uphold human rights norms.[94]

Therefore, she argues that "human rights are cultural" and that "what links officially sanctioned state practices and public pressure from civil society is cultural politics."[95] This reveals a view of law as being legitimate because it is culturally embedded, as well as legally enforceable. *Using* human rights in practice creates a human rights culture as much as responds to one. Practitioners change things simply by using it. And the *way* they use it counts in how it changes. Nash affirms that of course, human rights are enumerated in international human rights agreements as well as through state procedures. She alerts us to the fact that these procedures do provide clarity to their abstract formulations while maintaining latitude for interpretation. However, this does not fix meanings because through administrative and legal practices, human rights are constantly being defined and redefined.

The discursive and sociological approaches to practice intersect around the politics of language. There is tension between the work of activists and the institutions with which they engage. Language, Nash asserts, "is the most important structuring dimension of institutions";[96] however, the struggle for who will decide the language of rights is a political minefield. When states converge to set human rights standards, they are not just representing the dangers and obstacles to the realization of human rights; they are also necessary for the realization of human rights in practice. Nash observes that "officials in liberal-democratic states (UK & US) find it difficult, imprudent or unnecessary to adopt universal norms of human rights in practice, despite the fact that their leaders have been responsible for developing and promoting them."[97] This presents an interesting conundrum within the human rights culture. As Nash observes, the development of a global human rights regime is well under way, with state elites experiencing strong pressure from international agencies and domestic activists utilizing human rights ideals to push for change from below. However, in practice, the meaning of human rights depends heavily on the cultural politics of particular national contexts. Therefore, practice matters. It cannot be presumed that more activity around human rights in the international sphere, including an expansion in international law, will necessarily result in better forms of protection at both national and international levels.[98]

Nash's observations reinforce my argument that practitioners exert an important social influence on culture and politics because it is through their practices that human rights culture is created. The field of human rights is continuously reinvented by practices, which are in turn constructed by the field. How practitioners take positions within the field of human rights is a struggle for power over which interpretations of the meaning of human rights will prevail and the consequences each interpretation may carry. But the structuring power of the habitus often renders practitioners unable to reflect on their own practices, because they are also embroiled in their work to realize the impact their practice is having on the success of their own activism.[99] This is an intrinsic aspect of the creation of a human rights culture, which in turn has implications for the possibility of affirming the agency of those whose rights have been denied.

Agency in an important aspect of cultural power as there is agency in practice. Looking at agency in practice exposes how social practices produce meaning. The context of meaning and the relative power of activists determine the possible interpretations open at any given time. So the ability for the human rights discourse to empower any person or group is limited by the structures imposed and produced by the field at any given moment in time. A key variable for activists is timing. When particular areas of the field are being contested, this presents an opportunity for new interpretations that can lead to new ways of exercising human rights. However, as described earlier, these structured spaces are at the same time having an impact on interpretations, which means that the very act of recognizing a point of contention is going to affect whether there can be any such opportunity. This is made very clear when we look at the practice of visual representations of human rights. Moments of agency can be visual ones, in that in a particular visual moment numerous interpretations can be offered for an image and the battle for visual dominance, the struggle for structuring power, is won or lost depending on the position the image occupies in the field. However, during the contest, a whole host of interpretations will be tested and retested against the original ones. In these moments, agency is at play, because the suggestion of new possible interpretations creates new practices that can be empowering.

CONCLUSION

Discursive practice tells us that language is constitutive; it constructs, through language, what shall count as "reality." We determine the possibility (and impossibility) of particular meanings within a given context. The problem with discursive practice is that interpretations become normalized, fixing meaning in specific and often uncreative ways. So the challenge, then, for those seeking to exercise their human rights through discursive practices is to be in a position to decide what meanings will be normalized. The obstacle for human rights activism centered on discursive practices is that even if changing possible meanings within the discourse is achieved, the power to police these new meanings is tenuous when one seeks solutions in language alone.

The sociological framework tells us that discursive analysis of practice is too narrow because it focuses on the symbolic and does not account for the material. We understand our place within the field through habitus, and it is through habitus that culture is created. Within culture it is capital that legitimates activists' positions within the field and determines what opportunities will be available to them. If they are lacking in sufficient capital, they shall not be able to gain legitimacy (or recognition) for their campaigns. This is the ongoing struggle for human rights practitioners within the human rights culture. Exercising human rights relies on cultural capital within the field of human rights in order to obtain political capital to affect change. Increasing their cultural capital means reflecting on their own practice and understanding how they themselves are implicitly involved in constructing the cultural capital they seek to attain.

The discursive and sociological approaches to practice are in epistemological conflict, but I see a common critical purpose in both: their intersection around the politics of language. The tension between the work of activists and the institutions they engage with demonstrates the struggle for who will decide the language of human rights and thus who may exercise human rights. This struggle is political. Both analytical frameworks allow us to look at symbols in context—and I examine visual symbols in particular—and how these (visual) symbols are part of the production of culture in practice. The remainder of the book analyses discourse in practice: discourse as a logic of interpretation and social practice as the production of cultural power. Although I draw mainly upon the discourse analysis approach, the two frameworks may be used in a complementary sense to support a critical analysis of human rights practices.

In a human rights context, the analysis of discourse has to account for particular dynamics between activist discourses and that of international law. In a human rights context, meaning is produced largely via international law. As Chapter 5 demonstrates, international law is a context that produces a perpetrator of violence and a victim of abuse. The victim is shown to be without agency, while the perpetrator is shown to have agency. However, in the context of international law, the violence or abuse remains unproblematized. I argue that to overturn the dichotomous relationship between perpetrator and victim, the focus of analysis must shift to the violence enacted, which I argue is gendered, to understand why particular subjectivities are powerless.[100]

Drawing out another analytical theme discussed so far, I examine how the construction of subjectivities in discourse plays out in the meaning of embodiment, affecting agency in different contexts. Chapter 5 shows how, in the exclusionary discourse of international human rights, abuses are acted on bodies as the objects of torture, rape and mutilation, among others. Bodies as objects experience these abuses; hence, for explanations for causes of abuse, embodiment is a predictable response. Embodiment provides the body as an object of abuse. Furthermore, embodiment precludes agency, such that in the word–object relation, human–body, the body is merely a receptacle for violence. However, if we see bodies in a fluid context, then the word–word relation, human–body, implicates the body as subject of the abuses taking place. Thus, the body participates in the acts of violence and cannot be objectified or made absent because if one is intelligible as a subject, one has agency. Meaningful articulations of suffering and survival of human rights abuse requires the presence of intelligible subjects. Survival becomes meaningful when intelligible subjects can begin to speak of respect and dignity. Chapter 6 draws on this point when it examines the visual discourse of the Oka Crisis. What makes the Oka Crisis so pertinent is that because images of armed confrontation challenged normalized constructions of "Indian" in Canada, the visual language was continuously being disrupted by changes in context, which in turn provided space for "Warrior" to have multiple referents, hence an empowered Warrior identity.

In the case studies, I also draw on feminist discourse analysis by offering a reading of gender that promotes agency. Analyses of the processes of meaning production make evident the conflations of sex and gender in exclusive contexts. Interpreting gender as performative, and agency as an interface, avoids the traps of exclusionary discourses. If we expose the assumptions that underlie the representational logics that motivate such discourses, potential sites of lost agency are uncovered. Providing meaningful articulations of being human can locate those sites of respect and dignity and offer suggestions in how reinterpreting international law can provide agency for those who seek recognition.

Empirically, I examine agential discourses in practice by analyzing images, which take on a particularly influential symbolic power in human rights campaigns. I look at the implications of visual practice in two contexts: Amnesty International's 2004 *Stop Violence against Women* campaign and the aboriginal political protest in Oka, Quebec. These contexts portray very different photographic subjects, however; in both cases, exclusionary discourses are attempting to (and sometimes successfully) fix meaning. Whether it is "women" in the Amnesty case or "Indian" in the Oka case, both identities are constructed in an exclusionary discourse that requires viewers to interpret the photographic subject as object, and without agency. No matter what the photographic subject is intended to be, or what the photographer/videographer intended to capture, the context in which the viewer interprets the image structures its meaning. Hence, it is important to look at practice (taking context and power into account) when seeking to understand how modes of visual representation have an impact on understandings of "human" in human rights.

The content of the image—in the case studies this means the gendered identity of the photographic subject—is not what is at stake here. Instead, what I look at and argue is that the context produces the visual meaning. What I show is that exclusionary discourses interpret the photographic subject as embodied, as present, as represented. I argue, however, that the photographic subject is an incomplete representation and must remain so if the image is to be empowering.

NOTES

1. Anthony J. Langlois, "Human Rights: The Globalisation and Fragmentation of Moral Discourse," *Review of International Studies* 28, no. 3 (2002): 479–96.
2. Chris Brown, *Sovereignty, Rights and Justice: International Political Theory Today* (Cambridge, UK: Polity Press, 2002), 2.
3. Chris Brown, "Moral Agency and International Society," *Ethics and International Affairs* 15, no. 2 (2001), 87.
4. Brown, *Sovereignty*, 11.
5. Ibid.
6. Ken Booth, "Three Tyrannies," in *Human Rights in Global Politics*, ed. T. Dunne and N. Wheeler (Cambridge: Cambridge University Press, 2001), 45.
7. Ibid., 46.
8. David G. Chandler, "The Road to Military Humanitarianism: How Human Rights NGOs Shaped a New Humanitarian Agenda," *Human Rights Quarterly* 23, no. 3 (2001), 83.
9. David Jacobson and Galya Benarieh Ruffer, "Courts across Borders: The Implications of Judicial Agency for Human Rights and Democracy," *Human Rights Quarterly* 25 (2003), 75.
10. Ibid., 76.
11. Ibid., 75.
12. Ibid., 84.
13. Ibid., 81.
14. Norman Lewis, "Human Rights, Law and Democracy in an Unfree World," in *Human Rights Fifty Years On: A Reappraisal*, ed. T. Evans (Manchester, UK: Manchester University Press, 1998), 79.
15. Ibid., 80.
16. Ibid.
17. Ibid., 79.
18. Karl Marx, *Selected Writings in Sociology and Social Philosophy*, ed. T.B. Bottomore and M. Rubel (New York and London: McGraw-Hill, 1956).
19. Jiwei Ci, "Taking the Reasons for Human Rights Seriously," *Political Theory* 33, no. 2 (2005): 244.
20. Ibid., 247.
21. Ibid., 248.
22. Ibid., 249.
23. Ibid.
24. Ibid., 250.
25. Ibid.
26. Ibid.
27. See Urvashi Butalia, "Women and Communal Conflict: New Challenges for the Women's Movement in India," in *Victims, Perpetrators or Actors? Gender, Armed Conflict and Political Violence*, ed. C.O.N. Moser and F.C. Clark (London and New York: Zed Books, 2001), 99–113; Cynthia Cockburn, "The Gendered Dynamics of Armed Conflict and Political Violence," in *Victims, Perpetrators or Actors? Gender, Armed Conflict and Political Violence*, ed.

C. Moser and F. Clark (London: Zed Books. 2001), 13–29; Simona Sharoni, "Rethinking Women's Struggles in Israel-Palestine and the North of Ireland," in *Victims, Perpetrators or Actors? Gender, Armed Conflict and Political Violence*, ed. C.O.N. Moser and F.C. Clark (London and New York: Zed Books, 2001), 85–98; Meredeth Turshen, "The Political Economy of Rape: An Analysis of Systematic Rape and Sexual Abuse of Women during Armed Conflict in Africa," in *Victims, Perpetrators or Actors? Gender, Armed Conflict and Political Violence*, ed. C.O.N. Moser and F.C. Clark (London and New York: Zed Books, 2001), 55–68; and Dubravka Zarkov, "The Body of the Other Man: Sexual Violence and the Construction of Masculinity, Sexuality and Ethnicity in the Croatian Media," in *Victims, Perpetrators or Actors? Gender, Armed Conflict and Political Violence*, ed. C. Moser and F. Clark. (London: Zed Books, 2001), 69–82.

28. Caroline O. N. Moser, "The Gendered Continuum of Violence and Conflict: an Operational Framework," in *Victims, Perpetrators or Actors: Gender, Armed Conflict and Political Violence*, ed. C.O.N. Moser and F.C. Clark (London: Zed Books, 2001), 37.

29. Catherine, A. MacKinnon, *Are Women Human? And Other International Dialogues* (London: The Belknap Press of Harvard University Press, 2006), 51.

30. Ibid., 55.

31. Rachael Lorna Johnstone, "Feminist Influences on the United Nations Human Rights Treaty Bodies," *Human Rights Quarterly* 28 (2006): 152.

32. V. Spike Peterson and Laura Parisi, "Are Women Human? It's not an Academic Question," in *Human Rights Fifty Years On: A Reappraisal*, ed. T. Evans (Manchester: Manchester University Press, 1998), 141.

33. Ibid., 145.

34. Ibid., 146.

35. Georgina Ashworth, "The Silencing of Women," in *Human Rights in Global Politics*, ed. T. Dunne and N. Wheeler (Cambridge: Cambridge University Press, 2001), 261.

36. Véronique Pin-Fat, *Universality, Ethics and International Relations: A Grammatical Reading* (New York: Routledge, 2010).

37. Ludwig Wittgenstein, *Philosophical Investigations* (Oxford: Blackwell, 1958), §43.

38. Véronique Pin-Fat, "(Im)Possible Universalism: Reading Human Rights in World Politics," *Review of International Studies* 26 (2000): 664.

39. Ibid.

40. Ibid.

41. Ibid.

42. Véronique Pin-Fat and Maria Stern, "The Scripting of Private Lynch: Biopolitics, Gender and the 'Feminization' of the U.S. Military," *Alternatives: Global, Local, Political* 30, no. 1 (2005): 29.

43. Pin-Fat, "(Im)Possible Universalism," 664.

44. Zillah Eisenstein, *Against Empire: Feminism, Racism and the West* (London: Zed Books, 2004).

45. Pin-Fat, "(Im)Possible Universalism," 664.

46. Véronique Pin-Fat, "The Metaphysics of the National Interest and the 'Mysticism' of the Nation-state: Reading Hans J. Morgenthau," *Review of International Studies* 31, no. 2 (2005): 217–36.

47. Pin-Fat, "(Im)Possible Universalism," 668.

48. Ibid., 669.

49. V. Spike Peterson and Anne Sisson Runyan, *Global Gender Issues* (Boulder. CO: Westview Press, 1999).

50. Cynthia Enloe, *Bananas, Beaches and Bases: Making Feminist Sense of International Politics* (Berkeley: University of California, 1989), 197.
51. Vivienne Jabri, "Restyling the Subject of Responsibility in International Relations," *Millennium* 27, no. 3 (1998): 605.
52. Ibid.
53. Ibid.
54. Ibid., 604.
55. Jacobson and Benarieh Ruffer, "Courts across Borders," 82.
56. Ibid., 81.
57. Ibid., 76.
58. Ibid., 77.
59. Ibid., 84.
60. Ci, "Taking the Reasons."
61. Ibid.
62. Ibid., 249–50.
63. Ibid., 250.
64. Ibid.
65. Nietzsche in Ci, "Taking the Reasons," 250.
66. Ci, "Taking the Reasons," 259.
67. Judith Butler, *Undoing Gender* (London: Routledge, 2004), 198.
68. Ibid., 199.
69. Ibid., 209.
70. Ibid.
71. Ibid., 219.
72. Judith Butler, *Gender Trouble: Feminism and the Subversion of Identity* (London: Routledge, 1999), 179.
73. Butler, *Undoing Gender*, 219.
74. Ibid., 218.
75. Lois McNay, *Gender and Agency: Reconfiguring the Subject in Feminist and Social Theory* (Cambridge, UK: Polity Press, 2000), 14.
76. Ibid., 33.
77. Pierre Bourdieu, *Questions de sociologie* (Paris: Editions de Minuit, 1980), in David Swartz, *Culture and Power: The Sociology of Pierre Bourdieu* (Chicago: The University of Chicago Press, 1997), 96.
78. David Swartz, *Culture and Power: The Sociology of Pierre Bourdieu* (Chicago: The University of Chicago Press, 1997), 101.
79. Ibid., 103.
80. Ibid.
81. Pierre Bourdieu, *Distinction: A Social Critique of the Judgement of Taste* (Cambridge, MA: Harvard University Press, 1984), 226.
82. Swartz, *Culture and Power*, 126.
83. Kate Nash, *The Cultural Politics of Human Rights: Comparing the US and UK* (Cambridge: Cambridge University Press, 2009), 8.
84. Ibid.
85. See Pierre Bourdieu, *Outline of a Theory of Practice*, trans. Richard Nice (Cambridge: Cambridge University Press, 1977); and Pierre Bourdieu, *Language and Symbolic Power*, ed. John Thompson, trans. Gino Raymond and Matthew Adamson (Cambridge: Cambridge University Press, 1991), in Nash *Cultural Politics*, 30.
86. Ibid.
87. Ibid.
88. Swartz, *Culture and Power*, 142.
89. Ibid., 115.

90. Nash, *Cultural Politics*, 1.
91. Ibid.
92. Ibid., 2.
93. Ibid., 5.
94. Ibid., 6.
95. Ibid., 8.
96. Ibid., 3.
97. Ibid., 4.
98. Ibid., 19.
99. Robin Redhead and Nick Turnbull, "Towards a Study of Human Rights Practitioners," *Human Rights Review* 12, no. 2 (2010): 173–89.
100. Robin Redhead, "Imag(in)ing Women's Agency: Visual Representation in Amnesty International's 2004 Campaign 'Stop Violence against Women,'" *International Feminist Journal of Politics* 9, no. 2 (2007): 218–338.

Part II
Exercising Human Rights

4 Visual Methodology

Human rights is a prevalent tool in the conduct of international politics. It is used by many disparate actors to enforce, at the very basic level, respect for human dignity. Within the collective of advocates and skeptics (let's face it, there are some), a culture of human rights has emerged. This culture nurtures a commitment to human rights, both nationally and internationally, even though there is no agreement on the precise meaning of human rights. What makes this human rights culture so interesting is that actors with similar goals employ very different strategies and techniques for pursuing them. One such practice is the use of images depicting human rights abuses, and those involved in such abuse, to motivate an emotional response in an audience in the hopes of generating support for the "cause." This technique is widespread in the human rights culture because the use of images is a powerful, and often successful, tool in human rights activism. Images are interesting because they expose the political actions of several actors at once. There is the person capturing the image, the person who chooses that particular image from a whole host of others and the person who designs the visual material and sets the image in its human rights context. Then, there is the person who sees the campaign material or news footage and decides to act or not act. Finally, there is the person depicted in the image as a participant. Each of these positions reflects the internal politics of human rights practice, mainly the coming together of varied actors in the single purpose of seeking protection for victims of abuse. Because the human rights culture is morally driven, the political rhetoric that draws on the passions and emotions of the audience is fundamental to the success and future protection of people's lives. Without these images, human rights activism would falter. However, what is often neglected in analyses of images is the construction of the human rights context—those involved in the production of the image for general viewing—and how this practice generates and maintains dominant victim narratives, which in turn limits the ways people can exercise their rights. In the next two chapters of this book, I explore the practice of using images as a tool for representing human rights and critically evaluate how we interpret visual symbols in human rights discourse. There are many different analytical frameworks, broadly speaking, but I am interested in those that are contextual. Contextual perspectives are crucial because there are many actors with different perspectives making different interpretations. Furthermore, images are more open to interpretation than are highly detailed legal documents. This renders the meaning of images subjective and generates scope for significant agency in interpreting them.

By looking at how gender, agency and context relate to each other I have developed a framework through which to assess the practice of visual representation. Visual images are used to convey meaning:

> We live in a world of the image. The very idea of the self, the ways in which we make sense of the world, the means by which we communicate, have all become invested in, and developed through the visual. In many ways images have replaced the word as the defining aspect of cultural identity, and at the same time they have become part of the attempt to create a global culture.[1]

I have chosen two case studies (two contexts) to investigate the visual production of meaning for "human" in international human rights discourse. "Human" is a gendered identity against which other identities such as "woman" and "Indian" are constructed. Here I set out my methodology for interpreting visual logics in discourses of human rights and gender. Recognizing there is visual language—visual logic—further demonstrates the importance of context to interpreting visual meaning. Articulations of the photographic subject, and the role this subject plays in each context, provides a tool for assessing how particular meanings are policed and sustained through exclusive discourses. The construction of the viewer as an active interpreter of the image and the relationship between her interpretation and the photographic image are crucial to interpreting the visual. I consider concepts from studies of visual culture to establish a theoretical foundation for my methodology of interpreting visual logics. The relationship between the context, the image and the viewer are discussed in order to look at the practices of exercising human rights in the case studies that follow in Chapters 5 and 6. Meanwhile, this chapter engages the questions of how images function within human rights activism, specifically, and human rights culture, generally.

Using visual images to enhance or demonstrate particular positions or arguments occurs frequently in international politics.[2] However, understanding how images work in sociopolitical contexts is under-theorized as many scholars and activists are so preoccupied with the persuasive power of images they overlook or ignore their role in constructing the context through which the image will be interpreted. My focus is to explore the dynamics of how these visual contexts are generated and to expose the limiting forces context has on possible interpretations of the images. Visual images comprise a significant part of life everywhere, as the earlier quotation suggests. My concern lies with the impact of visual meaning on the protection of human rights. How "human" is produced visually, and interpreted contextually, determines whether a given identity will have subjectivity, agency and power. To begin unpacking the visual requires a discussion of visual logic.

INTERPRETING VISUAL LOGICS

Constructing, using and interpreting images are practices themselves: an *interpretive practice*. Photographs and video are visual representations that have their own unique visual logics as well as being part of the logic of international human rights discourse. Scholars have used a range of interpretive analytical frameworks to explain the production of meaning in international politics. For instance, Pin-Fat draws on Wittgenstein to conceive of a grammar that is constitutive in that it provides the rules of the language-game; it determines what possible meanings can exist.[3] The subsequent two case studies show how Amnesty International and the Canadian press employed images with the intention of showing the viewer what was really going on—in return, viewers have come to expect to gain knowledge of the real from what they see. It is a rhetorical device for *implying* a particular meaning rather than stipulating a strict interpretation of the action. The images used in the case studies are produced in specific sociopolitical contexts, which determine the parameters of possible interpretations, the visual logic. The *relation* between context and visual logic is productive and mutually reinforcing. Visual logics are constitutive, such as written language. Therefore, photography and video, as acts of recording visual language, when used in the context of international human rights are "not merely the act of an innocent bystander, but the involved participation of a perpetrator."[4] In other words, within human rights discourses, the use of photography and video as tools in visual logics are collaborative acts that recognize "evidence that a human life is at stake."[5] This notion of recognizing those human lives at stake impels many human rights advocates to use images in their campaigns.[6] Kozol explains that "the seeming transparency of photographic technologies legitimizes claims of the real in ways that ignore how gender categories are encoded within these visual perspectives."[7] As a result, the use of photographic technology is not without problems.[8]

Within visual logics, two forces are at work in relation to one another: (1) the image itself and (2) the viewer's interpretation of the image. The context in which the viewer operates will structure how he or she interpret the image while at the same time the context of the image will structure how the image can be interpreted. The viewer and the image are not always produced in the same context, however. When images are interpreted by the viewer the image becomes part of the viewer's context. Images "are the constitutive elements of visual culture; how we become spectators of them is what locates us within a visual culture."[9] The process of becoming a viewer is linked with the sociopolitical and economic elements of an individual's environment. Images do not simply exist; they must be made visual, rendered visible by the creation of a viewer. This is how "images come to exist, and, significantly, how they come to be seen as meaningful and the bearers of meaning."[10] No matter how powerful the image, it can be shaped and altered to fit within a particular context because it is not simply the creator of the image who determines visual meaning, but the viewer also necessarily shifts and contorts the image when interpreting it. The interpreter is always located within a range of forces that determine, and are determined by, the image.[11] The viewer is thus engaging in interpretive practice. In this case, practice means engaging with structured interpretations, *normative* or routinized ways of interpreting images. I argue that this relationship between the image and the viewer is where the potential for visual agency is located. The key to such interpretations is to be critical and reflective of one's own position as viewer. When a viewer is not critical, a viewer's interpretation is without agency. A look at how one becomes a critical viewer will be helpful in making this argument.

BECOMING A CRITICAL VIEWER

It is important to see the visual as exceeding the image itself. When we look at photographs or we watch images on television, we are engaging with other images and forming investments of power.[12] If we take the meaning of power from Foucault, who views power as "a technique or mechanism to be used in working out why and how we become subjects,"[13] then what becomes interesting is how power relations are produced to create certain subjectivities with specific reference to images. Applying Foucault's concepts to the visual results in the view that the viewer "struggles against the seduction of the image—the seduction of being placed, of being told how and what to view."[14] This theory of power links with gender and agency to bring together the key concepts of the book. I have already discussed agency as an interface between subjectivity and power, where subjectivity and power are each implicit in the other's constitution. Foucault's concept of power as a mechanism of subjectivity supports this idea of agency, in that he also sees power as constitutive of subjectivity and subjectivity as constitutive of power. The notion of gender performance accounts for power as a force that affects subjectivity. When gender, subjectivity and power are mapped onto this concept of agency, the relationship among subjectivity, agency and power can be clearly stated as fluid. In turn, this fluidity of subjectivity, agency and power may be understood as an interpretive practice used in a given context. This allows us to determine that the production of the viewer in a context, as a subject, within a visual logic, is a power relation but which includes, the possibility of agency. What this allows me to show is that certain logics attempt to fix subjectivity, having an impact on the interpretations the viewer can make and ultimately resulting in the loss of agency for both the viewer and the photographic subject. Chapters 5 and 6 explore this in detail. In summary, what is significant here is that these structured interpretations constitute interpretive practices, which have ongoing effects in the politics of human rights activism.

The seductive process articulated here is one I term *sedimentation*. Sedimentation is an explanation of how visual logics become interpretive practices. The viewer is seduced by an image "when being told what is meaningful is easier than assessing it critically for one's self."[15] In the larger context of international human rights discourse, sedimentation (seduction) occurs when an image is consistently repeated within the context to become representative of a particular political issue. The repetition of the image lulls the viewer into accepting the meaning of the image as unchanging, which limits the viewer's potential interpretations, in turn having an impact on the ability to empower the photographic subject within a human rights context. I have argued that when agency is fixed, so, too, are subjectivity and power. This explains my concern with the production of viewer subjectivity; without agency, visual cultures become passive collectives ingesting predetermined interpretations of images. When meaning becomes predetermined, then creativity is lost and, with it, the possibility of new meanings, new subjectivities, new images and new uses of the power of the visual.

Sedimentation is a result of representational logics, a belief that what is being shown is a true likeness of reality. The more the image is interpreted as being important and powerful in its given context, the more seductive it becomes, and the less agency the viewer exerts in his or her interpretation. In this way "an investment of power serves to strengthen the seduction of the image and ultimately its totalizing form."[16] What this indicates is that viewers tend to become less reflective of their own subjectivity as viewers in an unquestioning absorption of the dominant visual narratives present in the culture. In other words, viewers are able to contextualize themselves in relation to the image because the certainty of meaning is provided by the context and no longer needs negotiation. The "seduction to live out an uncritical and unquestioning existence forms part of the attraction to any image,"[17] and through this seduction, the viewer and the photographic subject become objectified.

This is problematic for political agency in human rights campaigns because when the viewer is objectified (via visual sedimentation) the identity of the photographic subject (the subject of the image) is also confined to singular interpretations. Hence, the potential for recognizing particular gendered identities such as "woman" and "Indian" remains difficult because the context of international human rights discourse does not provide the means to interpret these subjectivities as powerful. What this analysis aims to show is the importance of becoming *active subjects*, to resist the seduction of sedimentation and challenge interpretations that attempt to fix meaning, thereby resulting in the loss of agency. Becoming a critical viewer is a form of a new interpretive practice that opens possibilities within sociopolitical contexts, which permit agency for the viewer and the photographic subject in their own right. In human rights advocacy, the key to successful campaigns rides on how key images can be interpreted. Let us now look at how the photographic subject, who is often a victim of human rights abuse, can be empowered through images.

THE PHOTOGRAPHIC SUBJECT

Barbara Martinsons's discussion of the "human" subjects of photographs and of photography as a technology that represents "human" subjects reinforces that photography and video "[are technologies] of representation."[18] She explores questions of the *(un)representability* of photographic subjects by looking at the possibility of empowered photographic subjects. For Martinsons,

> [a]gency may be constructed by the photographer and the subject(s) in a joint dialogue; and it may be reconstructed by the viewer and the trace of the photographic subject in a second dialogic exchange. (All agency, like all meaning, is inscribed by power and must be invoked with dialogue, incantation, discussion, myth, story, and other constructed narrations) . . . the *oeuvre* lies here—in the space between the subject and the representation, between the work and the viewer formed, wrought, constructed, fabricated, by the narratives of possible—and plural—agency.[19]

Martinsons is articulating another way of looking at agency as interface, this time between the photographic subject and the visual power (impact) of the image. She is saying that "neither the photographer nor the viewer 'speak for' the photographic subject."[20] A photographic subject with agency "must have the ontological status to speak for her/himself and for a host of others."[21]

Photographic technology is a tool that fixes visual moments to film and, as such, is frequently read as a representative of the real. The media alter these discursive economies (representations of the real) by intervening in the delicate interplay of presence and absences.[22] Chapter 6 shows this in significant detail. What is important here is that the photographic subject is positioned within various contexts as being representative of this reality and is then assumed to *speak* to the viewer about the given situation in which the photographic subject finds itself. What appears as presence in representations of the real is actually absence[23] because attempts at representing reality are also attempts at fixing meaning, which I have shown disempower particular gendered subjectivities. Moreover, certain contexts—specifically exclusionary ones—perpetuate *speaking* of the real because the viewers' own subjectivity is secured through context, and as such, they interpret the photographic subject as representative of reality, in order to legitimate their own position as viewer. The possibilities of interpreting the photographic subject actively (reflectively) exist only when the viewer distinguishes between the photographic subject as an image and the photographic subject as a person who is portrayed in an image, because viewers consciously acknowledge their own interpretive practice. Within the image, there is a tendency for viewers to think of the photographic subject as embodied (corporally present). For example, this line of thinking would suggest that a photograph of an Indian Warrior is a representation of what an Indian Warrior would look like if he were standing next to the viewer. However, if we are engaged in visual interpretive practices, we can see active subjects through processes of reflection, which means that the identity of an Indian Warrior can never be fully fixed on film and can never be fully represented. In this way, the identity of the photographic subject is never complete—the image provides only a glimpse at the complexity of the situation, instead of its epitome. Martinsons clarifies that "we have learned that the results of the technology of visualization, including photographs, may cancel or distort the testimony of the subject."[24] She entreats that only when we see subjectivity and power as mutually constitutive are we "able to query the politics of the attributed meanings and judgments attached to photographs."[25] This meaning occurs in a social context.

We can extend this logic of interpretation by incorporating a sociological approach to understanding how interpretive practices are formed. Studying how images are interpreted in human rights allows us to see the effects this has on practices of human rights activism within the human rights culture.

My methodology of visual analysis requires that images be interpreted in context. I am not analyzing the photographic subject per se; instead, I am interested in which contexts the photographic subject appears. I argue that there is no ideal photograph or photographic subject but, instead, that there are contexts, and visual practices, that enable articulations of gendered identities, specifically "human" in human rights to have agency. My focus is not on the act of taking photographs or on the role of photojournalists. What concerns me is the process of image selection and its role in context construction, those people and situations that construct the visual logic through which the photographic subject will attempt to speak. Being aware of practice facilitates understanding processes of meaning production that engage with how people attempt to exercise their human rights.

The aim of the two case studies is twofold: first, to show how meaning is produced within particular visual logics and, second, to offer alternative interpretations of the images given an exposure of the problematic contentions apparent to exclusionary discourses. I begin with the case of Amnesty International's 2004 campaign *Stop Violence against Women* and follow up with the plight of the Mohawk Warriors in the 1990 Oka Crisis. The Amnesty International case is an example of a human rights campaign that sought to overturn the tendency of viewing women as victims within the human rights discourse. The Oka case is an example of the power of sovereignty and how not being legitimate under the law can be problematic when one needs the law to make a claim.

The two case studies that follow restrict themselves to analysis of photographs and video. These images appear in campaign documents, in national newspapers and on television news broadcasts. Within the context of both the Amnesty International campaign and the Oka Crisis, photographic subjects are assumed to represent participants in the politics of human rights.

NOTES

1. Patrick Fuery and Kelli Fuery, *Visual Cultures and Critical Theory* (London: Arnold/Hodder Headline Group, 2003), xiv.
2. See, for example, Michael J. Shapiro, *The Politics of Representation: Writing practices in bibliography, photography and policy analysis* (Madison: University of Wisconsin Press, 1988); Debbie Lisle, "Consuming Danger: Reimagining the War/Tourism Divide," *Alternatives* 25 (2000): 91–116; Patricia Molloy, "Theatrical Release: Catharsis and Spectacle in *Welcome to Sarajevo*," *Alternatives* 25 (2000): 75–90; David Campbell, "The Ones that Are Wanted: Communication and the Politics of Representation in Photographic Exhibition," *Journal of Modern African Studies* 41, no. 2 (2003): 331–32; and Christine Sylvester, "The Art of War/The War Question in (Feminist) IR," *Millennium* 33, no. 3 (2005): 855–78.
3. Véronique Pin-Fat, "The Metaphysics of the National Interest and the 'Mysticism' of the Nation-state: Reading Hans J. Morgenthau," *Review of International Studies* 31, no. 2 (2005): 217–36.
4. Barbara Martinsons, "The Possibility of Agency for Photographic Subjects," in *Technoscience and Cyberculture*, edited by S. Aronowitz et al. (London: Routledge, 1996), 243.
5. Ibid.
6. Mark Philip Bradley and Patrice Petro, eds., *Truth Claims: Representation and Human Rights* (London: Rutgers University Press, 2002); and Wendy S. Hesford, "*Kairos* and the Geopolitical Rhetorics of Global Sex Work and Video Advocacy," in *Just Advocacy? Women's Human Rights, Transnational Feminisms, and the Politics of Representation*, ed. W. S. Hesford and W. Kozol (London: Rutgers University Press, 2005), 146–72.
7. Wendy Kozol, "Domestication NATO's War in Kosovo(a): (In)Visible Bodies and the Dilemma of Photojournalism," *Meridians: Feminism, Race, Transnationalism* 4, no. 2 (1994): 4–5.
8. See Arabella Lyon, "Misrepresentations of Missing Women in the U.S. Press," in *Just Advocacy? Women's Human Rights, Transnational Feminisms, and the Politics of Representation*, ed. W. S. Hesford and W. Kozol (London: Rutgers University Press, 2005), 173–92.
9. Fuery and Fuery, *Visual Cultures*, xi.
10. Ibid., xii.
11. Ibid., xiii.
12. Ibid., 1.
13. Michel Foucault, "The Subject in Power," in *Michel Foucault: Beyond Structuralism and Hermeneutics* (Chicago: University of Chicago Press, 1983), 211.

14. Fuery and Fuery, *Visual Cultures*, 2.
15. Ibid., 3.
16. Ibid., 4.
17. Ibid., 8, 12.
18. Martinsons, "The Possibility of Agency," 236.
19. Ibid., 250.
20. Ibid.
21. Ibid.
22. Michael J. Shapiro, "Strategic Discourse/Discursive Strategy: The Representation of 'Security Policy' in the Video Age," *International Studies Quarterly* 34, no. 4 (1990): 333.
23. Douglas Crimp, "The Photographic Activity of Postmodernism," in *Postmodernism: A Reader*, ed. T. Docherty (London: Harvester Wheatsheaf, 1993), 173.
24. Martinsons, "The Possibility of Agency," 233.
25. Ibid.

5 Visualizing Women's Agency

Amnesty International's 2004 Campaign *Stop Violence against Women*

The purpose of our campaign is not to portray women as victims and stigmatize men as perpetrators; it is to condemn the act of violence itself.

Irene Khan, secretary general of Amnesty International[1]

Stating the aim of the 2004 campaign *Stop Violence against Women*, Irene Khan draws attention to how Amnesty International (AI)[2] views the relationship between gender and agency. Gender is expressed in the binary terms of men/women, while agency is implied in the gender relationship between victim (women) and perpetrator (men). Agency, for AI, means empowerment and is attributed to those who are no longer victims of violence. In this chapter I aim to demonstrate that AI's goal of disarming the stigma that associates women with victims ultimately remains unsuccessful because of its non-gendered concept of violence. This is not to say that its campaign did not raise awareness; it did, but in terms of disrupting a universal discourse that assumed gender-neutrality, it was unsuccessful because in the end it adhered to universalist language. AI's aim is to encourage support for the International Bill of Rights by stipulating that universalist language is the key to empowerment. However, when we look at its practice, we will see that this discursive strategy cannot fully accomplish its goal. A fundamental part of any AI campaign is the images used to document human rights abuses. In this chapter, issues of gender, agency and practice are explored by looking closely at how AI depicts women's agency through images of human rights in its campaign text *It's in our Hands: Stop Violence against Women*.[3] It will be shown that AI employs the exclusionary discourse of international human rights law. AI's adherence to this discourse limits its definition of gender, précised earlier, by reducing gender (woman) to an elaboration of sex (female). Looking at AI's visual representations of women's agency reveals a conflation of the terms *sex* and *gender*. Through interviews and contextualized readings of the campaign images the chapter shows that AI, in its attempt to empower women through universal human rights, is limited in practice because the universalist discourse privileges men over women. As shown in Chapter 2, the tension this privilege creates has an impact directly on the potential for women's agency in human rights discourse because what is provided in discourse is not provided in practice. Women do not have agency and, therefore, are repressed as victims. In response to Khan's address, neglecting to contextualize violence as gendered perpetuates conceptions of women as victims and clouds AI's perception of agency. It will be suggested that to empower women through human rights discourse, one must seek nonexclusive iterations that account for gendered interpretations of agency and practice.

In addressing AI's visual representations of women's agency, I do not make claims about appropriate definitions of agency, and I do not generalize beyond an AI context. Employing the theoretical framework outlined in Chapters 2 and 3, the approach I take looks at agency as a fluid interface between subjectivity and power, where agency, subjectivity and power are understood relationally, providing multiple referents for all terms and resisting the desire to represent reality as fixed, in other words, to look at the sociopolitical implications of language. This approach requires that we account for the impact context has on interpretations of existing visual logics. I argue that the possibilities for agency lie in interpretive practices that contextualize violence as gendered. This does not mean making claims about which images are good and which are not; the images I use here are those the interviewees chose themselves as successful examples of how AI wants to show women's agency. It is important to note that the photographic subject could be a man, and in some of the campaign images, men do appear. Nevertheless, the gender of the photographic subject is not what is at stake here. My analysis does not offer suggestions for how to take a better photograph of women's agency. Instead, what I propose is that interpreting visual images of human rights and gender in AI's 2004 campaign will bring to light the impact of exclusionary discourse on women's agency in the context of international human rights discourse. My focus is on how particular contexts limit viewers' interpretations of the images, which is subsequently reflected in how human rights are practiced. In this chapter, it is suggested that current visual logics do not exhaust understandings of gender and agency and highlights the need for contemplation of the processes of the production of meaning that shape our lives.

There are four main elements I claim are at work within AI's images of women's agency: context, the visual, gender and agency. This introduction provides a brief visual analysis in order to illustrate how all these elements have an impact on one another. Following this preliminary analysis, each element is discussed in detail, teasing out the nuances that remain frequently under-theorized in international politics. Through the interpretive practices undertaken throughout this chapter, what becomes apparent is how AI could adopt a more contextual understanding of women's agency; however, for reasons outlined in the following discussion, it remains committed to upholding the exclusionary discourse of international human rights law, instead of challenging it. To begin, let us consider Figure 5.1.

Figure 5.1   Refugees from the conflict in Kosovo.
©Andrew Testa/Panos Pictures

The image in Figure 5.1 appears on the front cover of the campaign publication under the title *It's in our Hands*. Placed on the cover of the campaign document, the image is an example of AI's visual logic, leaving the viewer to interpret the image of this woman as having experience of violence. The gestures of sitting on the ground, head in hands, facing away from the camera, and crying all become part of the visual logic as denoting representations of women who suffer violence. In attempting to break with victimization language, the photo researcher explained that "this image is more informative, more detailed, more shocking, than a typical one of overt brutality" (interview, August 6, 2004). Here AI tries to avoid what Hesford and Kozol termed "a simplistic spectacle of victimization" by choosing an image that does not shock its viewers through scenes of violence but that, instead, depicts "a post-traumatic moment."[4] The caption on the inside cover of the campaign document contextualizes this woman and child as refugees from the conflict in Kosovo.[5] AI's use of the pronoun *our* in the document title implicates the viewer in this discourse of violence.

The viewer is asked to interpret the conflict in Kosovo as relating to human rights and to regard this woman and child as survivors of the conflict—in that they are alive in the image. AI wants the photographic subject to tell her story through body language so that the viewer might begin to understand the brutality she has endured and how the viewer having now seen it, is implicated in the process: "violence against women will only end when each one of us is ready to make that pledge: not to do it, or permit others to do it, or tolerate it, or rest until it is eradicated."[6] No image can show all aspects of human rights. No image can capture all of what is understood as violence against women. But using a particular image in an AI campaign means that the content of the image will be interpreted in a human rights context. How the subject is positioned, the direction of the light, whether color film was used and what appears in the background all become elements of the visual logic viewers use to interpret the image as saying something about human rights. The possibility of women's agency does not depend on the correct combination of elements in a photograph. Instead, what is at stake are the possibilities for interpretation that exist within the visual logic. AI does provide instructions for what it is looking for from each image. What AI fails to do is question the context through which the image will be understood and its role in shaping it.

The cover image (Figure 5.1) says that this woman with her head in her hands, sitting on the ground and being comforted by a child, has been a victim of violence. As the campaign coordinator said, "images convey meaning" (interview August 5, 2004), then the meaning conveyed here is that women who are victims of human rights abuses look like this: they sit on the ground, head in hands; they do not look at the camera; they cover their faces; they cry. This is how AI wants the image to be interpreted. In order to better understand how AI uses images, we must look at the contexts in which the images appear, how gender and agency are constructed visually and what impact this has on how the viewer interprets the image. Now I turn to a discussion of these relationships.

AN AMNESTY INTERNATIONAL CONTEXT

Before analyzing AI's concepts of gender and agency, it is important to provide the context in which it operates as an international human rights organization. How AI comes to understand gender and agency is in part a reflection of what it perceives its role in human rights discourse to be. However, there is more at play here than just the context of AI's role as an international human rights organization. AI relies on international law to structure and support its advocacy, so it is necessary to explore how it employs international law as a context that codifies meaning. Furthermore, the images appear within a document, creating yet another context via the written text that seeks to explain the content of the image and how AI wants it to be understood by the viewer. As a result, there is a need to unpack three interrelated contexts in order to appreciate the influences that affect the visual elements of AI's 2004 campaign. I begin with a brief historical background.

AI was founded in 1961 "to translate human rights principles into practical action."[7] Historically, most of their campaigning has focused on

Prisoners of Conscience (PoCs).[8] However, because of the changing patterns of human rights violations in the world, AI found it necessary to also focus on mass violations in armed conflict because people are now more likely to be victims of abuse because of their membership in a particular community more than for their ideologies or their activism.[9] AI has "struggled to deal with the integration of 'difference' whether of gender, race or nationality, making it a surprisingly masculine, (culturally) white, Western and middle-class organization."[10] This is because, from the beginning, Peter Benenson, AI's founder, has tried to organize on a world scale around a set of particular Christian values taken to be transcendent principles.[11] In other words, AI operates like a brand; it became the face of globalization in human rights. This fixed set of principles (its brand) made it difficult for some members inside AI because much of the work was performed by volunteers who could afford not to spend all of their time and money protecting their own interests. Those who did not have such luxury found themselves marginalized.

As the first membership-based transnational human rights organization of its kind, AI was born into an environment in which human rights advocacy represented personal engagement with the world. The moral spirit that inspired the founders became an enormously successful example of ethical activism.[12] AI created a symbol—the candle in barbed wire—that, along with its name, became recognized globally as synonymous with human rights. Speaking the ethical language of universal human rights, AI contributed significantly to the construction of international human rights discourse. When AI spoke, it spoke of human rights, thus whatever issues it engages with are contextualized as having a human rights dimension. For instance, when AI uses an image to solicit a response from the public on a particular issue, the image, the issue and those who partake in supporting the campaign do so in a human rights context. Its campaigns show an acute awareness of the power of symbols and the potential for using the media.[13] AI has successfully branded itself as a human rights organization. However, AI is not a typical campaigning organization. Its members have always campaigned, and its researchers have always seen their work as campaigning, but rarely do members of AI march, or shout, or undertake publicity stunts or engage in direct action: AI's principle means of activism (in many sections) has remained the sending of letters and other forms of written communication, such as petitions.[14]

With the end of the cold war came an explosion in human rights organizations, which posed a direct threat to AI's identity and its capacity to dictate what human rights were. It no longer occupied the privileged position of being the principal human rights organization in the field. This new wave of human rights was more thematic and sub-universal and was linked to identity and interest (sexuality, gender, poverty).[15] AI's authority was being challenged by its reluctance to shift with trends in the human rights movement. While AI is certainly well aware of the threats of globalization, it is possible that its preference for promoting civil and political rights has itself been part of the problem, and this may continue to be the case if its efforts in defense of economic and social rights continue to be guided by the same liberal understanding of rights.[16] The campaigns to abolish torture track this historical shift and lead to further complications of how AI was to deal with the political issues surrounding homosexuality and women.

One of the biggest target areas for AI is torture. The frequency of torture in the PoC cases was particularly unsettling to researchers and members alike. Recognizing the need for trying to shape state behavior at a general level, "the organization devised a series of practical actions to promote the emergence of new norms to prohibit the use of torture by governments."[17] AI was shifting its practices.

Marking the twenty-fourth anniversary of the signing of the Universal Declaration of Human Rights, AI's 1972 Campaign for the Abolition of Torture (CAT) was the organization's first internationally coordinated publicity and lobbying effort. The aim of the campaign was to "raise public awareness of torture and the need for stronger international norms," with the potential "not only to create renewed international awareness of torture, but also to revive, deepen, and extend the international normative consensus against it."[18] The campaign strategy had three objectives: (1) to disseminate information on the international use of torture, (2) to enhance international legal means to fight torture, and (3) the development of new techniques of action to help victims of torture. AI published a report on torture in 1973. The report was "intended both to educate the public and generate a climate of public support for action on torture."[19] Concurrently, AI's members lobbied their governments for supportive action in the United Nations against torture. This was AI's first attempt to "identify a single problem which was global."[20]

Subsequent reports have further shaped AI's campaigns against torture. In 1995 AI published *Human Rights Are Women's Rights* in response to the 1993 Declaration of the UN World Conference on Human Rights, in which "the UN unequivocally stated that women's rights were human rights."[21] With this document AI acknowledged that

the extent and gravity of abuses against women such as domestic violence, genital mutilation, forced prostitution and other violent acts committed by private individuals and organizations . . . [but reinforced that] Amnesty International's mandate for action is directed at governments and armed political groups, not private individuals and organizations and therefore does not include such abuses.[22]

Five years later *Broken Bodies, Shattered Minds: Torture and Ill-Treatment of Women*[23] was published. AI had now taken up those issues not permitted under its 1995 mandate. Torture by private individuals, torture of women in the home and community, women bought and sold and torture by state agents and armed groups were all addressed. The publication

Combating Torture: A Manual for Action[24] is AI's main report on torture. Leaving behind the focus on women, this sizable document "draws on the ideas and experiences of human rights defenders around the world."[25] A collaboration of workers in the field and analysts of international law, this document reinstates AI's mandate toward identifying agents capable of committing torture, states and armed groups.

The International Council Meeting (ICM) is the supreme governing body of AI. It decides on AI's strategy, political, financial and organizational issues for the forthcoming years. It is for members only and is not open to the public or press. At the 1991 ICM in Mexico, a change was made to one of AI's statutes, allowing for the shift, noted earlier, in how AI to came incorporate women as an action category. The understanding of the word *sex* in the document was expanded to read as including "sexual orientation." Now, AI could adopt PoCs imprisoned because of homosexual acts or homosexual orientation. This mandate change was the catalyst that led to other significant changes, such as the decision to expand the focus of perpetrators of human rights abuses to include nonstate actors. The implication of this was profound because it created opportunities for campaigning for the protection of economic, social and cultural rights, which in turn allow AI to investigate relations between individuals, as well as between an individual and a state.

In 2004, AI launched the *Stop Violence against Women* campaign. One of the overarching aims of this campaign was to change the perception that human rights are abstract, and to bring them *home* (literally) for people, to make it evident that violence against women is "the most outrageous human rights scandal of our times."[26] For AI, respect for human life should begin at home.[27] AI presents the *Stop Violence against Women* campaign as an evolution in its conception of itself, from a prisoner-oriented organization, to one embracing economic, social and cultural rights.

The campaign has had a pervasive destabilizing effect on the organization. Not only did it uproot the origins of the organization; it also caused dissidence among those who work for AI. Since the 1984 *Campaign Against Torture*, a focus on women has been present in AI's human rights work, however sporadically and variable. In 1987, "of 33 prisoner cases carried in Amnesty's International Newsletter, only three were women, and eleven cases initially highlighted in 1988 as part of the *Human Rights Now! Tour* only one was of a woman."[28] It was not until 1995, for the UN's Fourth World Conference on Women, that AI put together a consistent campaign on women's human rights. As detailed earlier, this campaign dealt with issues of torture, state violence, abuses during armed conflict and disappearances but did not mention issues of domestic violence. A focus on domestic violence acknowledged individuals as potential perpetrators of violence. This complicated the public/private distinction around which AI had previously built its strategies, which is why it took the organization roughly nine years to clarify its own position on gender and human rights. Extending the concept of gender widened the scope of human rights to take in more political activism, so its organizational habitus changed, but by also being a leading human rights organization, it influences other actors in the field who can then follow its lead in gender activism.

Even though it was late to the game, by AI taking up gender as an issue, it changed the culture of human rights through its own practice. In this sense, the 2004 campaign *Stop Violence against Women* broke new ground. AI advocates that to stop violence, regard for women's human rights must take place. To accomplish this AI insists that the Universal Declaration of Human Rights (UDHR), which promises equal rights and equal protection for all, become a reality for all women.[29] Using the UDHR and other international law mechanisms, AI constructs a context for advocating that violence against women is the greatest human rights scandal of our times.[30] AI has claimed that women's rights have not been seen as human rights[31] and has struggled to overcome the division of men being associated with the public sphere and conversely, of women being associated with the private sphere.[32] Building on the work of women's organizations, the 2004 campaign, by acknowledging the individual as a potential perpetrator of human rights abuses, forced AI to move beyond the dichotomy of public/private and focus instead on empowering women.

From the point of view of context, AI wish to empower women by exercising international human rights law and demanding that states adopt and uphold these principles in their own domestic laws. AI feels that international human rights law, if applied globally, provides the necessary provisions to support human rights and prevent abuses.[33] Given its adherence to such a context, it remains important to look more closely at how AI uses international human rights law to advance its campaign goals. The following analysis brings this context to light.

Chapter 9 of the campaign document is titled "Organizing for Change—Making a Difference." The first image to appear is of two women standing and one man sitting on the ground in front of a building. The caption reads

The Masisukumeni women's crisis center, Tonga, South Africa. The center was established in 1994 in a poor rural area to support and assist survivors of violence against women, to uphold their human and legal rights, and to work against gender violence through education programs.[34]

In the context of AI, this image functions as documentary proof of the success in fighting violence against women gained through legal mechanisms. The image of a women's crisis center is a testament to good practice. For AI, using the international bill of rights to oppose violence against women lends its campaign credibility because it enforces its point that violence against women is a public responsibility requiring legal and social redress.[35] It also challenges the perspective that violence against women is cultural and thus overturns arguments about it being a legitimate practice.[36] This stance raises two issues. First, it asserts that violence against women requires legal and social redress—ramifications delivered through state procedures. Second, it declares that violence against women is not a legitimate practice—hence, no matter where it is found, no law should defend such practices. This is how AI balances the moral and legal aspects of human rights. It promotes international human rights mechanisms, while at the same time condemning practices of violence against women as illegitimate. Therefore, it becomes apparent that AI believes that the law can protect women, but only when violence against women is seen as a human rights abuse. This is the rationale behind Irene Khan's statement, highlighted at the opening of the chapter, that the aim of the *Stop Violence against Women* campaign is to condemn violence. To protect women from becoming victims, AI builds the case that when violence is seen as an illegitimate practice and perpetrators (states and individuals) are prosecuted using international legal mechanisms, then women will no longer be victims of abuse and can then be free to exercise their own rights (empowerment). Interestingly, of its own admission, AI's campaign was a late addition to this struggle to end violence against women.[37]

AI has always based its work on championing the rights of the individual, but not until the 2004 campaign had it taken up economic, social and cultural rights in such an explicit way. To do this, it relied on the voluntary work and assistance of several other women's rights activists, who were consulted as experts in the preparations for the campaign.[38] Gaining support for the campaign among members was difficult for the International Secretariat (IS) because not all AI members wanted to take on issues relating to gender—instead some members felt that it was extraneous because women's rights was not a regional priority in all regions (interview, campaign coordinator, August 5, 2004). However, the IS maintained that AI has a significant role to play because as an organization, AI would shape work on violence against women in a human rights context, which is often not the case for women's rights organizations because they do not have the international legitimacy AI has. To demonstrate its position within human rights culture as part of the wider activism going on around this issue, the campaign document included many examples of images depicting women demonstrating against state laws that discriminate or ignore women's complaints of violence and abuse.[39] No connection to AI is claimed in these captions, but instead, these women, as members of various women's organizations, are considered to be in partnership with AI. The goal here is for AI to gain cultural capital in the field and credibility among campaigners that it is not just a letter-writing organization.

With this in mind then, it is important to realize why AI uses these images of women campaigners. Consider the images in Figures 5.2 and 5.3.

The captions for Figures 5.2 and 5.3 express members of particular women's organizations who are demonstrating against discrimination, violence and injustice. The first image is of women in Port-au-Prince, Haiti; the second image is of women in Mexico.[40] Since the focus of the campaign is

Figure 5.2 Demonstrators protest violence against women Wednesday, November 25, 1998, in Port-au-Prince, Haiti, in front of the Palace of Justice.

©AP/PA Images

Figure 5.3 Daniela embraces her girlfriend Maura during the first Lesbian March in Mexico City Friday, March 21, 2003. Thousands of women march asking for their rights and against discrimination.

©AP/PA Images

to stop women being victims of violence through empowerment, AI uses these images to show women's agency. AI understands agency as groups of women working together to fight violence.

Images such as that in Figure 5.1 show victims of violence. The women campaigners, even if they too have experiences of violence, are constructed in this campaign to represent non-victims (survivors)—women with agency. These united voices of condemnation and searches for justice, in the eyes of AI, empower these women. Because AI itself rarely marches or demonstrates, it uses the work of women's organizations—typified as demonstrators—to present women as powerful instead of as victims. These images help shape how AI visually represents violence against women as producing either victims or survivors. Let us compare Figures 5.2 and 5.3 with Figure 5.1. According to AI, women who are yelling, marching and demonstrating cannot be victims. Women sitting alone, their head in their hands and crying, can. This visual logic persists throughout the interpretive practices of the campaign.

How AI positions itself within the international community of human rights advocates and alongside women's organizations is significant for interpreting images in the campaign document because it outlines what meanings are available to the viewer. AI asserts that it is

[i]ndependent of any government, political ideology, economic interest or religion. It does not support or oppose any government or political system, nor does it support or oppose the views of the victims whose rights it seeks to protect. It is concerned solely with the impartial protection of human rights.[41]

In upholding international law verbatim, AI constructs and maintains this impartiality. The name Amnesty International is then taken to be synonymous with international law, constructing AI as an organization with the same objectives as those it seeks to uphold. Its vision statement speaks to this point directly: "Amnesty International's vision is of a world in which every person enjoys all the human rights enshrined in the Universal Declaration of Human Rights and other international human rights standards."[42] AI agrees to pursue this vision through research and action targeting the prevention and end to grave abuses of human rights. All of its work is done in the spirit of promoting all human rights for everyone. AI has been awarded the Nobel Peace Prize for its work on torture (1977) and the United Nations Prize in the Field of Human Rights (1978). This context, which grants AI special status within the United Nations, is primarily concerned with protecting human rights through international legal mechanisms. In line with this, AI fully supports the wording of such mechanisms and their ability to provide for *every person*.

To better understand what this means, I show how AI's adherence to international law and legal solutions to political problems poses complications for successful campaigns that can empower women. The campaign document is divided into nine chapters, each raising different aspects of violence against women and discussing the legal mechanisms that exist to help prevent such violations. I trace AI's strategy through each chapter.

Chapter 1 of the campaign document sets out violence against women as a human rights scandal and introduces the human rights framework. In constructing violence against women as a human rights abuse, AI quotes the UN Declaration on the Elimination of Violence against Women to formulate the legal scope of the campaign because it lays out in legal terms definitions of violence against women, which AI can then mobilize as the basis for its claims. Accompanying the UN Declaration on the Elimination of Violence against Women, AI's first chapter also highlights four guiding principles from the UDHR. They appear as follows:

- Human rights are universal—they belong to all people equally.
- Human rights are indivisible—no one right is more important than another right. All rights are of equal value and urgency and they cannot be separated.
- Human rights cannot be taken away or abrogated. The exercise of some rights can be limited, but only temporarily under very exceptional circumstances.
- Human rights are interdependent, so that the promotion and protection of any one right requires the promotion and protection of all other rights.[43]

These principles are the backbone of the legal foundation for the campaign. Under no circumstances does AI waiver from defending these human rights. Each international legal mechanism invoked within the document is automatically linked with these principles, and as such, AI sees them as enhancing the principles rather than as contradictory or problematic.

The second chapter in the campaign document focuses on sexuality, violence and rights. Here AI takes time to look at how sexuality is controlled by violence. Paragraph 96 of the Beijing Platform for Action, the intergovernmental agreement reached at the end of the Fourth UN World Conference on Women, is used to illustrate that

> [t]he human rights of women include their right to have control over and decide freely and responsible on matters of their sexuality, including sexual and reproductive health, free of coercion, discrimination and violence. Equal relationships between women and men in matters of sexual relations and reproduction, including full respect for the integrity of the person, require mutual respect, consent and shared responsibility for sexual behavior and its consequences.[44]

Using this excerpt, AI constructs the framework in which women can be understood to have agency and how violence against women deprives women of such agency. Looking to the World Health Organization's working definition, AI identifies sexual rights as embracing human rights that are already recognized in international law. These include for all persons the right to

- the highest attainable standard of health in relation to sexuality, including access to sexual and reproductive health-care services;
- seek, receive and impart information in relation to sexuality;
- sexual education;
- respect for bodily integrity;
- choice of partner;
- decide to be sexually active or not;
- consensual sexual relations;
- consensual relations;
- decide whether or not, and when to have children; and
- pursue a satisfying, safe and pleasurable sexual life.[45]

When these rights are not met, then, according to AI, human rights abuses are taking place. The argument that human rights are universal is the topic of chapter 3 of the campaign document. Defending against relativist arguments, Amnesty cites the then UN special rapporteur on violence against women as confirming that "the greatest challenge to women's rights and the elimination of discriminatory laws and harmful practices comes from the doctrine of cultural relativism."[46] In promoting human rights as universal, AI ensures that "every person" includes "all women" despite their cultural situations. Hence, in the context of AI, there is no room for difference unless it is written in international law.

The question of women's discrimination is addressed with regard to poverty and articulated as a "stigma" in the language of human rights in chapter 4 of the campaign document. This stigma of shame or social disgrace "is often deployed in order to portray some groups of people as less deserving or even less than human and is used as an excuse for violence."[47] Chapter 5 concerns abuses by armed groups in wars and conflicts. Excerpts from the Geneva Convention are quoted to explain that basic rights must be protected even during conflict and that failure to do so can result in criminal charges of war crimes and crimes against humanity.[48] The UN Security Council Resolution 1325 is used here because it

reaffirms women's rights to protection in conflict and the need for all parties to armed conflict to take special measures to the effect; expresses willingness on the part of the Security Council to incorporate a gender perspective into peacekeeping operations; calls on all actors involved in negotiating and implementing peace agreements to adopt a gender perspective; and urges member states to ensure increased representation of women at all decision-making levels in national, regional and international mechanisms for the prevention, management and resolution of conflict.[49]

What becomes apparent in AI's use of all these international legal mechanisms is the belief AI shares that human rights are worth protecting and that the mechanisms are in place to protect them universally if only governments and armed groups would respect these laws. For the context of the campaign, this message contributes to the campaign slogan "It's in our hands." AI claims that if the laws are upheld, because human rights are universal and interpreted as such in these laws and legal mechanisms, then violence against women, which is seen as a human rights abuse, can be stopped. Incorporating the Convention on the Elimination of All Forms of Discrimination Against Women (CEDAW) into chapter 6 of the campaign document supports AI's claim because the CEDAW "expressly requires states parties (those governments that have agreed to bind themselves to the Convention) to 'take all appropriate measures to eliminate discrimination against women by any person, organization or enterprise' (Article 2 (e))."[50] For AI, eliminating discrimination against women serves to protect women's rights as guaranteed within the UDHR. And this has been shown to be its vision, its mission and its goal.

The final three chapters of the campaign document continue to use those legal mechanisms already discussed to broach issues of impunity, parallel legal systems and organization for change. The importance of going through AI's use of the legal mechanism is to establish, in specific detail, how AI legally constructs violence against women as a human rights abuse. This move plays a substantial part in how the images will convey meaning and how AI comes to be understood internationally.

At this point it is important to pause and reflect on some arguments from the previous chapters of this book. In Chapter 2, I showed, through the work of feminist scholars, that international human rights law was itself male oriented. Given that AI relies so heavily on international legal mechanisms to construct its campaign, I argue that even though AI seeks to use these legal mechanisms to advance issues of *gender* in human rights (understood as violence against women), it sets out to do so within a context that occludes such progress. AI's campaign goals remain unattainable because the organization fails to be critical of the legal framework it employs to protect human rights. What this shows is that the three contexts (international human rights discourse, AI's use of international law and the campaign document) are all at work in the construction of the *Stop Violence against Women* campaign's visual logic. What AI is as an organization, what international law it employs and how it understands violence against women as a human rights abuse influence the production of visual meaning and subsequently practices of human rights. I now look at the impact of these contexts on how campaign images are interpreted by the viewer, at whom the campaign is targeted.

IMAGES OF WOMEN'S AGENCY

Through interviews with the photo researchers who put together the images for the campaign, I explore how the practice of photograph selection has an impact on how the images are to be interpreted. This section engages with how context influences the viewer's interpretation of the campaign images. The AI photo researcher spoke of a requirement for assessing both the needs of the organization and what will suit the product, in this case the campaign document (interview, August 6, 2004). Photo researchers are not immune from social, cultural and political discourses taking place within society. Thus, putting the images on the table and choosing them for the editorial committee are not independent of existing discursive and sociological communities but, rather, contribute to the production and reproduction of certain assumptions apparent in the visual culture associated with human rights advocacy. Therefore, those images selected are thereby contextualized in the language of the campaign, which itself operates within a larger context of international human rights discourse.

What's more is that every campaign has a set of principles that define the scope for AI photo researchers (interview with audio-visual coordinator, August 6, 2004). Given the goal of overturning women as victims of violence, the main principle for the *Stop Violence against Women* campaign is women's agency (interview with campaign coordinator, August 5, 2004). The campaign coordinator works from the perspective that "images convey meanings as much as words" (interview with campaign coordinator, August 5, 2004). This means that she, and AI by extension, understands that images operate as a constitutive discourse. In this sense, photo researchers are working within a visual discourse that has its own representational logic, which I explained earlier with the comparison of Figures 5.2 and 5.3 with Figure 5.1. Thus, the role of the photo researcher is to find visual representations of the possibility of women's agency in AI's conception of international human rights discourse. However, the use of photographic technology, a tool in visual discourse, is not without problems.[51]

In outlining some of these problems, an AI researcher acknowledged that "the first thing human rights advocates must consider is that they cause no harm to those they want to help; images can cause harm so we must be very vigilant about how they are used" (interview, August 6, 2004). Photography, as an act of recording things, implicates the viewer in the process of producing the photographic subject.[52] In other words, within human rights discourses, photography as a tool in visual discourse is a collaborative act that recognizes "evidence that a human life is at stake."[53] This notion of recognizing those human lives at stake impels many human rights organizations, including AI, to use images of victims in their campaigns.[54]

It is useful here to pause and reconsider how interpretive practices work. Like context, visual discourse produces meaning. However, I argue that in the case of AI, discourse is decisive—it stipulates what stories can be told within the context; these are partial stories and therefore do not encapsulate all that is implicated in a context of gender and human rights. How the viewer interprets an image shapes the image itself. The context of the viewer provides the pool from which meaning can be derived. This in turn structures how the viewer will interpret the image. It is through visual discourse that we become visually literate as viewers. Discourses are useful because they provide a particular set of rules, which influences how and what interpretations can be made. Using international law as one discourse, AI chooses to adhere to those principles contained within the discourse and to accept the limitations of interpretation. In fact, its entire campaign is about how seeing international law as a limitation, which is why AI struggles to represent agency. AI relies on the discursive element of what Chandler calls "a hapless victim in distress" story. His argument follows Jonathon Benthall's moral *fairy story*, in which there are three key players. The first component is the hapless victim in distress. In the famine fairy story, this victim is always portrayed through film of the worst cases of child malnutrition in the worst feeding centers. In cases of civil conflict, the victims are often war refugees who have been "ethnically cleansed," as we see in Figure 5.4. The second component is the villain, the non-Western government or state authorities, the third component is the savior—the external aid agency, the international

Figure 5.4   Ethnic Albanians leave the woods where they had been hiding for three days to escape the shelling of their villages in Kosovo.

©Andrew Testa/Panos Pictures

institution or even the journalists covering the story whose interests were seen to be inseparable from those of the deserving victim.[55] Victimization stories used in this campaign "can be understood, in part, as a consequence of the primacy of violence against women as an organizing device in the international women's human rights movement."[56] In an AI context, the players are the victims of violence against women; the perpetrators, which implicate states and individuals; and the savior, AI, as a human rights organization. In contrast, Irene Khan affirmed the *Stop Violence against Women* campaign sought to break from typifying survivors of violence as victims. But as I show, AI visually produced a victimization story in order to represent agency as the alternative to victimization. In AI's case, the story is useful for manipulating the viewer into seeing violence against women as a human rights abuse because the viewer recognizes, within the images, his or her own humanity. I will pick up this line of argument later on, but first a look at how AI claims to circumvent stories of victimization.

As a first step in breaking the stigmatization of women as victims, AI obtains individual consent of the person in the photograph before the image is used (interview with campaign coordinator, August 5, 2004). This is not a unique practice; however, acquiring consent of the photographed implicates "the viewer, the reader and the witness within local and global communities."[57] AI desires to achieve this as the title of the campaign publication *It's in our Hands* acknowledges through the use of the pronoun *our*. For AI, consent allows the photographic subject to speak about experiences of violence. In this way, the images within AI's 2004 campaign aim to complicate a "simplistic spectacle of victimization by visualizing a post-traumatic space of public dissonance in which gender, violence, and recovery rub up against each other in discomforting ways."[58] As an example of this discomfort, consider Figure 5.4.

Figure 5.4 appears on page 5 of *It's in our Hands*. Placed within the campaign document, the image is an example of AI's visual discourse, leaving the viewer to interpret the image of this woman as having experience of violence against women. The gestures of sitting in a cart, hands reaching out, and crying are all components of the visual logic that denote visual representations of women who suffer violence. Here, as in Figure 5.1, AI tries to avoid what Hesford and Kozol termed *a simplistic spectacle of victimization* by choosing an image that does not shock its viewers through scenes of violence, but instead depicts a posttraumatic moment. The caption contextualizes these people as refugees from the conflict in Kosovo.[59]

The viewer is asked to interpret the conflict in Kosovo as relating to human rights and to regard this woman as a survivor of the conflict—in that each is alive in the image. Recalling Martinsons, neither the photographer nor the viewer can speak for the photographic subject. The subject of the photograph "must have the ontological status to speak for her/himself and for a host of others."[60] Through gaining consent to use her photograph, AI wants this photographic subject to speak of her experiences of violence.

Two assumptions are made here. First, AI assumes that consent of the photographic subject allows her to speak, giving her agency. Second, AI assumes that the viewer will be aware that consent was sought. AI wants the photographic subject to *tell* her story through body language so that the viewer might begin to understand the brutality she has endured and how the viewer having now *seen*, is implicated in the process: "violence against women will only end when each one of us is ready to make that pledge: not to do it, or permit others to do it, or tolerate it, or rest until it is eradicated."[61] This woman, with her arms reaching out to the viewer, embodies the hapless victim in distress because she is reaching out to the viewer crying for help. The caption says she is an ethnic Albanian fleeing her village in Kosovo to escape shelling.[62] Women fleeing their homes because of conflict is a global phenomenon, AI tells us, and as such, the plight of the individuals in this cart becomes representative of the plight of many around the globe.

The photographic subjects in this image speak of conflict, of displacement and of experiences of violence. They come to represent what really happens to people in times of civil unrest, conflict and war. This is an example of how AI utilizes a representational logic. AI uses this image as factual evidence that violence against women occurs. The visual discourse operates as a relationship between the viewer and the photographic image. The viewer has learned through context that this image speaks of violence against women. The viewer has also learned through context that women who are portrayed as crying and distressed are victims. Therefore, the viewer, via context and visual logic interprets the image as one of a victim of violence against women. As a result, the viewers focus their gaze on the plight of the woman in the foreground reaching out to the viewer. The gaze of the viewer in turn renders the woman—now singled out as the photographic subject— a victim and therefore without agency. According to the sources I interviewed, photo researchers must obtain approximately four hundred images for any large-scale campaign like *Stop Violence against Women* (interview with audio-visual coordinator, August 6, 2004). These images are obtained from a variety of sources: photo archives from within the organization itself, other media agencies such AS AP or Panos Pictures or photographers who either donate images or are commissioned for a specific purpose. The images must depict, in some way, the theme of the campaign (interview with audio-visual coordinator, August 6, 2004). For this particular campaign, images depict the possibility of women's agency in AI's concept of international human rights discourse. Given that the theme of the campaign is women's agency, it becomes obvious that gaining consent of the photographic subject is clearly not enough to undo the stigma of women as victims. Returning to Martinsons, the photographic subject of this image is not given the ontological status to speak for herself even though AI claims to be using her in this way because more than discursive freedom is needed. Interpretive practices encouraging agency require that the photographic subject remain incomplete rather than wholly representative of any one event or situation. AI's interpretive practices, because they are attempts to visualize legal discourse, are insufficient in accomplishing this goal.

One of the interesting lines of questioning in the interviews was how AI visually understands women's agency (interviews with audio-visual coordinator, photo researcher, August 6, 2004). By referencing the images from *It's in our Hands*, we discussed how AI constructs a visual discourse that conveys their understanding of women's agency. AI's visual intention is to empower women by letting the photographic subjects speak. I suggest that the Figures 5.1 and 5.4 are among photographs of refugees that

> fall easily into generic conventions that for much of the twentieth century have mobilized support for one side in the conflict by using images of mothers and children as metonyms for the innocent victims. This representation of innocence relies on heteronormative ideals expressed through the mother-child dyad.[63]

AI keeps to these forms of representation. AI's choice of images fits with generic conventions of depicting mothers and children as victims. The viewer is not certain whether the woman in the cover image is the mother of the child who is trying to comfort her or whether the young boys pictured behind the women in the cart are their sons. However, because representations within conventional heteronormative visual discourses rely on the reduction of woman to an articulation of a reproductive sex (mother–child dyad) to invoke responses, the viewer is left making this connection. AI wants the photographic subject to speak of experiences of victimization and violence against women to show she has agency. Her intended voice is her empowerment. However, the question remains: Does visual representation enable her to speak at all?

Figure 5.5 depicts a group of women and one girl sitting, their arms around each other at a table. The caption reads

> Following an earthquake in Turkey in 1999 the Women's Solidarity Foundation was formed to "provide all women with the means to be independent and stand on their own feet." This group has come together to contribute to this work.[64]

What can this visual discourse tell us about how AI understand agency? According to the photo researcher, groups of women working together have agency (interview, August 6, 2004). The linking of their arms shows a connection both physical and ideological (interview with photo researcher, August 6, 2004). In this context, agency means empowerment, as the caption reads "independence," the ability to "stand on your own two feet."[65] According to AI, working in groups helps achieve this independence. Most of the women are looking into the camera and smiling. This is a stark contrast to the cover photo of the woman with her head in her hands or the woman in the cart crying out to someone beyond the image. These women are sitting around a table, comfortable, indoors and visually free from violence. In this visual discourse, AI defines women with agency as being autonomous actors who are no longer under threat of violence, who are empowered and who are recognized as members of a sympathetic group. In the context of this campaign, these groups tend to form around common experiences of violence. This is a good example of how AI sees itself overturning the stigma of women as victims. For AI, the photographic subjects in the campaign document speak of common experiences of violence; they speak of victimization. The image of the Turkish women in Figure 5.5 also functions as another example of a posttraumatic moment in AI's visual discourse. These photographic subjects have experienced violence, as the caption reads, but they have survived and through solidarity are working toward independence. AI sees this independence as reflective of agency (interview with photo researcher, August 6, 2004). This image mirrors AI's own campaign strategy, which is to work with other women's activists to help AI acculturate itself into thematic campaigning. Therefore, it is not surprising that AI sees women working together as empowering, because they are practicing this idea themselves.

Figure 5.5 Following an earthquake in Turkey in 1999, the Women's Solidarity Foundation was formed to "provide women with the means to be independent and stand on their own two feet." This group has come together to contribute to this work.

However, AI's adherence to legal discourse limits the success of their campaign. As Kozol indicates, "the seeming transparency of photographic technologies legitimizes claims of the 'real' in ways that ignore how gender categories are encoded within these visual perspectives."[66] For AI to visually represent the possibility of women's agency, it should refuse to encode the photographic subject within binary gender categories.

How AI understands the relationship between subjectivity and power can be articulated as follows: make women a recognizable gender category and they will have power through existing provisions provided in human rights law; empowered women will no longer be victims; without the victim stigma, women are no longer the subject of violence. Consequently, making violence the focus (as the chapter-opening remark from Irene Khan indicates) means breaking down binary gender categories of women as victims and men as perpetrators. Unfortunately, more is going on here than AI realizes. In visual terms, agency lies at the interface between the photographic subject and what the image is meant to represent. Earlier, I explained that the viewer defines the photographic subject. This means that agency is only possible when the viewer distinguishes between the photographic subject as an image and the photographic subject as a presence beyond the image. AI wants the ethnic Albanian woman in the cart (Figure 5.4) to be present in the image and to tell her story as a photographic subject. AI also wants this ethnic Albanian woman in the cart to be known as present in the real world beyond the image, in Kosovo, after the photograph is taken. This dual presence seems genuine and on the surface does in fact accomplish AI's goal of allowing the photographic subject to speak. Nonetheless, this duality of presence is understood in a very specific context that employs limited expressions of agency. This means that for AI the ethnic Albanian woman is physically present at the time of the photograph and remains physically present after the photograph is taken. Physical presence for AI is embodied subjectivity, and once a subject is embodied, it can be represented as a complete entity. It continues to be the thrust of this argument, however, that representations that seek complete subjects are expressions of word–object relations, which results in the objectification of the subject. When a subject is objectified, meaning is fixed—as I showed with discussions of how AI constructs the viewer as part of a victimization story—and when meaning is fixed, the agency of the photographic subject is lost.

Photography, as a technology employed in AI's campaign, functions to capture the real of violence against women. The viewer is told how to interpret the visual image through context. Because AI invokes a victimization story, the viewer is seduced by the images and, as a result, accepts uncritically the meanings produced within the story and interprets them in the image. This seduction is how sedimentation works. AI consistently repeats variations of the same image in its context that says the image is representative of victims of violence against women, which lulls the viewer into passively accepting these representations as real. The viewer is convinced that these images are important because the context of universal human rights states that all human beings are entitled to rights because they are human, meaning that when these rights are abused, human lives are at stake. As such, viewers are confronted with their own humanity. Confronting their own humanity causes the viewer to momentarily—the decisive moment, as the photo researcher called it—place themselves in the image as photographic subject (interviews with photo researcher, August 6, 2004). In this way, the viewers are able to contextualize themselves in relation to the image and experience their own embodiment. The comfort of the sedimented images predetermines meaning. This degree of certainty of meaning gives the viewers a glimpse into their own humanity, which confirms the severity of the issue and reinforces AI's position as an international human rights organization. It seems that because sedimentation is part of visual culture, no viewers desire to place themselves at risk of violence; therefore, they resolve to accept the discourse without challenge. In summary, because AI uses images to show reality it is not only removing agency from the photographic subject (by fixing the photographic subject to an object) but also removing agency from the viewers (by objectifying their position as viewers). As Chapter 3 clarified, if agency is attempted in a fixed context, it will be unsuccessful. In order to speak of subjects with agency, I argue agency must be understood as an interface with power thus exposing subjectivity and power as mutually constituting processes. For these reasons, AI's desire for complete subjects makes it impossible for it to succeed in empowering women within universal human rights discourse.

To further expand this interpretive practice, I explore AI's appropriation of encoded gender categories as written in international law and how this has an impact on AI's understanding of agency. Through an analysis of the conflation of gender and sex, I demonstrate that AI has a limited concept of agency, such that it cannot empower women despite its best efforts to do so.

WOMAN AS VICTIM

In this section I show how AI conflates gender and sex and how this conflation produces the interpretation of woman as victim. I further link the association of woman with victim being derivative of a binary discourse found in international human rights law. I show that because AI takes its definition of gender from international law, it is unable to fully empower women. In the end, I claim that for AI, its campaign reduces woman (gender) to an elaboration of sex because, as Chapter 3 has shown, international human rights law adheres to exclusive binary gender codes. This presents a problem for AI because the tools they have chosen for the job—international law—are insufficient to address the root causes of violence against women as women are unequal to men in this discourse.

AI uses the UN Declaration on the Elimination of Violence against Women as support for its position that the "underlying cause of violence against women lies in discrimination which denies women equality with men in all areas of life."[67] Given that AI adopts and promotes the UDHR, which codifies equal rights of men and women, AI finds itself engaging with the roots of violence against women and, as such, with conceptions of gender in human rights discourse. Historically, gender (understood as women's) issues in international human rights was brought to the fore in 1979 and adopted in 1981 with the CEDAW. Described as an international bill of rights for women, the CEDAW "provides the basis for realizing equality between women and men."[68] The CEDAW laid the groundwork for subsequent legal mechanisms such as the UN Declaration on the Elimination of Violence against Women, on which AI bases its work on violence against women. As such, the organization is confined to the parameters set out by such legislation.[69] Article 1 of the UN Declaration on the Elimination of Violence against Women states that "the term 'violence against women' means any act of gender-based violence that results in, or is likely to result in, physical, sexual or psychological harm or suffering to women."[70] AI adopts the term *gender-based violence* and quotes the CEDAW General Recommendation No. 19 (1992), to solidify a working definition; violence "directed against a woman because she is a woman or that affects women disproportionately."[71]

In its extrapolation of the meaning provided by the UN documents, AI clarifies that

> not all acts which harm a woman are gender-based and not all victims of gender-based violence are female . . . men are victims of gender-based violence, for example gay men who are harassed, beaten and killed because they do not conform to socially approved views of masculinity.[72]

Therefore, according to AI's use of international law, gender-based violence is violence that occurs because of the presence of a particular gender. Subsequently, AI's use of this definition also establishes a link between the term *victim* and the concept of gender.

Let us look at how these moves are made. AI starts with international law as the foundation for its claims that violence against women is a human rights abuse. As I argued in Chapter 2, exclusive discourse assumes all relationships it describes are heterosexual and that they privilege male/masculine qualities and constructions over female/feminine ones. The rules for the language-game confirm what possible meanings are available as referents. In Chapter 2 I also established that in international law the term *woman* refers to the *object* adult female body because an exclusionary discourse engages with context through representational logic, which assumes the word–object relation is axiomatic. This explains why woman can only mean "female body" as the physical object referred to by the word *woman*. AI's desire for embodied subjects reflects a word–object relation (woman–female body), which in turn fixes meaning in this context. Therefore, when the term *woman* is invoked in international law, the axiomatic process of representational logic can only produce the meaning "female body" as referent, despite any efforts to do otherwise. This line of reasoning explains why AI makes a point of distinguishing that gay men can also be victims of gender-based violence. As I stated binary contexts privilege male/masculine over female/feminine and assume heterosexual relations. Therefore, applied to the term *man*, it is axiomatic that the referent be "male body." However, when considering the gender identity "gay man," the word–object relation man–male body is skewed because man is only capable of being heterosexual and masculine in a binary context, therefore precluding the possibility of a masculine homosexual man. This disrupts the word–object relation because the object (male body) is used to represent nonheterosexual masculine characteristics, usually associated with femininity. When femininity is confined to female bodies, the context cannot explain the presence of male bodies exhibiting femininity. This is an effect of the conflation of with sex and is the very reason why, in the context of this campaign, a link between gender and victim is established. In the following, I show that international law, being an exclusionary discourse, constructs men

Figure 5.6 Women using an official "writer" to help with their petition to a court in Kabul, Afghanistan. Women victims of crime are denied access to justice in Afghanistan, and there are few prosecutions for crimes against women. Cases which reach the criminal justice system usually do so where a woman or girl has the assistance of a male relative or supporter.

as those who carry out violence, as opposed to women on whom abuse is exercised. Interpreting Figure 5.6 discursively supports this point.

For AI, Figure 5.6 is an example of how photographic subjects speak as women who are victims of violence. The caption for this image reads

Women using an official 'writer' to help with their petition to a court in Kabul, Afghanistan. Women victims of crime are denied access to justice in Afghanistan and there are few prosecutions for crimes against women. Cases which reach the criminal justice system usually do so where a woman or has the assistance of a male relative or supporter.[73]

This example is particularly useful because it demonstrates the duplicity of mounting a campaign around the theme of women's agency in a binary context. The caption informs the viewer that the context in which these women live (Afghanistan) denies women the right to speak on their own behalf; however, AI chose this image with the aim of making these women's voices heard—allowing them to speak as photographic subjects. AI intends to give these women voices by using this photograph in their campaign. A binary definition of gender also comes out in AI's intended interpretation of the image, and I deal with this aspect momentarily. What is particularly important to note here is that AI supports the idea that violence against women is gender based and that those who experience violence against women, understood now as gender-based violence, are victims. The relationship between the term *victim* and the concept of gender begins to unfold. However, to understand this further, AI's concept of gender must first be established.

For AI, gender refers to

[t]he attributes associated with being male and female. Rather than being biologically determined, gender is a set of learned behaviors, shaped by expectations which stem from the idea that certain qualities, behaviors, characteristics needs and roles are 'natural' and desirable for men, while others are 'natural' and desirable for women. Gender is a critical element of power and inequality. Women's gender roles are generally accorded less political, economic, social and cultural value than those of men.[74]

From this definition, it seems that AI takes gender to mean socially constructed categories of behavior that are determined not by biological distinctions but through unequal power dimensions found in political, economic, social and cultural contexts. It also makes clear that "woman" does not operate on equal par with "man."

Here it is helpful to reevaluate AI's definition of gender in relation to the aim of the *Stop Violence against Women* campaign. The purpose of the campaign is stated negatively so as not to portray women as victims and stigmatize men as perpetrators but to condemn the act of violence itself. However, its definition of gender does not entirely disrupt discursive norms that establish differences between the gender roles of men and those of women because it still divides learned behavior as that "natural and desirable for men" and that "natural and desirable for women." Accordingly, it seems that even though behavior is learned (socially constructed), it must be learned in a particular way. If you are female, it is natural for you to desire to behave like a woman. If you are male, it is natural for you to desire to behave like a man. This definition of gender does not challenge the stigmatization of women as victims and of men as perpetrators because, of its own admission those behaviors that are natural and desirable, for men are attributed more power than are those behaviors natural and desirable for women. Put bluntly, this definition of gender reinforces women's association with victimhood by making women subordinate to men.

If, as AI claims, gender-based violence against women occurs because of the presence of a particular gender, (i.e., Article 1 of the UN Declaration on Elimination of All Forms of Violence Against Women), and women as a gender category are unequal to the gender category men,[75] then what is being elided in this focus on women as victims is the gendered aspect of violence itself. Not only is the aim of the campaign to dissolve a particular gendered stigma, but even more so, it is also to condemn the act of violence. However, in its attempt to condemn the act of violence, AI delineates between the act of violence and the victims of such violence. Using the language of international law AI constructs a discourse wherein violence exists outside the context of those who suffer the violence (as AI sees it). Therefore, for AI, the difference between a victim of violence and an act of violence is that the former is gendered, while the latter is not. Given AI's reproduction of a binary conception of gender, linking victim with gender discursively renders it impossible for Amnesty to visually represent a woman with agency. The women depicted in Figures 5.1, through 5.6 remain disempowered because the exclusionary discourse disables AI's attempts to represent empowered women in human rights discourse.

As a result, perpetrators are gendered beings but the act they perform is not. This is problematic because victims are only defined by the violence they endure, which leads perpetrators to being solely defined by the violence they enact (i.e., endorses men as perpetrators and women as victims). Because its concept of agency arises in a non-gendered understanding of violence, AI not only maintains the stigmatization of men as perpetrators and women as victims but also renders the campaign incapable of presenting an articulation of woman with agency. Figure 5.7 illustrates this point.

Figure 5.7 appears in the campaign document *It's in Our Hands*.[76] The caption reads "A survivor of sexual violence in Sierra Leone, where systematic rape and other forms of sexual violence have been used as weapons of war and to instill terror during a decade of internal conflict."[77] This image

Figure 5.7   A survivor of sexual violence in Sierra Leone, where systematic rape and other forms of sexual violence have been used as weapons of war and to instill terror during a decade of internal conflict.

©Nick Danziger/Contact Press Images

is another example of a posttraumatic moment. The visual discourse of the woman, facing away from the camera, head lowered and body limp, informs the viewer that the photographic subject is a victim of violence. Incorporated in the victimization stories of AI's visual discourse is the presence of a perpetrator of violence. In the case of the image in Figure 5.7, by committing acts of sexual violence against the photographic subject, the perpetrator renders the photographic subject a victim of violence against women. The perpetrator is absent from the visualization of the posttraumatic moment but is present as the cause of the photographic subject's traumatic experience. Sexual violence—as a weapon of war—is not part of the gendered binary of victim/perpetrator because AI does not explore the gendered aspects of war itself. AI's campaign focuses only on victims of violence. Perpetrators are defined by their ability to render the photographic subject a victim of violence, not by the violence they enact on the subject herself. It follows then that rape becomes a tool of the trade for perpetrators of violence against women, not the defining characteristic as it would if the term *rapist* were used to identify the perpetrator. In this way, AI's visual discourse interprets perpetrators as gendered beings who commit non-gendered acts of violence.

If we apply AI's delineation between gender and violence to Figure 5.7, then the woman in this image, having suffered gender-based violence, is a victim. Moreover, according to AI, a victim is a gendered being. Alternately, the violence endured by this victim is not gendered. Therefore, if we reinterpret Figure 5.7 and how AI use it, we see a case where AI applies the term *sexual violence* in a context that must consider rape as a non-gendered act. Rape, an act of violence that by its very definition is sexualized because of the biological element of both the crime and the body of the victim, is removed from a gendered interpretation.

AI uses the UN Declaration on the Elimination of Violence against Women to acknowledge that violence against women may be physical, psychological and sexual and that these are not mutually exclusive categories.[78] It seems then that AI's argument has four components. First, gender is socially constructed but is limited to behaviors deemed natural and desirable. Second, violence against women is taken to mean gender-based violence. Third, gender-based violence occurs because of the sex of the gender women. Finally, women who suffer gender-based violence are victims. However, violence is still missing from this gendered analysis.

To clarify, let us consider how these claims relate to each other. The first claim *violence against women is gender-based* works because AI has established that women are understood as a gender category. The problem arises in the relationship between claims 2 and 3: *violence against women means gender-based violence* but *gender-based violence occurs because of the sex of the gender woman*. AI explains that the gendered woman has a particular sex (female) that can be a target for violent perpetrators. The violence described herein is discussed in sexualized but not in gendered terms. The stigma victim/perpetrator genders both the victim and the perpetrator but not the violence. It seems then that gender-based violence is sexualized but not gendered. Furthermore, violence is sexualized in exclusively heteronormative and male-oriented ways. It becomes clear then, that AI's use of the term *sexual violence* is problematic because it produces a gendered victim from a non-gendered act. A closer look at AI's adherence to international law will help expand this interpretation.

For AI to condemn violence in the context of violence against women, it needs to condemn women as victims. Attempts to do this are made through visually representing women survivors of violence against women as having agency. Unfortunately, simply juxtaposing images of victims with images intended to show empowered women does not challenge the victimization story. Rather, it simply succeeds in producing more images of victims.

Furthermore, if the victim is gendered, and the victim is produced as such by the violence she endures, then it becomes apparent that the violence being acted out on the victim must also be gendered. We know this to be the case by looking at the international law AI supports. AI obtained the term *gender-based violence* from the use of the UN Declaration on the Elimination of Violence against Women.[79] Furthermore, AI, with CEDAW, enhances its concept of violence against women, accepting the definition as violence directed against a woman or that affects women disproportionately.[80] Both of these legal mechanisms draw a link between gender and violence. Thus, AI's attempt to represent women as having agency in human rights discourse fails because AI does not engage with violence against women as gendered. Without contextualizing violence as gendered, AI maintains woman as victim, and therefore, agency is lost.

What is needed for an agential articulation of woman in human rights discourse is a concept of agency that accounts for both an expanded understanding of gender that is not reduced to sex and a consideration for the context in which this gendered being expresses itself. The final part of this section uses the work of Judith Butler to illustrate another way of engaging with women's agency that attempts to create the possibility for women to have agency.

Judith Butler uses the concept of performance to break away from conflations of sex and gender she finds inherent in many social discourses. She asks the reader to

> [c]onsider that a sedimentation of gender norms produce the peculiar phenomenon of a 'natural sex' or a 'real woman' or any number of prevalent and compelling social fictions, and that this is a sedimentation that over time has produced a set of corporeal styles which, in reified form, appear as the natural configuration of bodies into sexes existing in a binary relation to one another.[81]

According to Butler, "the action of gender requires a performance that is repeated," and this repetition is simultaneously a reenactment and reexperiencing of already socially established meanings.[82] Legitimacy for these repetitions lies within their mundane and ritualized enactments.

AI's definition of gender is evidence of this point. For AI, gender refers to characteristic needs and roles that are *natural* and desirable for women and men, independent of each other.[83] Gender humanizes individuals within contemporary culture and thus as a strategy of survival within compulsory systems, gender is a performance with clearly punitive consequences.[84] The compulsory notion of performance is evidenced by AI's definition of gender: inclusion in the realm of human rights is determined by the gender you perform. The reference AI makes to gay men suffering violence for their sexuality is case and point: "some men are victims of gender-based violence . . . gay men who are harassed, beaten and killed because they do not conform to socially approved views of masculinity."[85] AI claims that gay men do not perform the compulsory heteronormative gender identity scripted in international law and, as a result of their exclusion, become subjects of violence. The humanizing effect of gender in human rights discourse is that it excludes particular gender performances and thus renders them outside the scope of documentation and international law. This is problematic because, as Butler asserts, gender norms are impossible to embody.[86] The repetitive performance of a particular identity normalizes that identity within a specific context but does not require the performed identity to be static or unchanging. In the cases AI present violence against women is repeatedly associated with their sex, and as such they are victimized for it (e.g., rape as a weapon of war). Gay men are also victimized because they are understood to have female characteristics, and thus, their bodies are not those of heterosexual masculinity. Only two corporeal identities are possible: male body or female body. Thus, if gay men cannot have male bodies because of their particular gender identity, they become by default female bodies. This is why AI is able to include gay men in its conception of gender-based violence, because gay men, in AI's concept, have female bodies, and gender-based violence happens because of the presence of female bodies.

However, Butler asserts that there will be certain identities whose performance challenges the norm in a way in which it is unable to be normalized. This discontinuity is integral to a fluid construction of gender, one that is not fixed or limited by a binary discourse. Gender then becomes constituted by social temporality, within the time and space of a given society.[87] The implications for this in human rights discourse are troublesome, in that if adopted by policy makers, a performative concept of gender would challenge the foundation on which international legal human rights discourse rests because it would disrupt the fixed terms of *man* and *woman* by offering multiple referents for the term *human* in human rights. AI has helped and upheld the exclusionary discourse by appropriating international legal human rights discourse as a key element of its advocacy. It remains impossible for AI to escape the sex–gender articulations of woman and man that are so prominent in their current campaign *Stop Violence against Women* because it uses this binary discourse, as part of a visual discourse, to construct its definition of gender. Therefore, in terms of the possibility of visual representations of women's agency, imagining a new discourse that accounts for the potential of performative gender renders the impossible possible by opening up the context through which the photographic subject can speak her experience. Applying Butler's concept of gender means the photographic subjects in Figures 5.1, through 5.7 are no longer limited to speaking stories of victimization, which conflate gender and sex, but instead are given both visual and discursive spaces to tell their gendered stories in a manner that, with the viewer having the necessary discursive tools, can now interpret them as possible.

Until gender is understood as a fluid concept, which can be detached from a narrow focus on sex, the human rights of some women and men will continue to be disregarded, overlooked and ignored.

GENDERED VIOLENCE

In order to move beyond discursive frameworks that see women as victims of violence must be contextualized as gendered. This section exposes the discursive challenges of visually representing women's agency in the *Stop Violence against Women* campaign. It shows that AI conceptualizes the photographic subject as an embodied gendered agent, thus limiting the possibility of woman's agency and reproducing gender norms in a context that fails to contextualize violence as gendered. As I stated previously, agency involves mutually constitutive relationships between subjectivity and power. Interpreting agency discursively opens up possibilities for gendering subjectivity and power in discourses of violence against women because it resists the need to represent reality in corporeal form by seeing woman as the subject of violence, not merely as the object of violence. I argue that when violence against women is gendered, the victim/perpetrator stigma is broken because the acts of violence against women are gendered. A gendered notion of agency in a context that interprets violence as gendered provides for the possibility of empowerment for women in human rights discourse.

I begin by returning to AI's conception of women's agency. For AI, agency is about independence; it is about being an empowered autonomous actor who is no longer under threat of violence. In AI's visual discourse, agency is marked in the posttraumatic moment, read as survivors of violence. Acquiring permission from the photographic subject before using her photograph is one way AI attempts to attribute agency to the photographic subject. As stated earlier, there is an assumption that viewers will be privy to this process of consent. Obtaining permission is a method of recognizing the autonomy of the photographic subject. Letting her speak her story through body language is another device AI uses. In the *Stop Violence against Women* campaign, images work as canvases on which AI applies agency to photographic subjects by creating a context that allows these women to speak through visual representations.

AI, via this campaign, wants to stop women being perceived as victims by providing empowered articulations of woman in human rights discourse. It seeks to transform this stigma through recontextualizing images of victims. AI desires an embodied account of agency that the viewer can see—represented visually—in order to know—provide evidence—that violence against women, considered a human rights abuse, continues to occur (interview with photo researcher, August 6, 2004). Herein lies the problem. Butler tells us that gender norms are impossible to embody.[88] And, as I have argued, AI's use of the term *gender* reproduces binary gender norms. It follows then that an ontological desire for embodiment (corporeal reality) as proof is counterintuitive to Butler's notion of gender performance because it fixes (objectifies) woman to female body, denying her subjectivity, power and agency. To avoid gender conflation and to conceive of gender as performative, one needs to resist seeing as knowing and work toward interpretations that increase what becomes possible by resisting the desire to represent the real. Acquiring permission of the photographic subject is not in itself problematic, nor is the desire to visually represent agency. However, given that context determines how the viewer will interpret the image, the inadequate accounts of consent and agency expressed in AI's visual discourse remains problematic. Hence, mounting a campaign in the context of international human rights law, which is steeped in an exclusionary discourse, prevents AI from succeeding in their aim to stop violence against women because the viewer has yet to be fully implicated as a potential perpetrator. I argue that an interpretive practice that has agency requires implicating the viewer, and it is to this point that I now turn.

AI's international recognition as a human rights nongovernmental organization places it within an international discourse of human rights that continues to battle with concepts of sex and gender.[89] For AI to advocate effectively for women's agency, it would need to begin by challenging the binary discourse of international human rights discourse, instead of seeking to uphold it. This begins with contextualizing violence as gendered.

If the victim is gendered, and the victim is produced as such by the violence he or she endured, then it becomes apparent that the violence being acted out on the victim must also be gendered. In a context of gendered violence, the perpetrator is not read narrowly through the process of victimization that fixes the meaning of perpetrator to men. Instead, a context of gendered violence reads the perpetrator as a gender-performing being, a fluid gendered identity with agency constituted through relationships of subjectivity and power. Once the perpetrator is understood to have agency, then the words *it's in our hands* begin to resonate with us, the viewers. Avoiding the victim/perpetrator stigma implicates all people as potential perpetrators because it realizes that men are not the only gender category capable of violence. We, the viewers, are now implicated in the discourse of violence against women as a potential perpetrator because our presence in the visual discourse is recognized as a gendered relationship. As viewers, we become potential agents of violence, opening the concept of victim to multiple referents (subjectivities), thus invoking a fluid concept of agency. The photographic subject as a gender-performing being need not be strictly defined by the violence enacted on her; she may also be a gendered agent, whose subjectivity as a survivor can now have power to speak of experiences of violence as gendered acts.

By putting violence in context, agency is contextualized because violence needs an agent: an individual or a state to partake in enacting violence against women. An un-gendered notion of violence means that AI cannot escape the binary discourse in international law. Furthermore, only non-contextualized notions of violence create victims because they define victim through violence, thus eradicating the agent from view. For AI to condemn violence and see individuals as responsible, it needs to contextualize violence so that the notion of victim is not attributed to sex but is, instead, a performing gendered individual, which can then explain why particular acts of violence are more prevalent or directed disproportionately toward women. In this sense, the aim of condemning violence begins to appear as a possibility. Until AI contextualizes violence against women as gendered, it cannot begin advocating for women's agency in a way that empowers women.

CONCLUSION

In her forward to the campaign's publication *It's in our Hands*, Irene Khan writes, "[T]his campaign is like no other that we have organized before because it calls on each of us to take responsibility."[90] AI, in breaking away from only targeting states as the perpetrator of violence, broadens the scope of agents of violence against women to include all of humanity. The result of this new direction is an attempt to look at the relationship between gender and agency in human rights. Using international law as support for its position, AI puts forward a definition of gender and gender-based violence that seeks to dissolve the stigmatization of women as victims and men as perpetrators. The strategy AI uses to attempt to escape from this gendered stigma is to advocate for women's agency. The aim of the campaign is to empower women by showing them not as victims but as emancipated agents. And as the statement from Irene Khan at the beginning of this section indicates, the campaign implicates every individual as a perpetrator of violence whether passively (by permitting others to do it, by tolerating it) or actively (by enacting violence), and accepts nothing less than the eradication of said violence. According to the slogan, stopping violence against women is in our hands.

However, if AI seeks to condemn the act of violence itself, it must contextualize violence as gendered to fully target all individuals as responsible. A fluid concept of gender and agency creates individuals who can be understood to enact or endure violence. Accounting for the social, cultural, historical, political and economic contexts of gendered individuals can help with understanding what causes individuals to resort to violence and how violence may be perpetrated because of the presence of particular gender performances.

I argue that AI needs to turn its critical eye inward to its own use of international human rights mechanisms. When AI begins to question its own involvement in constructing the context in which these images appear, then gender can be understood as performative. Gender when understood as performative does not conflate sex and gender, such that AI can break away from stigmatizing women as victims and men as perpetrators because the focus is a gendered individual rather than a biological sex. It becomes possible to empower such an individual only when the socially constructed roles that were previously assigned according to biological sex are invalidated, thus providing the performing gendered being with agency. Therefore, for AI to focus on violence and to move away from gender stigmas, it would need to move away from binary conceptions of gender and to seek to operate within a practical understanding of gender and agency.

Juxtaposing images of victims, constructed as such by the violence they experience, with images claimed to show women's agency does not allow AI to disentangle itself from the gendered stigma it so desperately wants to exceed. The conflation of sex and gender prohibits AI from avoiding the construction of woman as victim, because it ties a victim to the violence she endured. Moreover, a failure to contextualize violence as gendered limits articulations of agency because violence must have an agent. Without an agent to enact violence, the focus remains on the victim who is defined by sex. Given the binary context, women are always going to be the victims of violence in a campaign targeted at violence against women.

The gender of the photographic subject is not what is at stake here. Instead, what I have looked at and have argued is that the possibilities for agency lie in visual discourses that contextualize violence as gendered. This context produces visual meaning. Only in a context of gendered violence are we, as viewers, implicated in violence against women. Only then is it understood to be in *our hands*. Hence, I do not offer guidance for AI on ways of producing new or better images. What I do in this chapter is provide a critique of interpretive practices used in AI's *Stop Violence against Women* campaign. Looking at interpretive practice allows us to identify the relationships between gender, agency and context that influence how "human" is visually constructed in AI's campaign specifically and in international human rights discourse more generally. If AI were to take a sociological approach to visual representations of gender in human rights, it would be able to honor the words of Irene Khan and make such a campaign "like no other [it] has organized before,"[91] because it would interpret women as gender-performing beings who are subjected to gendered violence. The lives of photographic subjects expressed in the visual images used within the campaign have agency when interpreted through practices which see agency as a fluid interface between subjectivity and power, such that agency is no longer lost to women.

In 2010, AI commissioned an independent review of the campaign in order to "identify key areas learning and recommendations that can be used in their future work."[92] The report *A Synthesis of the Learning from the Stop Violence against Women Campaign 2004–2010* identifies two critical learning areas: women's rights and global campaigning. The general critical learning required about women's rights was that women's rights were seen as human rights and that economic, social and cultural rights were integrated into AI's thinking and work much more than before the campaign.[93] However, there was insufficient dissemination of the women's rights and gender dimensions of human rights throughout other areas within the organization. So it seems that AI's binary conception of gender expressed in the campaign is also reflected in its own practice as an organization. Its current work still looks at women specifically and is organized around the theme *My Body, My Rights*.[94] Chapter 6 moves away from a focus on gender to demonstrate how "Indian" in human rights is visually constructed in the context of the crisis at Oka, Quebec.

NOTES

1. Amnesty International, *It's in our Hands: Stop Violence against Women* (London: Amnesty International Publications, 2004), v.
2. The research conducted in this case study deals directly with Amnesty International's International Secretariat, the central body of the organization, located in London, England. Thus, when AI is referred to it will denote only the International Secretariat and not all the country specific sections.
3. Amnesty International, *It's in our Hands*.
4. Wendy S. Hesford and Wendy Kozol, "Introduction," in *Just Advocacy? Women's Human Rights, Transnational Feminisms, and the Politics of Representation*, ed. W. S. Hesford and W. Kozol (London: Rutgers University Press, 2005), 13.
5. Amnesty International, *It's in our Hands*.
6. Ibid., v.
7. Ann Marie Clark, *Diplomacy of Conscience: Amnesty International and Changing Human Rights Norms* (Princeton, NJ: Princeton University Press, 2001), 3.
8. Tom Buchanan, "The Truth Will Set You Free: The Making of Amnesty International," *Journal of Contemporary History* 37, no. 4 (2002): 575–97.
9. Amnesty International, *It's in our Hands*.
10. Stephen Hopgood, *Keepers of the Flame: Understanding Amnesty International* (Ithaca, NY: Cornell University, 2006), 174.
11. Ibid., 175.
12. Ibid., 10.
13. Buchanan, "The Truth," 596.
14. Hopgood, *Keepers*, 128.
15. Ibid., 129.
16. Fiona Robinson, "NGOs and the Advancement of Economic and Social Rights: Philosophical and Practical Controversies," *International Relations* 17, no. 1 (2003): 87.
17. Clark, *Diplomacy of Conscience*, 37.
18. Ibid., 43–44.
19. Ibid., 45.
20. Ibid.
21. Amnesty International, *Human Rights are Women's Rights* (London: Amnesty International Publications, 1995).
22. Ibid.
23. Amnesty International, *Broken Bodies, Shattered Minds: Torture and Ill-Treatment of Women* (London: Amnesty International Publications, 2001).

24. Amnesty International, *Combating Torture: A Manual for Action* (London: Amnesty International Publications, 2003).
25. Ibid.
26. Amnesty International, *It's in our hands*, iii.
27. Ibid.
28. Hopgood, *Keepers*, 179.
29. Amnesty International, *It's in our Hands*, 111.
30. Ibid., iii.
31. Ibid.; Amnesty International, *Broken Bodies*; and Amnesty International, *Women's Rights*.
32. Gillian Youngs, "Private Pain/Public Peace: Women's Rights as Human Rights and Amnesty International's Report on Violence against Women (Women and World Peace)," *Signs* 28, no. 4 (2003): 209–22.
33. Amnesty International, *It's in our Hands*.
34. Ibid., 103.
35. Ibid., 101.
36. Ibid.
37. Ibid.
38. Ibid., inside cover.
39. Ibid., 17, 21, 34, 45, 53, 70, 82, 112.
40. Ibid., 82, 21.
41. Ibid., back cover.
42. Ibid.
43. Ibid., 12.
44. Ibid., 18.
45. Ibid., 20.
46. Ibid., 32.
47. Ibid., 43.
48. Ibid., 56.
49. Ibid., 64.
50. Ibid., 68.
51. Arabella Lyon, "Misrepresentations of Missing Women in the U.S. Press," in *Just Advocacy? Women's Human Rights, Transnational Feminisms, and the Politics of Representation*, ed. W.S. Hesford and W. Kozol (London: Rutgers University Press, 2005), 173–92.
52. Barbara Martinsons, "The Possibility of Agency for Photographic Subjects," in *Technoscience and Cyberculture*, edited by S. Aronowitz, B. Martinsons, and M. Menser (London: Routledge, 1996), 243, 248.
53. Ibid., 248.
54. Mark Philip Bradley and Patrice Petro, eds., *Truth Claims: Representation and Human Rights* (London: Rutgers University Press, 2002); and Wendy S. Hesford, "*Kairos* and the Geopolitical Rhetorics of Global Sex Work and Video Advocacy," in *Just Advocacy? Women's Human Rights, Transnational Feminisms, and the Politics of Representation*, ed. W.S. Hesford and W. Kozol (London: Rutgers University Press, 2005), 146–72.
55. David G. Chandler, "The Road to Military Humanitarianism: How Human Rights NGOs Shaped a New Humanitarian Agenda," *Human Rights Quarterly* 23, no. 3 (2001): 700.
56. Hesford, "*Kairos* and Geopolitical Rhetorics," 150.
57. Hesford and Kozol, "Introduction," 11.
58. Ibid., 13.
59. Amnesty International, *It's in our Hands*, 5.
60. Martinsons, "The Possibility of Agency," 250.
61. Amnesty International, *It's in our Hands*, v.

62. Ibid., 5.
63. Wendy Kozol, "Domesticating NATO's War in Kosovo(a): (In)Visible Bodies and the Dilemma of Photojournalism," *Meridians: Feminism, Race, Transnationalism* 4, no. 2 (1994), 5.
64. Amnesty International, *It's in our Hands*, 46.
65. Ibid., 46.
66. Kozol, "Domesticating NATO's War," 4–5.
67. Amnesty International, *It's in our Hands*, 5.
68. United Nations, 1979. *The Convention on the Elimination of Descrimination Against Women*, accessed March 28, 2014, available from www.un.org/womenwatch/daw/cedaw/.
69. Amnesty International, *It's in our Hands*, 4.
70. United Nations, 1993, *Declaration on the Elimination of Violence Against Women*, accessed March 28, 2014, available at www.un.org/en/ga/search/view_doc.asp?symbol=A/RES/48/104.
71. Amnesty International, *It's in our Hands*.
72. Ibid.
73. Ibid., 36.
74. Ibid., 29.
75. Ibid.
76. Ibid., 2.
77. Ibid.
78. Ibid., 3.
79. Ibid., 4.
80. Ibid.
81. Judith Butler, *Gender Trouble: Feminism and the Subversion of Identity* (London: Routledge, 1999), 178.
82. Ibid.
83. Amnesty International, *It's in our Hands*, 29.
84. Butler, *Gender Trouble*, 178.
85. Amnesty International, *It's in our Hands*, 4.
86. Butler, *Gender Trouble*, 179.
87. Ibid., 180.
88. Ibid.
89. Amrita Basu, "Globalization of the Local/Localization of the Global: Mapping Transnational Women's Movements," *Meridians: Feminism, Race, Transnationalism* 1, no. 1 (2000): 68–84; and Ara Wilson, "The Transnational Geography of Sexual Rights," in *Truth Claims: Representations and Human Rights*, ed. M.P. Bradley and P. Petro (London: Rutgers University Press, 2002), 251–65.
90. Amnesty International, *It's in our Hands*, v.
91. Revisit Khan in ibid.
92. Tim Walace and Helen Baños Smith, *A Synthesis of the Learning from the Stop Violence against Women Campaign 2004–10* (London: Amnesty International, 2010), accessed 23 March 2014, www.amnesty.org/sites/impact.amnesty.org/files/PUBLIC/FINAL%20SVAW%20REVIEW%20SYNTHESIS%20act770082010en.pdf.
93. Ibid., 16.
94. Amnesty International, *My Body, My Rights*, 2014, accessed March 23, 2014, https://campaigns.amnesty.org/campaigns/my-body-my-rights.

6 Not in Our Backyard
Visual Agency in the Oka Crisis

In the summer of 1990 tanks rolled into the quiet Canadian town of Oka, Quebec, as the last move in a standoff between Mohawk Warriors (Warriors) and the Sûreté Québec (SQ). Media coverage of this event shocked the Canadian public and challenged the Canadian consciousness about its peaceful coexistence with peoples. Tarnishing Canada's international reputation, the standoff brought to the fore controversial aboriginal rights issues, branding the event the Oka Crisis (Oka). The Warriors are the military branch of the Mohawk people (the Mohawk), the aboriginal peoples living in Quebec and Ontario (Canada) and in New York State (USA). The SQ is the Quebec provincial police force and was the first armed service to confront the Warriors.

In this chapter, I look at key instances of Canadian Broadcasting Corporation (CBC) news footage covering the Oka Crisis aired on Canadian national television between July 12, 1990, and September 26, 1990. An analysis of how these images contributed to an ongoing Canadian governmental policy of reducing the number of people who can claim an "Indian" identity demonstrates the impossibility of an embodied aboriginal identity with agency because the legislation used to legitimate (give status to) that identity is defined and assigned in an exclusionary discourse. Constructions of femininities and masculinities are integral to understanding what it means to be "Indian" in the Canadian human rights discourse. I continue to argue that visual representations of human rights are gendered and show how the production of visual meaning is a gendered process through which the possibility of recognition, respect and dignity for some becomes limited, if not impossible.

The focus of this case study is the destabilizing effect of images of armed confrontation on both the Mohawk and the Canadian discourses. Aboriginal rights are considered minority rights in international human rights discourse. Thus, as this case study looks at the construction of an "Indian" identity, it is also looking at another form of "human" in human rights. Like "human," "Indian" is a complex gendered identity. In showing the historical construction of the term *Indian* and how it forms part of a Canadian context, the potential for agency is uncovered. The term *Indian*, as this discursive analysis shows, applies to many different aboriginal peoples. For the purpose of this chapter, I am particularly interested in the Mohawk people from Kanasatake and Kahnawake, more specifically the Warriors. Their lands are located in the Canadian province of Quebec just outside Montreal, near the towns of Oka and Châteauguay, respectively.

This case study is restricted to images from the CBC, which at the time was a state-run television and radio conglomerate. I focus on the CBC reports because its reporters maintained a presence among the Mohawk Warriors longer than did any other television news crew at the time. I also use newspaper articles from *The Globe and Mail*, the national newspaper, to provide more details and complement the opinions expressed in the TV broadcasts. My interest in Oka is to demonstrate how these examples of national news media visually constructed the issue of aboriginal rights in Canada. Aboriginal rights claims are usually structured around land claims and the right to self-government. Land-claim issues have been prevalent throughout Canadian history; however, what makes Oka such a renowned case is that the Canadian armed forces were deployed against the Mohawk. The sight of tanks rolling along quiet village roads upset many Canadians' view of Canada. The entire issue of human rights in Canada was challenged because of debates about "Indian" identity. As the images shown in this chapter were being watched in Canadian living rooms across the country, a nation was simultaneously confronted with its past, its present and its future. Unlike the sedimentation seen in the Amnesty International case study, Oka provides an example of how images can be disruptive to viewers' visual discourses and how new sedimentations occur.

As in Chapter 5, I begin with a brief introductory analysis of visual images to show how all four elements—gender, context, visual and agency—had an impact on the interpretation of an "Indian" identity in Canada. I begin by tracing the difficult trajectory of an "Indian" identity historically from the time of British rule to contemporary Canadian legislation. This historical course forms the background for what comes to be understood in this case study as Canadian discourse. I then shift the focus to Mohawk discourse and provide the historical background for the Oka Crisis from the point of view of the Mohawk. To show the power of interpretive practices, I explore how the battle for control of visual context between Canadian and Mohawk sovereignties provided moments of agency. Finally, by way of conclusion, I take the analytical elements discussed throughout the chapter and demonstrate how this struggle between the sovereignties still continues in how Canada deals with aboriginal rights. I argue that the visual challenges invoked by the Oka Crisis have become sedimented and, as such, are representative in the Canadian context as a definitive relationship between aboriginal peoples and the Canadian state. I show that it was not the case that Oka was a foregone conclusion. A Canadian discourse of sovereignty is not as stable as people might think. Looking at how interpretive practices produce meaning emphasizes the point that Canadian state sovereignty is a practice itself. The visual analysis provided here highlights how elements of both Mohawk and Canadian sovereignties are being reconstituted at different times throughout the crisis. I argue that these features are only made visible when looking at practice.

The image in Figure 6.1 is a still taken from the CBC broadcast aired August 12, 1990, one month into the siege.

In the footage, the news broadcaster opens with an explanation of the events:

> Here at home a breakthrough in the month old dispute between Mohawks and Quebec Police. An agreement has been reached to get negotiations going again. Tonight's deal is complex but it goes something like this: food, water and other basic necessities will be allowed to flow freely across the barricades. Mohawk advisors will also be allowed to cross unimpeded, and an international team of 24 observers will be chosen to monitor the talks.[1]

Scenes of men in suits and men dressed in traditional Indian dress are seen passing over the barricade, under a banner that reads *Are you aware that this is Mohawk land?* The banner sets the context for the dispute: the municipality of Oka, Quebec, granted permission for the expansion of a local golf course on land claimed sacred by Mohawks.[2] Not only is this is a local dispute, but the banner also questions the broader issue of Canadians' awareness and knowledge of their colonial history and the continued battle between Canadian governments and aboriginals for return of aboriginal

Figure 6.1   Signing ceremony behind the Mohawk barricade in Kanesatake. Quebec Native Affairs Minister John Ciaccia (left), Judge Alan Gold (holding the flag of the Mohawk Nation) and Federal Indian Affairs Minister Tom Siddon (not pictured) meet with Mohawk leaders to sign an agreement to seek agreement.

© CBC News August 12, 1990. Neil Macdonald reporting.

lands. The comments of the news broadcaster bring the international context into play when she announces the presence of twenty-four international observers at the talks. In brief then, it seems that these images of the Oka Crisis are located simultaneously in local, provincial, national and international contexts. Later in the chapter, I develop the impact of relationships among these different levels of government and how it affects what viewers come to understand as aboriginal rights in Canada.

In the broadcast, the Warriors are referred to as paramilitaries and are shown wearing masks and army fatigues. Plain-clothed aboriginals also appear in the footage. The masked Warriors do not speak in this footage; rather, spokespeople speak instead on their behalf. Ellen Gabriel, a Mohawk spokeswoman, appears unmasked and asserts that "this agreement shows that we were right."[3] The agency asserted in this comment is linked to the complicated gender relationship between the armed Warriors and the voiceover of CBC reporter Neil Macdonald that follows Gabriel's comment. Macdonald states that the deal "is less than the Indians had wanted" and that "phrases that from the Canadian government that would have eroded Canadian sovereignty have been completely sniffed out of the final version."[4] Agency is articulated in terms of winning or losing, and Macdonald implies that the Mohawks have not won as much as they claim. The battle for agency is fought not only through legislation and legal agreements but also through visual images. What became apparent in the Oka Crisis is that both the Mohawks and the various levels of government officials were highly aware of the impact these media images were having on Canadian viewers. Exposing interpretive practices as producing meaning indicates that certain images in a given context can challenge a visual discourse. The images of violence that marked the battle at Oka challenged the peaceful concept many Canadians held of their country and created a new visual discourse that continues to be seen in media coverage of aboriginal rights in Canada.[5] This visual struggle is exemplified in the footage of federal Indian Affairs minister Tom Siddon sitting down with a masked Warrior. The voice of the reporter is heard clarifying that

> [t]oday after nearly two hours of ceremonies and speeches, the deal was produced. A deal that allows for all sides to sit down and negotiate an end to the dispute . . . Federal Indian Affairs Minister Tom Siddon, who vowed never to negotiate at gunpoint, sat at the same table as a paramilitary Warrior. And he didn't have much to say about the substance of the deal.[6]

Mr. Siddon then says he is "not here to debate the past, the past is the past, we are here to take charge of the future."[7] His comment indicated that the Canadian government was not willing to reopen previous aboriginal issues; however, they would be a part of future relations. This statement was more damaging than it first appeared because historically the identity "Indian" was created to identify certain groups of people who were not considered full citizens. What is important here is to recognize that the struggle for control of the visual media is entangled within historically constructed expressions of gender and continually renegotiated agency.

THE DIFFICULT TRAJECTORY OF AN "INDIAN" IDENTITY

How the Canadian state discursively constructs an "Indian" identity through legislation is crucial to the events at Oka because it explains the frustration and determination the Mohawk exhibit with regard to the disputed land. The Oka Crisis is not only about land; it is also about the survival of a people who have been subject to colonialism. I reveal the gender dynamics of the difficult trajectory of an "Indian" identity to expose the historical background of the various legislative procedures through which an "Indian" identity is constructed in Canada and to show how it reinforces encoded binary gender terms in Canadian discourse. As I demonstrate, this discourse privileges patriarchy, it privileges the male body, and it privileges the protection of Canadian sovereignty. The ramifications of this exclusive process are integral to the struggle for control of context observed in this analysis of the Oka Crisis. Unlike the Amnesty International case study, in which gender was the driving force of the campaign, in this case, gender is implicit in the construction of "Indian" identity but is not the primary motivator of the conflict. Because an "Indian" identity in Canada is constructed in an exclusionary discourse, the term functions to reinforce what I have been referring to as the conflation of sex and gender. This conflation originates from the time of colonization and remains systemic throughout relationships between the Canadian government and aboriginal peoples. What I show is the pervasiveness of exclusionary discourse and the long-term effects it creates in terms of aboriginal peoples' ability to identify themselves. Specifically, this means limited possibilities for the term *Indian*. I establish that an "Indian" identity in Canada is gendered, and as such, the context in which this identity is policed must also be gendered. Moving toward a focus on the construction of the Mohawk Warrior identity, I first establish the historical background that led to the Oka Crisis. It begins, like all discursive analyses, with language.

Becoming Indian

Many terms are used to describe the peoples who inhabited North America before the arrival of the Europeans: Indians, Natives, Aboriginals, Indigenous Peoples and First Nations. This section provides a short account of the origin of each term to clarify which terms I use in my analysis. The term *Indian* was imposed on the heterogeneous groups of peoples and cultures on the North American continent by those European settlers who became colonizers. These diverse groups with their own cultures and languages have been written historically as Indians, *peaux-rouge, sauvages* or worse.[8] The term *native*, used frequently in the Canadian media, typically denotes a condition of birth; people are native to their culture, city or nation of birth.[9] Derived from the Latin phrase *ab origine*, which means "from the beginning," *aborigine* is used in its adjective construction to become *aboriginal*, which is then used to modify the noun *peoples*, to produce *aboriginal peoples*. In some contexts, it may adequately acknowledge the people who were present from the beginning of history. However, "such a reference may become imbued with ambiguity because of the priority given to one perspective of history," usually the perspective of the colonizers.[10] *Indigenous people* is the term usually associated with international discussions and protocol agreements. As general categories go, neither is better nor worse than the other. Like all generic terms, these invariably disguise diversity for the sake of convenience.

Anthropologists and linguists classified all aboriginal peoples of North America according to linguistic families.[11] The linguistic groups were then subdivided by the territory they inhabited. When the newly formed government of the Dominion of Canada began to assign ownership of the land, the aboriginal peoples entered into treaties with the budding Canadian state to ensure their rights to parcels of the land they occupied. In its search for a "clearer idea of the heirs to these rights [treaty rights], the federal government created three subcategories of aboriginal peoples in Canada: Indians, Inuit and Métis."[12] If an aboriginal person could not be categorized as one of these three, then that person would not be considered aboriginal.

First Nations is the preferred term today because it implies many separate, formerly sovereign entities. However, this term is not legally recognized in Canadian law and refers only to those individuals and groups defined as "Indian" under the Indian Act. Before I continue to illustrate the various moves the Canadian federal government made to continuously reconstruct an "Indian" identity with the express purpose of reducing the numbers of claimants, it is important to clarify which terms I use in the chapter. Even though *First Nations* is the preferred colloquial term, I choose to use *aboriginal peoples (aboriginals)* in this discursive analysis because it is the legally recognized term. While I acknowledge the imperialist contentions implied in the use of *aboriginal peoples*—a term prescribed to various groups of indigenous communities that implies homogeneity with the express purpose of controlling access to claims of diversity—I maintain the use of *aboriginal peoples* because the term plays a specific role in the discourse. For it is through aboriginal status that one can claim to be "Indian." The ability to claim aboriginal status is a crucial component in the land dispute at the core of the Oka Crisis and is at the heart of determining an "Indian" identity in Canada. It is also important to acknowledge the frequent use of the term *native* in Canadian media. When I quote directly from such sources, the word *native* is used in reference to "Indians."

The Indian Act

Before the 1800s, Europeans were a minority population and viewed aboriginal peoples as vital to their survival. Aboriginal peoples were valued for their skills in locating, skinning and trading valuable beaver pelts as well as their abilities as warriors and diplomats. However, after the war of 1812, fought between the British Empire and the United States on land in North America and at sea, and the decline of the fur trade, aboriginal peoples, even though many of them had fought on both sides of the war, were no longer desirable to Europeans. There was a significant shift in attitude: "Europeans now saw Indians as obstacles to their own economic development and as a people who were becoming dependent economically as a result of the collapse of their traditional hunter-gathering way of life."[13] Aboriginal populations suffered huge losses due to disease and poverty because of British immigration from the 1820s onward. A once-thriving group of distinct cultures was being destroyed by processes of colonization. In the 1830s, the newly developing Canadian state placed new emphasis on taking traditional lands from the aboriginal peoples by convincing them to enter into treaties. Over a period of four decades in the late 1800s and early 1900s, eleven treaties were signed between the federal government and the various aboriginal tribes.[14] Aboriginal tribes "ceded all of their rights to large tracts of land (and resources therein) in return for reserve land and various forms of government assistance."[15] The basic purpose of the land cession treaty was to *extinguish* Indian title to a specified area in order to clear any obstructions to the Crown's title.[16]

The *reserve* was born. The legal definition for reserve is a tract of land, the legal title to which belongs to the British Crown, which has been set apart by Her Majesty the Queen of England for the use and benefit of a band.[17] Not only were aboriginals subjected to diminished and sometimes less fruitful lands, but they also encountered evangelization, Western education and prescribed agriculture, which permanently altered their traditional cultures. The non-aboriginal population began to see aboriginals as an undifferentiated "Indian" population whose Indianness ought to be eliminated.[18] With the creation of the reserve, the budding Canadian state was able to control "Indian" identity by restricting being "Indian" to living on a reservation. If one ventured off the agreed territory, one could not be legally recognized as "Indian." The intrinsic link that government made between land and "Indian" identity was legislated in 1850.

The first definition of "Indian" was written into legislation in 1850 (and then was revised in 1851). In the Act for the Better Protection of the Lands and Property of Indians in Lower Canada [Quebec], "Indian" refers to a

> [p]erson of Indian blood, reputed to belong to the particular Body or Tribe of Indians interested in such lands and their descendents [*sic*] . . . persons intermarried with any such Indians and residing among them,

and the descendents of all such persons . . . persons residing among such Indians, whose parents on either side were or are Indians of such Body or Tribe, or entitled to be considered as such: And . . . persons adopted in infancy by any such Indians, and residing in the village or upon the lands of such Tribe or Body of Indians and their Descendents.[19]

An "Indian" identity was linked not only with bloodline but also with parentage. A child adopted by "Indians" became "Indian" regardless of his or her genetic parentage, as well as any spouse of non-aboriginal origins who married into an aboriginal community. To be "Indian" was not considered a privilege among the Euro-Canadians, and as such, the founding fathers of a new country sought ways to ensure the purity of their own British and French identities by defining "Indian" as broadly as possible. Hence, the Act for the Better Protection of Lands and Property of Indians in Lower Canada provided a very inclusive definition.

In search of new methods of containing aboriginal peoples and recovering more land, the Gradual Civilization Act of 1857 "went on to spell out how an "Indian" could cease to be an "Indian"—or, in legal language, become enfranchised—in colonial law."[20] Enfranchisement offered assimilation into mainstream society and was designed to remove "Indians" off reservations to progressively integrate them into the dominant culture. The government withdrew the right to live on a reservation and membership in an aboriginal community by denying them status.[21] A non-status "Indian" was not privileged to treaty rights; therefore, if the government were to unmake "Indians," then aboriginal land claims could be questioned. The language of the Gradual Civilization Act 1869, Section 16 stated that those Indians that enfranchised "shall no longer be deemed Indians within the law relating to Indians."[22]

The continuous reconstruction of "Indian" identity became the trend in Canadian legislative procedures toward aboriginals. One of the processes was enfranchisement, which meant that male members of aboriginal communities could acquire all the rights of male Euro-Canadian citizenship. At this time, neither European nor Euro-Canadian women had the right to vote. This exclusive feature of European and Euro-Canadian society contributed significantly to the view expressed by colonizers that aboriginal lineage be traced through the man. However, this meant not only losing his "Indian" status, but his wife, his children and all subsequent descendants would become assimilated as Euro-Canadians. Once enfranchised, there was no method of regaining or acknowledging one's aboriginal status. Needless to say, this strategy was not popular with those who identified as "Indian." The Gradual Civilization Act was proposed as a *solution* to the *Indian problem*, because it was intended to free up land by dissolving reservations, but it was a failure. In 1867 The British North American Act (now known as the Constitution Act) saw the birth of the Dominion of Canada and the jurisdiction over "Indians" and their land assigned to the national level of government in Canada's newly fashioned federal state.²³ Two years later, the Gradual Enfranchisement Act added a *blood quantum* to the definition of "Indian." Now, no person of less than one-fourth Indian blood born after the passing of this Act, "shall be deemed entitled to share in any annuity, interest or rents of the band to which that person belonged."²⁴

The constant reconstruction of an "Indian" identity was becoming more prevalent as the vise of federal legislation was tightened around aboriginal peoples. An overpowering blow was dealt in 1869 with the Canadian Indian Policy, which restricted identity further and imposed a gender divide on aboriginal peoples that would have lasting consequences on the futures of "Indian" women in Canada.

The Canadian Indian Policy confronted an already debated "Indian" identity. It legislated that an "Indian" woman who married a non-"Indian" man would lose her—and all her subsequent descendants—"Indian" status as recognized by the Canadian state. The purpose of the provision was clear: "to unmake Indians and reduce the total number of Indians over time."²⁵ The provision discriminated only against women because if "Indian" men were to marry non-"Indian" women, their status would not be affected, and their wife was given "Indian" status. Thus, a woman who was born "Indian" lost her status through marriage, while a woman who was born non-"Indian" gained her status through marriage. This is an example of how Canadian discourse is constructed in binary terms. The Euro-Canadians relied on a dichotomous conception of man and women, which privileged the masculine over the feminine in that only men could carry on a lineage. An "Indian" identity during this time was subjected to the same process of exclusion. The result was the prevention of aboriginal women from passing on status to their children, hence the construction of an "Indian" identity on binary gender terms. This gender division struck at the core of aboriginal communities, especially the Mohawk. Traditionally, Mohawk communities were matrilineal, meaning that all children belonged to the mother's clan; young men could not inherit their father's property or position; it was passed from their mother's brothers.²⁶ This discrimination remained central in Canadian Indian Affairs policy until 1985.

Contributing to the gender division laid out in the 1869 Canadian Indian Policy, the first Indian Act was passed in 1876. The purpose of the Indian Act was to codify various scattered legislative provisions of pre-Confederation Quebec and Ontario involving aboriginal peoples into a single comprehensive statute. Once again, a definition for "Indian" was written into Canadian legislation and, subsequently, into Canadian culture. An "Indian" was now classified as the following:

1. Any male person of Indian blood reputed to belong to a particular band.
2. Any child of such person.
3. Any woman who is or was lawfully married to such a person.²⁷

The acquisition of an "Indian" identity became reliant on aboriginal males, where it had traditionally rested with clan mothers.

In 1951, the Indian Registry was brought into effect. This formalized the process of constructing an "Indian" identity, as it was through the registry that one's status or non-status was determined. If a person was on the list, he or she had status; if a person was not, he or she did not have status. The Indian Registry was another way of further dividing aboriginal peoples and minimizing claimants. The government was required to provide for those who were given status but was not obliged to respond to those with non-status. Nine years later, the Bill of Rights was enacted by the Diefenbaker government.[28] The Bill of Rights laid out the rights of each Canadian citizen and was the precursor to the Constitution Act 1982. With newfound rights under the Bill Jeannette Lavell, an "Indian" woman, took her case to court to try to reclaim her "Indian" status after being stripped of it by marrying a non-aboriginal.[29] Her goal was to overthrow the Indian Act. The Supreme Court of Canada did not find for Lavell in 1973, and it was not until Sandra Lovelace, a Maliseet[30] woman, took her similar case to the UN Human Rights Commission in July 1979 that inroads began to be made toward aboriginal women's reacquisition of "Indian" status. In 1981, the UN committee decided the gender discrimination inherent in the Indian Act was a denial of Sandra Lovelace's rights under the UN International Covenant on Civil and Political Rights. Lovelace made her experience public, and the issue of gender discrimination toward "Indian" women became prominent in Canadian press. Lovelace had international backing through the United Nations. However, she still needed to have the Canadian government recognize her status. The government's response was enshrined in the renewal of the Canadian Constitution in 1982, in which was "included a Charter of Rights and Freedoms that explicitly outlawed discrimination on several grounds, gender among them."[31] Now, any court would have to strike down that portion of the Indian Act because of the gender equality guarantee found within the Charter of Rights. This seemingly newfound success was short-lived.

Canadian legislative methods of defining "Indian" privileged patriarchal constructions over the traditional matriarchal structures of aboriginal peoples, specifically Mohawk communities. These exclusive practices were designed to facilitate the containment of aboriginal peoples and the emergent Canadian state's acquisition of "Indian" lands. Of most importance to how Canadian discourse is understood is the discursive aspect that historically "Indian" has been constructed as an imposed category of identity constituted through gendered legislation.

The Constitution Act 1982

Highlighting another component of Canadian discourse, this section explores how legislating patriarchal practices results in privileging the male-body.

The Constitution Act 1982 legally recognized aboriginal peoples as an identity deserving of *rights*, providing for the possibility of aboriginal self-government. However, the way Canadian discourse defines aboriginal peoples by their ancestral land adheres to a representational logic, meaning it can only produce "aboriginal male body" as the referent to "Indian," preventing Canadian legislation from overcoming its gendered colonial past.

Section 35 of the Constitution Act, 1982 states,

> The existing aboriginal and treaty rights of the aboriginal peoples of Canada are hereby recognized and affirmed.
>
> In this act, 'aboriginal peoples of Canada' includes the Indian, Inuit and Métis peoples of Canada.[32]

Through these words, the Canadian state expressly acknowledged for the first time the existence of an aboriginal identity to whom rights can be assigned.[33] This term reflects the ideology of original peoples while reflecting the heterogeneous communities to which it applies. However, even as the choice of term had been decided, what it meant was still and continues to be debated: "although all parties agreed to put 'aboriginal rights' into the [Constitution] Act, there was no consensus regarding its meaning."[34] The production of meaning that takes place via writing aboriginal peoples of Canada into the Canadian Constitution Act makes evident the representational logic inherent in exclusionary discourse. This legal discourse references claimants as embodied subjects.

Distinguishing a person as *aboriginal* is a complex process that involves making a connection between ancestry and land. For aboriginals, the affirmation of ancestry was determined by territory; most aboriginal peoples were bonded to parcels of land allocated to them by the settlers. Lists of the names of occupants were kept to keep track of those eligible for state benefits. The issue of autonomy concerning allocated lands is at the heart of the process of producing aboriginal persons in Canada. When drafting the Constitution Act 1982, discussions between the prime minister, provincial premiers and aboriginal representatives identified one central area of concern, "whether or not the definition of aboriginal rights included 'special' political rights such as the right to self-determination for aboriginal peoples."[35] At first glance, the presence of the term *aboriginal peoples* in the Canadian constitution meant an end to continual reconstructions of "Indian" identity, in that the disputed aboriginal rights provided the opportunity for self-government and self-determination. Those claiming to be aboriginal would be given the power to determine their own existence through recognition of self-government.

Wrapped up in the implications of having legally recognized aboriginal peoples in Canada is the definition of "Indian." As one of three subcategories of aboriginal peoples, "Indian" was now a reference to those whose ancestors were defined as "Indians" at the time of the Indian Act of 1876. It would include non-aboriginal wives of registered "Indian" men but exclude aboriginals who enfranchised, and those "Indian" women who married non-aboriginal men. The Constitution Act 1982 created an overarching aboriginal identity under which it was assumed "Indian" fit as one of three subcategories (the other two being Inuit and Métis).

The Indian Act of 1876 established the male-oriented lineage of an "Indian" by claiming "Indian" to mean

1. male person of Indian blood reputed to belong to a particular band;
2. any child of such person;
3. any woman who is lawfully married to such a person.[36]

The phrase "male person of Indian blood" refers to the object "aboriginal male body" because an exclusionary discourse adheres to a representational logic, which assumes the word–object relation is self-evident. The primacy attributed to "male person of Indian blood" over the subsequent child and woman is exemplary of an exclusionary discourse. Furthermore, because "Indian" is a subcategory of aboriginal, "Indian" can only mean "aboriginal male body" as the physical object referred to by the word *Indian*. The Canadian government's desire for embodied subjects reflects a word–object relation (Indian–aboriginal male body), which in turn fixes meaning in this context. This becomes more evident when looking at the construction of a Warrior identity. Therefore, when the term *Indian* is invoked in Canadian legislation, the self-evident process of representational logic can only produce the meaning "aboriginal male-body" as referent, despite efforts to do otherwise.

Bill C-31 was the Canadian state's effort to remove gender discrimination from legislation dealing with an "Indian" identity. An examination of the Bill emphasizes the particular discourse of Canadian sovereignty. It also shows how difficult it is to "correct" gendered legislation because Bill C-31 resulted in bureaucratic confusion, leaving "Indian" women in legal limbo. Building on the provisions in the Constitution Act 1982, Bill C-31, as I show, was another way for the Canadian state to reinforce patriarchal processes through the exercise of protecting state sovereignty.

In 1985, Bill C-31: An Act to Amend the Indian Act was passed as the government's "solution" to discrimination in the Indian Act of 1876. Its aim was to dissolve the distinction between status and non-status "Indian." The bill distinguished between "Indian" status, which was granted by the federal government, and "band membership," which was to be granted by individual bands. This differentiation resulted in "Indian" women being granted "Indian" status by the government but then being denied membership from their bands. Without membership, these women had no rights to live on the reserve or partake in reserve benefits. A new category was created for those "Indian" women who found themselves in legal limbo; they became known as "C-31s." Bill C-31 was a hollow victory over gender discrimination. The tension between those rights gained in the 1982 constitution and those mis-appropriated in Bill C-31 remains in the Canadian public as points of contention and confusion.

When put into practice, Bill C-31 had three objectives:

1. to remove all discrimination (including gender) from the original 1876 Indian Act;
2. to ensure that Indian status within the meaning of the 1876 Indian Act and band membership rights be restored to persons (primarily women) who had lost them;
3. that Indian bands have the right to control their own membership.[37]

The most important changes of this new provision were women no longer gain or lose entitlement to registration as a result of marriage; the practice of enfranchisement, a process by which Indians could apply to give up status and band membership, is abolished; the marriage of parents is no longer a factor in the entitlement of children; and bands can now choose to control their own membership.[38] Under these new amendments, an "Indian" refers to a person who is registered or entitled to be registered on the Indian Registry. The Indian Registry, created in 1951, is a centralized record of all persons registered as "Indians" in Canada. This registry determines whether an "Indian" has status (legal recognition of being "Indian"). *Indian status* is a term commonly applied to a person who is registered as an "Indian" under both the Indian Act of 1876 and Bill C-31, which became the new Indian Act of 1985.[39] To become registered one must be a member of a band.[40] The band list is a list of persons who are members of a particular band. This list, kept either by the band leader or by what was then known as the Department of Indian Affairs, determined those understood to be status "Indians" in Canada. Therefore, at the time of Oka, whether one was an "Indian" was determined by band membership.

The problem was this: to have "Indian" status, one needed to be a member of a band, but to be a member of a band, one already needed to be registered as "Indian" in the Indian Registry. The federal government bestowed "Indian" status on those who could confirm a link to ancestral (or reserve) lands. What Bill C-31 did was delegate the power of determining access to these ancestral lands, and hence be a legitimate "Indian," to individual bands. This gave the appearance of self-determination, for "Indians" would decide who was "Indian." However, this was not as straightforward as it appeared. What the Canadian state had done was solve the "Indian" problem by making *being* "Indian" the problem. In other words, because the Constitution Act 1982 only affirmed existing aboriginal rights, and self-determination was not at this time an existing aboriginal right, the federal government managed to provide a loophole in which an "Indian" identity would remain subordinate to the Canadian state. There was no legal measure in place in which an "Indian" identity could be self-determined.

Therefore, there was no way a subcategory of aboriginal people could legally challenge the sovereignty of the Canadian state. Thus, a discourse of Canadian sovereignty was affirmed.

Bill C-31 was a clever means by which the federal government could appear to be acting in the interest of the "Indians" while ensuring measures to protect Canadian interests. These cloak-and-dagger tactics reappear later when I discuss the specifics of the Oka Crisis in terms of agency and the visual. However, the purpose here is to reveal how sovereignty is a vital aspect of Canadian discourse.

MOHAWK SOVEREIGNTY

Mohawk sovereignty is complex. I explore aspects of Mohawk discourse and illustrate, using visual images, how the Mohawk discursively position themselves in relation to the Canadian state. Specifically, I look at Kanesatake and Kahnawake, the two Mohawk communities directly involved in the standoff at Oka. I offer a historical background of the Mohawk people and develop the parameters of the land-claim dispute at the center of the Oka Crisis. Through this history, it becomes evident that land rights are a key aspect of Mohawk discourse. I reveal the struggle to recover traditional longhouse practices as another aspect of Mohawk discourse. Longhouse supporters are not ruled by the Indian Act and believe that one cannot be at once Mohawk and Canadian. This interpretive aspect is central to the Oka Crisis because, as I show, it produces a Mohawk discourse at odds with Canadian discourse. I use images to illustrate how the Mohawk Warriors are constructed in Mohawk discourse as defenders of Mohawk land. It emphasizes Mohawk sovereignty as a feature of the Mohawk discourse and forecasts discussions of visual agency that take place. Overall, it provides details of discursive aspects that continue to resurface as my analysis of the Oka Crisis unfolds.

Disputed Land

The Mohawk are part of the Iroquois Nations. They feature prominently in Canadian history because they were among the first aboriginal peoples encountered by settlers. Members of Mohawk communities were skilled politicians and diplomats but are remembered most as warriors. In the early sixteenth century, the League of Iroquois, known to its members as the Haudenosaunee, "The People of the Longhouse," united the Five Nations as a military force.[41] The Haudenosaunee was composed of the Seneca, the Cayuga, the Onondaga, the Oneida and the Mohawk peoples. Later, the Tuscarora community from South Carolina moved north and was adopted into the league to become the Six Nations. The leader of the Six Nations was Joseph Brant, and from his time, "the Iroquois at Six Nations have maintained that they are sovereign people."[42] For the Mohawk, *nation* means a people who have their own government and their own territory.[43] Accordingly, "they have strongly opposed the Indian Act, which allows little in the way of autonomous decisions, because they assert that they are a separate nation with their own political constitution."[44] The Mohawk account for about two-thirds of the total number of Six Nations present in Canada, and Mohawk is the only Iroquois language not highly endangered.[45]

For the Mohawk to have their land rights recognized under the federal land claims process, they must prove that they are not merely early immigrants to the region but that they have lived there since *time immemorial*. Archaeological evidence shows that the Mohawk of Kanesatake, meaning "place of the crusty sand," have inhabited this territory for more than two thousand years. However, anthropologists have not determined conclusively that the Mohawk are related to the Indians who populated the shores of Lac des Deux Montagnes in 1535 when Jacques Cartier first visited the St. Lawrence valley.[46] Cartier called them the St. Lawrence Iroquoians, but unfortunately little is known about them because their settlement had disappeared by the time Samuel de Champlain retraced Cartier's voyage up the St. Lawrence some seventy years later.[47] What is known, however, is that their language and culture were similar to those of the Mohawk and others in the alliance of nations known collectively by the French as the Iroquois. The Iroquois were corn farmers who supplemented their food by hunting and fishing. Scholars have surmised that in the late 1500s, the Mohawk moved north to gain control of the fur trade, driving the St. Lawrence Iroquoians out of the St. Lawrence Valley.[48] It is thought that some of the defeated St. Lawrence Iroquoians were absorbed into the Mohawk clans through adoption and intermarriage. As a result, it remains likely that the Kanesatake Mohawks of today do have blood links to the earliest-known inhabitants of the region.[49] The problem the Mohawk face in determining their presence since *time immemorial* is that their traditions were passed down orally or were captured through symbols woven into wampum belts. These forms of historical transcripts were not accepted by colonial and subsequent Canadian governments. It is for this reason that the Kanesatake land in Oka remains disputed to this day. The following traces the legacy of legislation that shapes the Mohawk discourse.

The disputed land for the golf course expansion at Oka is located on the north shore of the Lake of Two Mountains, where it meets the Ottawa River, 53 kilometers west of Montreal. According to the Department of Indian Affairs, the lands allocated to the Mohawks of Kanesatake "do not constitute a reserve, and are interwoven with lands belonging to the non-aboriginal people of the village and parish of Oka."[50] However, the Mohawk of Kanesatake claim that these have been their lands long before the white man came.

The Seminary of St. Sulpice of Paris became the seigneury of the region known as the Lake of Two Mountains in 1717 under the orders of the governor of New France, Philippe de Rigaud de Vaudreuil. Louis XV confirmed this grant for use in building a Catholic mission for the Indians in the spring of 1718.[51] The Sulpicians aim was to convert the Mohawks to Christianity. With the promise of a deed to the seigneury, the Mohawk settled there in 1721; however, the Sulpicians never provided these written documents, nor did the grant from Louis XV provide explicit recognition of the Mohawk's right to the land. When more funds were needed to build the new settlement, a new grant was confirmed in 1735. In the case of both grants, the land was turned over to the Sulpicians "for the use and benefit of the Indians of the mission, on the express condition that title would revert to the Crown if the Indians vacated the mission."[52] This meant that if the Mohawk left the mission, the land would become the property of France. The Sulpicians began imposing their will on the Mohawk community and claimed ownership of the land. Plots were allocated to individual Mohawks for building homes and growing crops; however, the Mohawk were not permitted to sell either the land or the wood, or the hay and crops they harvested on that land, without the approval of the director of the mission.[53]

The Mohawk fashioned a wampum[54] belt to cement their agreement to settle at Lake of Two Mountains, in accordance with Iroquois tradition. The belt symbolized their adherence to the faith of the Sulpicians by showing men on either side of a cross. A long white band in the background was meant to symbolize the limits of their territory. At each end of the belt was the figure of a dog, which was to stand guard over the seigneury, barking warnings to the Mohawks if anyone disturbed them in their lands.[55] The Mohawk wampum belt presented to the superintendent of Indian Affairs in 1781 as proof of the Mohawk title to the land and was rejected by the government as worthless. Subsequently, the Mohawk of Kanesatake delivered a steady stream of petitions (1781, 1788, 1794, 1802, 1818, 1839, 1848, 1869—and on into modern times) to successive colonial administrators and Canadian politicians, demanding recognition of their claim to the seigneurial lands.[56] In response to countless petitions brought before successive governments, beginning soon after the British conquest of New France in 1760, the Sulpicians testified that without strict tutelage, the Mohawk would return to being *savages*, thus confirming their role as administrators of Mohawk rights.

King George III's Royal Proclamation of 1763 offered protection of Indian lands unless those lands were formerly surrendered to the Crown.[57] Aboriginal peoples across Canada accepted this document to be a kind of charter of aboriginal land rights, and the Mohawk believed this, too, solidified their claims to Kanesatake. However, their dealings with the Sulpicians were far from over. In 1840, for their assistance in quelling the rebellion of 1837–38, the British government passed an act confirming the Sulpician seminary's title to the land. The British ordinance reinforced the 1718 and 1735 grants, confirming the land titles were in the name of the Sulpician seminary. In this act, the government dealt a huge blow to the Mohawk of Kanesatake because it undermined their legal recognition of their land claim. Government efforts to appease the Mohawks were made in the form of new lands offered in Ontario; however, the Mohawk resisted this pressure and held firm to their belief in their rights to Kanesatake. To make matters worse, the Sulpicians were selling large tracts of land to white settlers, despite Mohawk objections, and the town of Oka was being populated by a growing number of French Canadians.[58] Oka became incorporated as a municipality in 1875 and the Mohawk were confined to the tiny plots they had received "at the pleasure" of the Sulpicians.[59]

Convinced that the priests were trying to force them out of the seigneury, the Mohawk converted en masse to Protestantism in 1869.[60] They hoped to finally expel the priests and gain undisputed control of the forests and fields of the region. By 1877, tensions in the seigneury were nearing a breaking point. Police continuously arrested Mohawks for cutting down wood and for fencing off common lands. Chief Joseph was imprisoned for appropriating a piece of land in 1876, which caused tempers to flare. The few Mohawks who had remained faithful to the priests were threatened by some of the Protestant Mohawks, who warned that the settlement was on the verge of war and that those who sided with the seminary would be exterminated. In October 1878, the federal Indian agent in Oka warned his government that the Mohawks were no longer willing to tolerate the prosecution and persecutions of the Sulpicians and were preparing to take up arms if necessary.[61] Other attempts to relocate the Mohawk were made, but the Mohawk fell doubtful of the Sulpicians' promises and refused to leave Kanesatake. In 1905, the Sulpicians wanted to sell the federal government the remnants of the seigneury, including the forest, the common lands and the lands already occupied by the Mohawks in an attempt to settle the land question once and for all. Unwilling to accept the scraps left them by the priests, the Mohawks demanded that all the original land grants be honored. They appealed to the government to test their claim again in court. Three Mohawk chiefs—Angus Corinthe, Baptiste Gaspé and Peter Oka—brought their claim before the Court of King's Bench. It reached the Privy Council in London, England in 1912, where it was subsequently rejected on the grounds that the Ordinance of 1840 and subsequent legislation placed beyond question the Sulpician's title to the seigneury.[62] The ruling of the lords of the Privy Council did leave room for the government to acknowledge that the Sulpicians did have obligations to the Mohawks that could be enforced by federal legislation, but the government did nothing to honor this at the time.

It was not until 1945 that the federal government stepped up to resolve the question. The Sulpicians had sold the remnants of the seigneury to a wealthy Belgian, Baron Empain in 1936, so the federal government purchased what was left: 132 lots scattered throughout the town of Oka and the farmlands west of the town. It amounted to about four square kilometers—one percent of the size of the original Two Mountains seigneury of 1718 and 1735. It remained Crown land, and the Mohawks were given "certificates of possession," which allowed them to stay on the land they occupied. Because the land did not have the status of a reserve, this did nothing to solve the problem because it gave the Mohawk no legal rights to the land. The land purchase was made without consulting the Mohawks and made no attempt to secure the Commons, the land most important to the Mohawks. The Quebec provincial government authorized the town of Oka to expropriate some of the baron's land, including the Pines and the land now occupied by the golf course, in 1947.[63]

The Mohawk continued their fight through the 1950s, challenging private landowners and the municipality of Oka who sought to develop the disputed land it expropriated in 1947. In 1959, a private nonprofit corporation, the Club de Golf Oka Inc., leased part of the Pines to build a nine-hole golf course.[64] Desperate to put a stop to this development, Jeffrey Gabriel, a young Mohawk, convinced prominent Montreal lawyers Émile Colas and Frank Scott to take his case. He asked them to try to block a private member's bill put before the Quebec National Assembly confirming the municipality's title to the property. Recommending a swift settlement to the 240-year-old Oka land question, the joint Senate–Commons Committee on Indian Affairs recommended the government set up an Indian Claims Commission and name the Oka claim as one of the priority cases.[65] Unfortunately, the advice went unheeded.

Contrary to accusations, the Mohawk were not opposed to progress. They were, however, opposed to having their land base whittled down to nothing. In 1975, another attempt to claim land rights was launched. This time, the Kanesatake, the Kahnawake and the Akwesasne submitted a comprehensive land claim to the federal and Quebec governments, asserting their right to lands along the St. Lawrence and Ottawa rivers, including the Lake of Two Mountains seigneury. Only four months after it was submitted, the Department of Indian Affairs rejected the claim on the grounds that the Mohawks could not prove they had occupied the territory from time immemorial. Moreover, the department asserted that any aboriginal title that may have existed had been extinguished by the French Kings when they made their seigneurial grants and later by the British Crown when it opened the lands to settlement.[66] Determined not to lose their land, the Kanesatake Mohawks tried once more in 1977 to make a specific claim for the original seigneury of the Lake of Two Mountains. It was their intent to prove that the royal grants of 1718 and 1735 had indeed been intended as a reserve for the Indians who had settled there and that their rights to the land had never been extinguished. Almost ten years later, in 1986, the federal government decided against the Mohawk claim. It ruled that while the government recognized that Mohawks faced a serious land shortage, it had no legal obligation to the Kanesatake Mohawks on the land issues. In a fruitless gesture, the government offered to consider other ways of resolving the Mohawks' grievances; the Kanesatake band council was provided with funds to hire a consulting firm to study the settlement's land needs—but by then, the land issue was overshadowed by political infighting over the system of government in the settlement.[67]

Claim to the land at Kanesatake is a prominent aspect of Mohawk discourse. Both the Sulpicians and the federal government of Canada tried unsuccessfully to relocate the Mohawks of Kanesatake.[68] After years of unsuccessful legal battles with the white man, the Mohawk community found itself struggling to maintain unity amongst itself. The impact of two centuries of colonial rule had taken their toll, dividing the Kanesatake into factions. Not only did the Mohawk have a battle with the various branches of government; they also faced a battle within. Because of this division, the Warriors arrived in Kanesatake and decided to force the government to take action regarding the outstanding land claim.[69] The following shows the consequences of colonial history on the Kanesatake Mohawk community.

A Community Divided

We need to look at the history of the divisions within the community to understand why they ended up in a dispute. The arrival of the Mohawk Warriors raised tensions between followers of the longhouse tradition and those who did not. This internal struggle of competing traditions caused friction between members and made strategizing difficult. The struggle to recover traditional longhouse practices is an important aspect of Mohawk discourse, because longhouse supporters are not ruled by the Indian Act and believe that one cannot at once be Mohawk *and* Canadian. This discursive aspect is central to the Oka Crisis because it produces a Mohawk discourse at odds with Canadian discourse. Internal divisions within Kanesatake led to the arrival of the Mohawk Warriors and the escalation of the land dispute. The overwhelming influence of Christianity, dating back to the time of the Sulpician missionaries, almost completely wiped out the traditional spiritual and political institutions of the Mohawk people. The church and the state had suppressed longhouse religious festivals and council fires, forcing them to become secret underground practices. The majority of Kanesatake Mohawks forgot or rejected these old customs. A small group remained allied with the Catholic priests, while the rest, in hopes of driving the priests out, became Protestants. It was not until Kanesatake Mohawks began traveling to Onondaga and Akwesasne, territories of the Iroquois Confederacy, that a new interest in learning the traditional beliefs flourished. A small number of families renewed their faith in the longhouse and discarded Christianity. The following develops the return of longhouse tradition to Kanesatake.

A longhouse was constructed at Kanesatake in 1964, and eight chiefs and clan mothers were appointed. Christian Mohawks shunned those who raised their children in the longhouse tradition, meaning that those who adhered to it had little influence over Kanesatake affairs. Official power rested with the band council, which conformed to the rules and regulations of the Indian Act. Longhouse followers refuse to recognize the jurisdiction of the Indian Act, they refuse to accept social assistance either provincial or federal and they refuse to accept employment that requires them to swear an oath of allegiance to the Canadian government.[70] Instead, longhouse followers reaffirm the ancient principles of the Two Row Wampum, set in a treaty between the Iroquois and the Dutch in 1645. The principle holds that a birch-bark canoe and a European sailing vessel can share the same waterway, meaning that Iroquois and Europeans can coexist peacefully without interfering with each other's traditions. However, the principle warns that if one tries to keep one foot in the canoe and another on the ship, the person would meet a disastrous end.[71] Thus, one cannot call oneself Mohawk while practicing a European religion or submitting to European-based government. For the staunch longhouse supporters, in Mohawk discourse, one could not at once be Mohawk and Canadian.

By the late 1960s, even the Kanesatake band council began lobbying for a model of government that reflected more of the old ways. Previously, chiefs were elected; however, in 1969, the community adopted a new system loosely based on the Iroquois Confederacy laid out in the Great Law of Peace.[72] Three clan mothers representing the Turtle, Bear and Wolf clans were appointed and given the responsibility of choosing three chiefs, one from each of the three clans. Both clan mothers and chiefs now held their positions until they died. The new band council called itself the Six Nations Traditional Hereditary Chiefs of the Iroquois Confederacy. This angered the Longhouse people, who saw themselves as the only true Confederacy members because they rejected the Indian Act. It was their view that a band council under any name is merely an arm of a foreign government and therefore against the ideology of ancient Mohawk tradition. Having lost their clans through intermarriage with whites, many Kanesatake Mohawks who supported the Six Nations Traditional Hereditary Chiefs of the Iroquois Confederacy did not have the right to speak at clan meetings. Almost immediately after the federal government agreed to recognize the new system of *custom* band government (for which the Six Nations Traditional Hereditary Chiefs would have qualified), a rival group called Kanesatakeron Indian League for Democracy surfaced to challenge the legitimacy of the new band council. Their complaint was that without elections, the new system was undemocratic and that because so many members could not speak, it failed to represent the wishes of the majority of the community. In hopes of resolving the internal tension, in 1973 the Department of Indian Affairs surveyed the Kanesatake Mohawks in order to determine the level of support for the custom band council. By a slim margin, the Six Nations Traditional Hereditary Chiefs of the Iroquois Confederacy gained most support and confirmed the government's recognition of the council. Unfortunately, continued internal disputes raged over how to govern Kanesatake.

In 1977 the Kanesatakeron Indian League for Democracy filed a lawsuit against the Six Nations Traditional Hereditary Chiefs of the Iroquois Confederacy, which resulted in a group of chiefs whom the clan mothers had dismissed, refusing to step down. By the spring of that year, Kanesatake had two sets of traditional clan mothers and chiefs claiming legitimacy. A multitude of petitions challenging the legitimacy of the custom band leadership was received by the Department of Indian Affairs. One departmental representative commented,

> After three centuries of having one form of government or another imposed on them and their own clan system of government suppressed, it [is] not surprising that the Mohawks [are] having difficulty resurrecting old customs and modifying them to comply with both the regulations of the Indian Act and the expectations of the community for a modern-day government.[73]

In 1985, when Bill C-31 returned Indian status to hundreds of Kanesatake Mohawks the band list of legitimate members almost doubled. This exacerbated the internal rift because many newly recognized Kanesatake Mohawks had lost their link to Mohawk culture and tradition. To complicate matters further, linguistic divisions, harking back to the time of the Sulpicians, began to cause problems. Catholic Mohawks spoke French, while Protestant Mohawks spoke English. The internal feuding divided the community along many lines. However, the one issue that remained a uniting force was the belief that Kanesatake was Mohawk land. By 1990 Kanesatake was still not recognized as Mohawk territory, as longhouse people claimed it was, nor was it recognized as a federal Indian reserve, which was the desire of those who accepted federal jurisdiction of the Indian Act. What remained to be seen was that within the Mohawk community of Kanesatake there were three main factions: the Longhouse people, the custom band council and the Kanesatakeron. Each had their own view of how to govern the Mohawk people. Each believed the land at Oka belong to the Mohawk. However, the longhouse people proved to be the only ones willing to take violent action for their land rights, for the Warriors were born out of a return to longhouse tradition.

In refusing to accept federal or provincial jurisdiction or to be governed by the Indian Act, longhouse supporters discursively construct being Mohawk as incompatible with being Canadian. Looking at this journey over several decades reveals the internal importance of Mohawk discourse to the community itself. Mohawk identity is not homogeneous, even though it is often perceived as such. The images of the Warriors challenged the Mohawk's own perception of themselves, challenging their community to appreciate its own representation of itself. As we see, this was not a unified voice.

Warrior Nation

Within a divided community, the Warrior Nation carries a particular weight. Warriors are the male protectors of the community. They have a strong sense of duty that has a long history for the Mohawk people. The televised images of armed Warriors fighting for their land communicate to those within the community a particular identity. It is problematic because not all Mohawk are supporters of the Warriors but, at the same time, all recognize that these images are evidence of the conflict they have with the Canadian state. The Warrior Nation not only represents a time of war but also brings the chance for resolution and peace. In this sense, visual images are instrumental in the struggle for control over the context between the Mohawk and the Canadian government, because the images affect the Mohawk's self-image as much as they do Canada's. This fight for visual primacy affected the outcome of the crisis because it changed the way aboriginal rights are perceived by the Mohawk and by Canadians alike.

The Warrior Society grew out of a long tradition of Mohawk militancy in Kahnawake and Akwesasne, a Mohawk reservation sitting on the southern border of Ontario and Quebec (Canada) and the northern border of New York State (USA). With the growth of Mohawk nationalism in those communities had come a rebirth of the men's societies of the longhouse, whose role it was to defend Mohawk rights and territory.[74] The longhouse is the location of both worship and government in Mohawk culture. The Warrior Society was formed in the early 1960s and is built on the teachings of the Great Law, which is the ethical code of the longhouse otherwise known as the Constitution of the Iroquois Nations. Three interwoven concepts make up the Great Law: peace, power, and righteousness. It is believed that power, understood as authority, is necessary to enforce the peace and to protect the righteousness of the law; "peace will endure only if men recognize the sovereignty of a common law and are prepared to back that law with force."[75] The longhouse people of Kahnawake believe in "peace through strength," which is not incongruous with mainstream American political philosophy, in which violence and capital punishment are legitimate and justifiable to preserve the security of communities. The Warriors are seen as a domestic army for protecting peace in Mohawk territory. The barricades and weapons of the summer of 1990 were legitimized in the Mohawk discourse by Wampum 91 of the Constitution of Iroquois Nations:

> 91. A certain wampum belt of black beads shall be the emblem of the authority of the Five War Chiefs to take up the weapons of war and with their men to resist invasion. This shall be called a war in defense of the territory.[76]

Because non-aboriginal Canadian society fails to grasp the profound attachment between an "Indian" identity and the land, non-aboriginal Canadians cannot seem to accept the Warrior's willingness to sacrifice anything, including life, for it.[77]

There was no formal Warrior Society at Kanesatake; therefore, the Warrior societies of Kahnawake and Akwesasne were relied on for technical support and expertise during the armed standoff between the SQ and the Warriors at Oka, Quebec. Warriors express their sovereignty as being part of a single

Mohawk nation, and it is for this reason that the standoff posed a serious political threat to the federal government. Previous to the July 11, 1990, SQ advance on the Warriors that resulted in the shooting of SQ officer Corporal Marcel Lemay marking the beginning the Oka Crisis, Indian bands were supposed to wait patiently for Ottawa to provide a solution to their land grievances. This bureaucratic process could take a decade or longer.[78] However, in refusing to follow the established rules, the Warriors threatened the status quo—exposing the weakness of the federal land-claims policies. The frustrations of aboriginal people across Canada were dramatized in the events at Oka. The Warriors focused attention on Ottawa's failings in aboriginal issues.

For days after the shooting of Corporal Marcel Lemay, the catalyst for the crisis, images of masked Warriors (see Figure 6.2) appeared on the front

Figure 6.2   A warrior raises his weapon as he stands on an overturned police vehicle blocking a highway at the Kahnesetake reserve near Oka, Quebec July 11, 1990.

© Tom Hanson/Canadian Press/*The Globe and Mail*, July 11, 1990, A1

page of Canada's national newspaper, *The Globe and Mail*, providing an embodied subject onto which non-aboriginals could project their fears.

In this image, Warriors are expressed visually as defiant Mohawks who wear masks, army fatigues and carry rifles. In the exclusionary discourse employed by the Canadian and Quebec governments, Warrior means "Indian" paramilitary, criminal and terrorist. On July 16, 1990, Gilles Landreville, mayor of Châteauguay, denounced the Warriors as terrorists and criminals.[79] Prime Minister Brian Mulroney also referred to the Warriors as criminals several times.[80] In contrast, the Mohawk discourse understands a Warrior to be a soldier legitimately defending Mohawk territory. This is an example of how context influences the production of meaning. Images such as Figure 6.2 can be interpreted in different ways depending on the context in which they are used.

The production of meaning that occurred through the manipulation of context resulted in moments that interrupted the exclusive language of the Indian Act and the Canadian constitution. If we recall that in an exclusionary discourse, sex and gender are conflated such that the term *masculine* comes only to denote male, while *femininity* is limited to female. As well, exclusionary discourses construct words in relation to objects, such that masculinity correlates to male body and femininity correlates to female body. The exclusive language of the Indian Act confines "Indian" to mean aboriginal male body. Because Warrior is a Mohawk identity and Mohawk is an "Indian" identity, the conflation of sex and gender that takes place in the word–object relation "Indian"–aboriginal male body influences the construction of a Warrior identity in the Oka Crisis. Images interpreted in an exclusive context identify Warriors as male "Indian" paramilitary.[81] Given that articulations (whether visual or linguistic) in an exclusive context occurs as word–object relations, then it follows that in this circumstance an image of a Warrior is interpreted as a masked, male "Indian" body dressed and armed as a paramilitary fighter. Even though other Mohawk spokespeople addressed the Canadian public via the media, this construction of masked, militant Warriors came to dominate Canadian conceptions of "Indian" identity in Canada. In Canadian discourse, Warriors were constructed as violent criminals to be feared.

In the broadcast aired August 22, 1990, on the CBC national evening news program *The Journal,* an in-depth look at public opinion and Mohawk opinion on both sides of the debate was presented. The barricades at Oka and the Mercier Bridge had been up for forty-one days, and Quebec premier Robert Bourassa had asked the Canadian government to intervene. Prime Minister Brian Mulroney had said the Canadian military would replace the SQ at the barricades. International observers had arrived in Oka; however, talks had stalled between the Mohawks and government officials because Mohawks claimed the military had come too close to their barricades in Pines. The Pines is the name for disputed land, occupied by the Warriors, on which the golf course was authorized to be built. It is named for the forest of pine trees that grows in this sandy environment. Among these trees Mohawk ancestors are buried, explaining the determination the Mohawk to claim it.

Susan Reisler's (SR) report[82] focused on Yvon Poitra (YP), pictured in Figure 6.3, a retired SQ officer and leader of Solidarité Châteauguay, a pressure group of angry Châteauguay residents. Châteauguay is a small Quebec suburb of Montreal, adjacent to the Khanawake reserve, connected by the Mercier Bridge. The Mercier Bridge itself is constructed on Mohawk land and is a major artery for commuters who work in Montreal. The Mohawks at Khanawake closed the Mercier Bridge on July 11, 1990 in solidarity with the Mohawks in Kanasatake. Mr. Poitra spoke in French, while English subtitles appeared beneath him. Following is a transcription of the interview:

SR: Who are the warriors?
YP: Who are the Warriors? They are international terrorists. 80% or 90% come from the US.[83] It's the mafia, the Indian mafia.
SR: Are you afraid?
YP: What about you? Aren't you afraid? You have to live here in Châteauguay to understand the problem.[84]

The overwhelming affirmative response to Mr. Poitra's question, "Are you afraid of the Warriors?" to the townspeople gathered around him reinforces the interpretation of Warriors as criminals (mafia) and terrorists. He mentions that 80 to 90 percent of them are from the US, further distancing

Figure 6.3   Yvon Poitra a retired Sureté Québec police officer and leader of Solidarité Châteauguay speaks out against the Mohawk Warriors. The subtitle reads, "Are you afraid of the Warriors?"

©CBC *The Journal* August 22, 1990. Susan Reisler reporting.

the Warriors from a Canadian context. Without showing any images of Warriors, the interview with Mr. Poitra constructs the meaning of Warrior as something alien to Canada and something to be feared. Mr. Poitra's comment also expresses the position of many non-aboriginals who understood that being Canadian did not mean taking arms against other Canadians. At its most extreme, being Canadian meant not being "Indian."

In addition to Mr. Poitra, the words of the broadcaster at the beginning of *The Journal* report also contributed to the polarization of the standoff by lumping the people of Oka and Châteauguay into one group and the people of Kahnawake and Kanesatake into another. This report, we are told, shows "both sides of the barricades."[85] In the visual context of this report, the exclusionary discourse enshrined in Canadian law is expressed through the non-aboriginal views reinforcing Canadian discourse while, in contrast, aboriginal views reinforce Mohawk discourse. The non-aboriginal perspective is shown to be motivated primarily by military intervention and the cessation of the standoff by force. This perspective of Canadian discourse denies legitimacy to the Mohawk and condemns the Warriors' tactics. The discursive aspect most at odds with the Mohawk discourse is Canadian sovereignty. Rooted in exclusive language of the Indian Act and the Constitution Act 1982, Canadian sovereignty is what the Canadian and Quebec governments seek to uphold by denying Mohawk sovereignty. The inverse argument exists within Mohawk discourse: the Warriors believe that the land is Mohawk land, and as a sovereign aboriginal nation, it is their duty and right to defend it with force. The Warriors derive their legitimacy from Wampum 91 of the Constitution of the Iroquois Nations as previously discussed.

For the purpose of clarification, I would like to note that not all non-aboriginals upheld the exclusive aspects of Canadian discourse, nor did all aboriginals support Mohawk sovereignty at Oka. However, what I am concerned with here is how the discourses played out visually, and as I show, this tension between discourses is evidenced in the CBC reporting. What is of particular interest to me here is the notion that living in a state of siege seemed "unreal to many Canadians" and that "armed confrontations and troops in the streets are alien to our image of Canada."[86] The focus of this case study is the destabilizing effect of images of armed confrontation on both Mohawk and Canadian sovereignties. Therefore, the contention between how the Warrior is interpreted visually in both discourses reinforces the importance of controlling context, because it is through context that visual discourses control meaning. The visual process of meaning production occurred in a dynamic context that was being shaped and reshaped almost instantaneously as the crisis unfolded. Television crews and print media journalists were on both sides of the barricades, creating an open battle for visual dominance between the Mohawk Warriors and the Canadian state.

The historical colonial discourse of an "Indian" in Canada collides with the contemporary visual presence of armed Warriors standing off against

Quebec provincial police, a product of which is the unanchoring of reality. Images of hostile gun violence within Canada are atypical for Canadians, who had been known to advocate peaceful and nonviolent solutions to conflicts. Depicting the Warrior view of the standoff, Warrior historian Louis Hall identified the Warriors as every Mohawk other than chiefs and clan mothers.[87] This disrupts the exclusive definition that only associates "Indian" with aboriginal male body by providing other referents including the Warrior and the Mohawk. This discursive aspect offers a gendered articulation of "Indian" that does not rely on sex. These aspects demonstrate that when expressed in Mohawk discourse, Warrior is neither exclusive, nor embodied. In other words, in Mohawk discourse, the meaning of Warrior is interpreted discursively as a word–word relation that is constantly negotiated within the language-game. Interpreting Warrior discursively recognizes that context is always fluid, leaving room for multiple referents and gender performance. When the Warrior is performative, then gender conflation is overturned, and the desire inherent in Canadian discourse to represent the real "Indian" as an embodied subject is avoided.

Let us consider Figure 6.2 again. This image plays an important role in the visual logic. It demonstrates how moments of agency in the Oka Crisis are visual moments, meaning that the presence of the Warriors in the visual discourse disrupts historical attempts the Canadian state has made to fix the context in which "Indian" is understood. Moreover, the gendered meaning of the Warrior articulated in Mohawk discourse allows the subject of Figure 6.2 to be interpreted as a male Warrior without precluding other possible referents. However, it is easier to disrupt context than to disrupt exclusionary discourses. To address this point further, we must first look at how the visual discourse of Oka produces the meaning of Warrior.

Returning to *The Journal* report and the interviews given by Warriors, a Warrior spokesman from the Khanawake reserve articulated the place of Warriors in Mohawk society in terms of a man's role:

> In our constitution and by our own laws we have the right to protect our people and our territory. And under our constitution that is the main function of the Warriors, or the men of our society. They are just fulfilling their obligations of our constitution and our society.[88]

The CBC journalist Susan Riesler interviewed this Mohawk on the Khanawake reserve, with the Mercier Bridge in the background and the Warrior flag flying above. The Kahnawake Warriors captured this bridge on July 11, 1990, after reports of the police assault on the Warriors at the Pines (Kanesatake). The Mohawk discourse dominates this visual context precluding the Canadian discourse from fixing it to exclusive terms. Instead, the assumed reality of an embodied Warrior subject of exclusionary discourse is challenged because *Warrior* functions in word–word relations. The visual discourse providing the possibility of interpreting Warrior performance is signaled by the CBC news anchor at the beginning of the segment. He remarks,

For 41 days now the people of Oka and Châteauguay, Kahnawake and Kanasatake, have been living in a state of siege that still seems unreal to many Canadians. Armed confrontations and troops in the streets are alien to our image of Canada.[89]

Given how he contextualizes the footage intended to show views on "both sides of the barricades," it remains impossible for Warrior to be confined to exclusive conceptions because in acknowledging "both sides" the broadcaster acknowledges the presence of Mohawk discourse, which undermines attempts by the Canadian state to maintain control of context.[90]

In this same report, the interview between CBC journalist Susan Harada (SH) and the Warrior called "Wizard" (WW) makes further reference to the historical constructions of "Indian" in Canadian society, but does so through Mohawk discourse. The Mohawk maintain control of the context as the journalist is brought deeper into the lands for which Warriors are willing to give their lives:

> WW: The White Man has come and taken all of it, that we were willing to share in good faith. Now there is only crumbs left. They want that so now we must draw the line and say wait a minute here. What is going to be left for our people? Our children? To become a Warrior you have to be self-disciplined. You have to be willing to go so far as to give up your own life.
>
> SH: I have talked with many Canadians who have told me they understand your position, and they respect the way you feel; until the violence started, until Châteauguay[91] started, till those started happening.
>
> WW: We are a nation, within another nation; we will never change that position. So if they are upset at us they should think a minute. They should try to understand that this is all we got left, and we're not going to give it up.[92]

In contrast to Mr. Poitra's comments, Wizard provides an interpretation of the standoff from the Mohawk perspective. The visual image of a masked, armed Warrior (Figure 6.4), similarly dressed to that in Figure 6.2, is produced in a context that allows for the meaning of the Warrior to be performative because it is interpreted through Mohawk discourse.

Here a Warrior identity can speak of injustice done by the white man to a people who were willing to, "in good faith," share access to their lands. Because the white man is not willing to share, the Warrior is left no choice but to take up arms and defend what remains of the Mohawk land. Expressing Canadians' fear of the violent measures the Warriors' defiance provoked, Susan Harada provoked the Wizard's confirmation that sovereignty is an aspect of Mohawk discourse: "we are a nation, within another nation." The Mohawk see themselves as a distinct people living among Canadians. The

Figure 6.4 Masked and armed Mohawk Warrior "Wizard" explains the plight of the Kanesatake Mohawks to CBC reporter.

© CBC *The Journal* August 22, 1990. Susan Harada reporting.

images of Wizard explaining the plight of the Kanesatake Mohawk people challenge the Warrior construction (Indian–mafia, international terrorists) presented in Mr. Poitra's interview. The Mohawk controlled the context, and with it how Warrior is interpreted, when reports were broadcast from their side of the barricade. The Mohawk lost control of the context, allowing the Warrior to be interpreted as "international terrorist," when reports were broadcast from the SQ side of the barricade. This polarization, between a Mohawk discourse and a Canadian discourse constantly at odds with one another throughout the crisis, provides constant reinterpretations of the Warrior as either a terrorist or a defender of sacred lands. The two competing discourses struggle for control of context in order to police how the Warrior is interpreted in the visual discourse. As a result, the standoff is seen as having only two sides, aboriginal and non-aboriginal, which further polarizes interpretations of the Warrior and with it the meaning of "Indian" in Canada.

Colonial processes of constructing an "Indian" identity in Canada are exclusionary. The conflations of sex and gender inherent in exclusionary discourse produce the desire for embodied "Indian" subjects. Exclusive contexts fix meaning. When context is being continuously negotiated, so are the meanings of the terms. Therefore, the struggles of recognition of land rights and of self-government, which are at the heart of the Oka dispute, have an impact on the production of meaning insofar as it delineates the possibility of agency through fluid contexts. Fluid contexts allow for performative gender identities, which can have agency. The Mohawk context is not exclusive and thus contains more possibilities for agency. The Warriors believe the Mohawk have a legitimate claim to the land at Oka and are willing to give their lives to protect it. Contrary to interpretations of the Warrior in Canadian discourse that see the Warriors as international terrorists, Mohawk discourse stipulates that one cannot be at once Mohawk and Canadian, hence positioning the Mohawk as an independent nation living within the nation of Canada. I have demonstrated three main elements of Mohawk discourse: the importance of land rights; Warriors are not ruled by the Indian Act, which makes them distinct among some Mohawk; and Mohawk sovereignty is an integral aspect of Mohawk discourse. Because Mohawk discourse is at odds with Canadian discourse in the Oka Crisis, these elements of the Mohawk discourse resurface time and again as a means of exercising aboriginal rights. What I go on to show is that in the Oka Crisis, there were creative moments in which performance led to agency. These moments were visual ones.

VISUAL MOMENTS OF AGENCY

The elements of the Canadian discourse (exclusivity and sovereignty) and the Mohawk discourse (land rights, incompatibility of Mohawk and Canadian identities and sovereignty) are at work at different stages in Oka Crisis. Chapter 3 explained that how we understand bodily presence is a function of context. The being of bodies is constantly negotiated in the language game, which provides interlocutors with the meanings available to them. I suggested that within exclusionary discourses meaning is restricted to word–object articulations, thus fixing meaning to single referents. Butler's notion of performance interprets identity as a word–word relation, thus creating openings for multiple referents. Therefore, identity interpreted in exclusionary discourse cannot be performative. What makes the Oka case so interesting is that because images of armed confrontation challenged sedimented constructions of "Indian" in Canada, the visual language is continuously disrupted by changes in context, which in turn provides space for the Warrior to have multiple referents, hence a performative Warrior identity. Butler's notion of performance is thus central to understanding the construction of Warrior in the images of Oka.

The moments of agency for a Warrior identity in the Oka Crisis are visual ones. Media coverage of the events provides witnesses in terms of the reporters and the viewing public at large. With witnesses, the photographic subject, the Warrior, gains a presence in the visual discourse and is able to disrupt the Canadian context, which has historically interpreted the Warrior without agency. The presence of competing discourses, the Mohawk discourse and the Canadian discourse, creates an unfixed context by disrupting predetermined meanings resulting in spaces for agency. Although both discourses fight for control over context, only the context changes; both discourses remain intact. Furthermore, the Mohawk discourse and the Canadian discourse are mutually exclusive. This has a direct impact on how the viewer interprets the images. The Mohawks used the presence of television cameras to their advantage to pressure to both the Quebec and the Canadian government to take action in finding a resolution to the land-claim dispute. In response, the Quebec government uploaded responsibility to the federal government, which in turn reinforced itself by deploying the armed forces, a sight unfamiliar to Canadian citizens. The standoff became symbolic of aboriginal rights in Canada because, at its pinnacle, the Warriors succeeded in forcing Canadians to ask, "What is Canada?" and ultimately compelled the federal government to defend its statehood both nationally and internationally. This is why Oka was so traumatic for the Canadian discourse.

To track the moments of agency for Warriors through the visual I have analyzed the CBC reports in chronological order. In this way, the sequence of images is experienced in similar fashion to how the viewers watching the news broadcasts in 1990 would have received them. There is no methodological advantage implied in this move, in that the images can still be interpreted if seen in a different sequence. Therefore, it is only on preferential grounds that I employ a teleological telling of this story. I begin, therefore, at the beginning.

Under Siege

On March 11, 1990, Mohawks from the Kanasatake settlement "set up a blockade in a bid to stop the Township of Oka from expanding a golf course on land the natives claim as theirs."[93] The land in question is a small part of a larger portion of land in the region claimed by the Mohawks. Four months later, on July 11, 1990, a force of one hundred SQ officers attacked the blockade with assault rifles, concussion grenades and tear gas. Corporal Marcel Lemay was shot and died later in the hospital.[94] The SQ surrounded Kanesatake, blocking off all food and medical supplies. In a show of solidarity, Mohawks at the Kahnawake reserve near Châteauguay blocked highways leading to the Mercier Bridge that links South Shore communities to Montreal. A standoff began that would last the summer and that would thrust aboriginal issues into the limelight of Canadian politics.

On July 12, 1990, the CBC evening news program *The Journal* reported that on the previous evening there were shots fired between SQ officers and Mohawk Warriors, as tensions mounted in the land dispute about the Oka golf course. The attack resulted in the shooting of SQ officer Corporal Lemay. Images taken the next morning from atop the Mohawk barricade looking down the hill to the SQ barricade were shown. CBC reporter Eric Rankin was trapped, along with Mohawks and other journalists, behind these barricades. His report visually recorded the Warriors' reactions to the escalation of violence. CBC journalists, such as Eric Rankin, wrote down what they heard and saw at any given time, while the videographer captured the images on film.[95] Before a story is aired, the uncut footage is fed to the video librarians who edit the raw visual images into seven-minute reports. These video librarians keep track of the footage and manage the visual images that are aired. Video librarians adhere to CBC guidelines as to what is admissible for broadcast. By keeping track of the images, the video library contributes to the production of visual meaning because its editorial process determines which images will come to document events.[96] The presence of CBC journalists throughout the standoff had a significant impact on how the issue of Mohawk land claims, and aboriginal rights more broadly, has come to be understood among Canadians. Even the Warriors relied on news broadcasts to find out what was going on because at many stages of the crisis they were prevented from communicating with their communities. Eric Rankin captured this sentiment in the following remark: "It's hard to say who has the most invested in this land now, the police who lost a man yesterday or the Mohawks who say this has been their land for 300 years."[97]

What Figure 6.5 and Rankin's comment show is the discursive element of sovereignty, akin to both discourses, being played out. Sovereignty is practiced in the unfamiliarity with civil armed conflict stated in Canadian discourse and the desire for legitimacy at all costs in the Mohawk discourse. The struggle between both discourses to control the context in which the parameters of the land dispute were articulated signifies the constant unfixing of what it means to be "Indian" in Canada. As the exclusive element of the Canadian discourse tried to fix the Warrior as an embodied subject, the element of incompatibility of Mohawk and Canadian discourses offered agency to a Warrior identity that challenged historically sedimented

Figure 6.5   Sûrêté Québec police car spray painted with "Mohawk Nation # 1"
©CBC *The National* July 12, 1990. Paul Adams reporting.

meanings. Evidence of this initial upheaval is presented again in Eric Rankin's report: "at the end of the war zone, this bizarre monument; earlier yesterday morning these fully equipped patrol cars were symbols of police power, now they are symbols of native power."[98]

The shift in power mentioned here marks an example of visual agency. The killing of Corporal Lemay destabilized the Canadian context because armed confrontation on Canadian soil is foreign to Canadians' concept of Canada as a peaceful country. This in turn gave the Warriors a presence as an armed paramilitary group in the visual discourse. They were also present as photographic subjects. Once the Warrior subjectivity was present in the visual discourse, agency became possible and, with agency, came a potential for power. In this case what this means is that Warrior subjectivity interfaced with agency to demonstrate power (as the visual image of the spray-painted car in Figure 6.5 depicts). For the photographic subject to gain presence in the visual discourse, a viewer is required to bear witness to this presence. In the Oka Crisis, the media fulfilled the role of recording the Warrior presence.

The circumstances of Corporal Lemay's death brought the Oka land dispute into the public eye, disrupting the Canadian context of sovereignty and allowing for articulations of "Indian"–Warrior with agency through visual discourse. Twenty-three seconds of gunfire between the SQ and the Warriors turned a roadblock into a standoff: "[i]t is incidents like this that make the Mohawk believe they are at war. No one here is optimistic that war will end soon, as the Mohawks prepare for another night."[99] Visual presence in the form of unsettling images of masked, armed Warriors provided the Mohawk discourse with the opportunity to express agency by asserting their sovereignty and land rights. In Eric Rankin's report, he explained that "the constant threat of violence has everybody on edge, and for those involved in this dispute, no act, no matter how ordinary is without meaning."[100] This statement indicates that the Canadian context was challenged and that the Mohawk discourse was making a claim of presence through the visual. We know this because the broadcaster asserts that "no act, no matter how ordinary is without meaning."[101] The presence of a competing discourse (Mohawk) unfixes Canadian sovereignty in this context, thus opening spaces for moments of agency. Disrupting Canadian sovereignty renders the context fluid and thus allows for the production of new meaning. When the context is challenged, the sedimented meanings (produced through repetition within the discourse) are once again defied and the viewer is left searching within the competing discourses for meaning. In other words, an empowered "Indian" identity is problematic for the Canadian discourse because it cuts to the heart of state sovereignty. Bill C-31 does not provide for the element of sovereignty seen as having agency in Mohawk discourse, which defines the Mohawk people as a nation within a nation. Instead, Bill C-31 encourages the Mohawk to assimilate as Canadians. Karonhiokta, a Mohawk from Kanesatake, summarized this plight in her interview with *The Journal*:

> Nobody wanted this war, we just wanted everybody to recognize this is our land and to recognize we were here and we will always be here. I mean they have always been fighting against Indians, and why don't they just leave us alone?[102]

This is why the Oka Crisis was so traumatic for the Canadian discourse, because it forced Canadians to ask, "What is Canada?" and ultimately compelled the federal government to defend its statehood both nationally and internationally. As the next two news segments show, a clever bit of context policing allowed the representatives of government to avoid this potentially devastating discursive attack on Canadian sovereignty by manipulating the visual, thus putting the Warrior agency at risk.

The Military Moves In

Just more than a month after the standoff began, the Quebec government had grown weary of stalled negotiations. Federal Indian Affairs minister Thomas Siddon announced that the federal government would not be involved in talks because it did not want to jeopardize negotiations between Quebec and the Warriors. Angry residents of Châteauguay responded by burning effigies of Mohawks and by demanding military intervention. Despite its claim to remain uninvolved, Mr. Siddon made it known that the federal government was trying to buy the disputed Oka land. Negotiations between Quebec and the Mohawk broke off. Prime Minister Brian Mulroney appointed the chief justice of the Quebec Superior Court, Alan Gold, to mediate an agreement, with preconditions of resuming full negotiations. Mr. Mulroney also said that the army would be made available to the Quebec government if needed. Mr. Gold succeeded in reaching a deal on the preconditions involving the free movement of food and supplies in and out of Kanesatake and Kahnawake. This deal also allowed for the free movement of Mohawk advisers over the barricades as well as the creation of an international team of observers to monitor events. The riots in Châteauguay were escalating, provoking the SQ to use tear gas to disperse hundreds of local residents who were throwing rocks and bottles at police. Responding to Quebec's request, General John de Chastelain, chief of defense staff, announced that 2,500 Canadian soldiers had been deployed to locations near Oka and were awaiting orders to replace the SQ at the barricades. CBC reports from August 14, 1990, show the military moving into the small town of St. Benoit. A line of tanks was juxtaposed with a local resident riding his bike alongside them.
CBC reporter Neil Macdonald remarks,

> The government's big stick rolled across Quebec all night and by dawn this morning, military armor and heavy firepower was in place, only

minutes away from the barricades at Oka and Khanawake. The soldier in charge of the operation was talking tough, but he carefully avoided making any threats.[103]

The Quebec government, failing to make headway with the Mohawk, uploaded responsibility for ending the standoff to the federal government. Fuelled by the Mohawk's sense of being "at war," the federal government responded with a show of military force.

At this point in the crisis, the military presence acted as a real threat to the Warriors, but there had been no order to deploy troops toward the barricades. As a result, media focus shifted from the Warriors to the Canadian military because the sight of tanks rolling through small rural Canadian towns is something to which Canadian citizens are not accustomed:

> Against the peaceful countryside of St. Benoit near Oka, the army's arrival was a stark show of force. Residents suddenly found themselves picking their way around armored vehicles, while in the fields outside town soldiers set up a small tent city.[104]

Military presence on Canadian soil contradicts the popularly held view of Canada as a peaceful nation.[105] With the SQ and the Quebec government failing to end the standoff, the federal government strategically policed a Canadian context through this visual disruption in order to send the message to the Mohawks (and Canadians) that the federal government will not tolerate sovereign "Indian" identities in Canada. However, as Brigadier-General Armand Roy expressed, with a French accent, the show of force was not stated outright to be against the Warriors: "we are prepared to do whatever military mission, but I would not qualify this to be against anyone."[106] By not stating that the increased military presence was aimed at the Warriors rendered them invisible within the visual discourse and thus without agency. This move of making Warriors absent is what is meant by context policing. The federal government, and the military, did not acknowledge the Warriors as opponents, which in turn recaptured the media's attention and reinvigorated federal control over the Canadian context.

The federal government's refusal to declare war against the Warriors functioned to reinforce government presence through absence. Government presence was invoked by the threat of military engagement. The delivery of a threat, and no actual military engagement, is how the federal government had presence (threat) through absence (lack of engagement). By positioning the military nearby Oka, the federal government treated the Warriors as a threat to national security. What happens then is a reversal of agency through policing of context. The Mohawk context portrays the Canadian government as a threat to Mohawk identity and provides the Warriors with moments of visual agency. However, the uploading of the land-dispute resolution to the federal government invoked the exclusive element of the Canadian discourse, which protects a Canadian context by reinforcing Canadian sovereignty. As I have established before, the Canadian discourse can only provide a fixed meaning of "Indian," which cannot be performative and thus cannot have agency. Neil Macdonald speaks to this point:

> In Quebec City the [federal] government is now taking a stricter line towards negotiations with the Indians. It's concerned about negative public reaction to these images from last Sunday. Pictures of ministers signing a deal with masked paramilitary Warriors [see Figure 6.1] is an apparent rapprochement with people who were denounced as criminals.[107]

Therefore, instead of being the ones under threat, as the initial SQ attack would suggest, the Warriors were then contextualized as those posing the threat, not just a threat to the people of Oka and Châteauguay but also a threat to the entire concept of Canada.

Internationally, the federal government's show of force was being interpreted differently. The Mohawk had taken their land-rights claim to the UN Commission on Racial Discrimination, in hope of gaining international support for their position. Articles in the Canadian national newspaper, *The Globe and Mail*, reported that "Canada's international image as a tolerant society is being tarnished by the stand-off at Oka, according to numerous media reports across the United States and elsewhere in the world."[108] Images accompanying such articles depicted tired Warriors still struggling to hold their line. The pressure of the federal government is expressed visually in the crouched position of the Warrior. The once-defiant image of the Warriors as seen in Figures 6.2 was replaced with images showing fatigue and strain on the Warriors' side.

With this shift in visual discourse, it is becoming evident that while context may be changing, the competing discourses are not. Inherent in both discourses is a contradiction that cannot be overcome. For the Mohawk discourse to have agency, Canada, in its current formulation, must cease to exist because the Mohawk see themselves as a sovereign nation within another sovereign nation. On the other hand, for a Canadian discourse to continue to prevail, it must refute any other discourses that challenge its sovereignty because the Canadian constitution does not provide the legal framework to fully accept the sovereignty of the Mohawk people. Therefore, producing a meaningful Warrior identity (interpreted as having agency) was under threat because the Canadian discourse could not overcome its own element of sovereignty to accept the competing claim to sovereignty present in Mohawk discourse.

International observers have taken up places at the barricades and negotiations involving the Mohawks and provincial and federal governments have resumed. The Canadian forces announced that troops and equipment would be deployed to replace the SQ at the barricades. This caused the talks to stall because the Warriors claimed that the military had come too close to their barricades. Quebec premier Robert Bourassa promised Châteauguay residents that the government would "look to other measures" if the Mercier Bridge did not opened soon. Talks resumed the following day, but Prime Minister Brian Mulroney warned that the federal government's patience was wearing thin. Hopes for a settlement were dashed after talks reached an impasse over terms for dismantling the barricades. There were questions concerning surrendering of Warrior weapons and a demand for immunity from criminal prosecution for acts committed since the beginning of the crisis. The observers from the International Federation of Human Rights criticized both the Quebec and federal governments for failing to honor preconditions previously agreed on. Mr. Bourassa suspended negotiations and asked the army to move in and dismantle the barricades at Kanesatake and Kahnawake. At a news conference in Ottawa later that day, General de Chastelain said that soldiers would use force only if obliged to do so by Warriors.[109] The Kahnawake blockades continued to be dismantled, but the troops at Kanesatake maintained their standoff. Mohawk and government negotiators blamed each other for another stall in negotiations. Mohawk factions met separately, and Mr. Siddon said that Ottawa had begun laying the groundwork for a land-claims settlement in Oka. On September 1, 1990, troops moved into Kanesatake. The military moved in with tanks and infantry to dismantle the Warrior barricades and to push them back toward the Treatment Centre located in the Pines, where it had all started. Reluctantly, the Warriors moved back, but not without a confrontation with soldiers.

In the September 3, 1990, evening broadcast, the news anchor explains that

[i]t was a weekend of taking things to the limit in Oka. The army's advance was methodical, the warrior's response a series of angry confrontations, and eventual withdrawals. 55 days of armed barricades came down in less than 72 hours. Throughout the weekend the potential for a breakout of gunfire was always present.[110]

The images of an armed soldier face-to-face with an armed Warrior (Figure 6.6), which was the feature story that night, became iconic of the Oka Crisis. Anticipation of another gun battle weighed heavy on both sides of the barricades. It marked the pinnacle of the standoff: the Mohawks were losing ground daily as the soldiers pushed them back toward the Treatment Centre situated on the land at the origin of this dispute. The "face-off" image made the soldiers "appear courageous and unflinching in their defiance of the Warriors—an image that soon embedded itself in the consciousness of millions of Canadian television viewers."[111] Support for the Warriors started to wane and, with it, their agency. The visual presence of the military—understood here as the threat

Figure 6.6   A Canadian soldier Patrick Cloutier and Saskatchewan native Brad Larocque alias "Freddy Krueger" come face to face in a tense standoff at the Kahnesatake reserve in Oka, Quebec, Saturday, September 1, 1990.

CP PHOTO/str-Shaney Komulainen

of military attack—reinforces the federal government's control of context. Acting as a mouthpiece for the federal government, the military followed a masterful strategy to maintain its control of the news flow by mobilizing twenty public relations experts from military units across the country to prepare briefing documents for army spokespersons.[112] In contrast, media coverage of the Warriors was limited; only media already behind the barricades were permitted to stay. As part of military operations, the Warriors were slowly deprived of telephone lines and electricity. Cellular telephones[113] belonging to CBC reporters ended up being their only link to people outside the Pines. At the end of the final advance, four hundred soldiers surrounded the Treatment Centre at the Pines—inside Mohawk territory, thirty warriors, seventeen women, seven children and a handful of journalists and advisors remained.

One of the interesting aspects of the September 3, 1990, news segment is that it shows the transfer of context control through its various stages. Starting with the first military advance and ending with the Mohawk confined to the Pines. As reporter Eric Rankin observed,

> 3PM Saturday, the army moves in. Its first objective, the west barricade of the Kanasatake Mohawk. The natives are caught unawares. The advance is met by a lone Warrior in a golf cart.[114]

The image of the lone Warrior addresses the waning agency of the Warrior in the visual discourse. When the tanks have reached the blockade a soldier (S) confirms his orders with the Warrior known as Mad-Jap (MJ):

(S): We have an agreement that in 15 minutes we will bring the bulldozers forward.

(MJ): I just have to check it out, I won't be a moment. We waited a lifetime for our land; you can wait a few minutes.

Herein lies the crux of this standoff. A Mohawk discourse has existed for lifetimes with the hope of getting the moments of agency experienced throughout the standoff, and now as the federal government re-sedimented (fixed) the meaning by taking control of the Mohawk context, the "Indian" was once again silenced and, like his claim to the land, was buried in legislative jargon. The point is further driven home with the comment of Jenny Jacks, an aboriginal woman from the Canadian province of British Colombia:

We try to negotiate with the government to get some sort of a deal. Where there is going to be a peaceful resolution, and at this point it doesn't look like this is going to happen. Every time the Mohawk people have tried to go to the table, the governments found one reason or another to pull away. As long as the cameras are here, they are going to be civil, but as soon as they are not, they're going to walk in and do whatever they want.[115]

Jenny Jacks's statement summarizes not only the position of the federal government toward the Mohawk people but also the relationship between the Canadian discourse and the Mohawk discourse. The conflicting elements of sovereignty akin to both discourses, and the capture of Mohawk context by the Canadian armed forces, resulted from a reassertion of sovereignty within Canadian discourse and a rendering of agency lost from Mohawk discourse and, with it, the Mohawk people. To sustain moments of agency, the Warriors must remain visible in the media; they must remain present within the visual discourse. With the barricades coming down, the Canadian public's attention would be focused elsewhere as the media refocused their attention on other newsworthy issues. Knowing this, the federal government took measures to ensure that the Warriors had little opportunity to maintain presence in the visual discourse, thus reestablishing Canadian discourse as the interpretive tool for the land claims context. For without the cameras, the Warriors became re-sedimented as embodied subjects, returning their interpretation to the historical disempowered position within Canadian discourse. The words of a Mohawk woman being removed by a military bulldozer, shown in the September 3, 1990, broadcast, echo the return to this historical reinterpretation:

I think democracy has failed us in this land because, if they don't manage to bring us under control politically then they use guns and threats of death. And I think our ancestors must have gone through this as well a long time ago and that's why the treaties were made and to the disadvantage of our people. We want the people to see that this is the way it was done then and that's the way it's done today.[116]

She pleads for the viewer to act as witness for the Mohawk people so that their struggle and defiance will not go unheeded and that Mohawk agency will not disappear along with the barricades.

It is through the work of journalists, such as those at the CBC, that Canadian citizens became witnesses to the events at Kanesatake. In the September 3, 1990, broadcast, Eric Rankin and his videographer became trapped between the advancing military and the retreating Warriors.[117] Images of armed Canadian soldiers advancing through the forest toward the armed and masked Warriors wearing army fatigues were given several minutes of airtime. The military officer shouts to the Warriors, "Nobody has nothing to gain as killing somebody. Move out."[118] A Warrior defiantly answers, "This is Indian land."[119] This exchange locates two photographic subjects: the Canadian military soldier and the Warrior. Both photographic subjects are armed and dressed in camouflage. The only significant difference between the two is that the Warrior is masked. Unlike Amnesty International's campaign document, these photographic subjects were being viewed as the image captured by the CBC reporters trapped only meters behind the subjects. The televised news broadcast constructed the images as evidence of what is actually going on at that moment in Kanesatake. According to Bourdieu,

> dangers inherent in the ordinary use of television have to do with the fact that images have the peculiar capacity to produce what literary critiques call a *reality effect*. They show things and make people believe in what they show . . . The simple report, the very fact of reporting, of *putting on record* as a reporter, always implies social construction of reality that can mobilize (or demobilize) individuals or groups.[120]

Because these televised images produce a reality effect, the viewer understands the photographic subjects according to the context in which they are presented to them. In the case of this segment, the predominance of the military feeds into the reemerging dominance of the Canadian discourse, and this recaptured Canadian context is interpreted as exclusive. It follows then that the viewer, because of the polarizing tendencies inherent in exclusionary discourses, will be persuaded to make a distinction between the photographic subject "soldier" and the photographic subject "Warrior" (see Figure 6.6). Moreover, in this recaptured Canadian context, the viewer is limited to interpreting "soldier" as upholding Canadian values by taking a nonviolent (nobody-has-anything-to-gain-in-killing-anyone) stand against armed threats to Canada, while "Warrior" is reduced to the embodiment of this threat. What results is the loss of Warrior agency. As the federal government manages to regain control of the context in which the viewer interprets the images of Warriors, the possibility for agency is shut down because an exclusionary discourse does not allow for Warriors to express agency. Instead, the photographic subject "Warrior" is interpreted as an embodied subject, again fixing meaning in the word–object relation Warrior–aboriginal male-body. This loss of Warrior agency in interpretations of visual context is echoed in the footage of the methodical military advance toward the Warriors in the Pines.

At this point in the Oka Crisis, when the roads were opened and life, for most, seemed to be returning to the way it was before the standoff, Lieutenant General Ken Foster, speaking from the site where the military advanced stopped, confirmed that

> The army goes no farther. The perimeter is closed, there is no strategic value to this particular land and the routes are going to be open.[121]

His admission to the press that there was "no strategic value" to the land the Warriors still occupied reinforced the loss of Warrior agency. For the Warrior's retort to the soldier, "This is Indian land," no longer had the same meaning it held two months before.

Footage from the September 9, 1990, broadcast illustrates that the situation in Kanesatake remained, as Eric Rankin reports, that "after a 55 day stand-off the Mohawk Warriors now hold little more than their weapons and the conviction that they will not unconditionally surrender."[122] Interpreted without agency, the Warriors became invisible and, as such, disappeared into the back pages of *The Globe and Mail* and into the video archive at the CBC. However, their unwillingness to surrender prolonged the standoff for almost another month. Regardless of their loss of media coverage, the Warriors remained defiant to the end.

Defiant to the End

It has been almost a month since the army moved in and surrounded the Treatment Centre. Worried about the danger of another deadly gun battle, CBC senior executives decided to pull their reporters and technicians from the Mohawk encampment. They were the last remaining television crew inside the Warrior headquarters. However, news was still getting out. The European Parliament had passed a series of resolutions condemning Canada and Quebec for violating the August 12, 1990, agreement on international observers and human rights. In his letter to Prime Minister Brian Mulroney, the vice-president of the European Parliament, Wilfred Telkamper, protested the human rights violations taking place at Oka and wrote that "the cut-off of telephone lines is an unjustifiable attempt to turn away international attendance and to resolve this conflict without any witnesses."[123] The federal government refused to discuss the land-claim issue until the Warriors had disengaged and placed themselves in military custody. The Warriors took this as the final insult. Already frustrated with the lack of progress in the negotiations with the army, the Warriors gave up in disgust. The new session of the Parliament opened on September 24, 1990, during which Liberal and New Democrat members of Parliament accused the Mulroney government of abdicating its responsibility to aboriginal people by leaving it to the army to settle the conflict. Realizing they are losing their spot on the national stage, and with fears of being left with no witnesses, the Warriors decided on terms of disengagement. Warriors would lay down their guns and enter military custody if Quebec agreed to appoint an independent prosecutor to review the criminal charges faced by some of the Warriors. On September 26, the Mohawks left the Pines, unbeknownst to the military and captured one last moment of agency.

Peter Mansbridge's opening remarks on *The National*, on September 26, 1990, allude to the fleeting agency Warriors reclaim as the journalists act as witness to their surrender:

> A stunning chaotic end tonight to the bitter drawn out siege at Oka, Mohawk Warriors put down their weapons and sprang out of the woods, into the hands of surprised soldiers. Soldiers who were expecting a more orderly surrender, and that element of surprise has turned the end of the stand-off into a series of wild scuffles, but no shots were fired and there are no reports of serious injury.[124]

Using the element of surprise, the Warriors had managed to disrupt the context enough to regain presence in the visual discourse. Their disorganized exit meant that soldiers were not prepared, and in the soldiers' attempts to establish control, those surrendering were able to manipulate the visual discourse so that the army's efforts to detain the Warriors were interpreted as brutality.

Once interpreted as brutality, the force used by soldiers came under international human rights codes of conduct, a fact the Warriors did not overlook and used to their advantage. International viewers would be watching, and with a claim to the UN Committee on Racial Discrimination already under investigation, the Warriors were aware of the importance of visual discourse to their pending incarceration. Making the army and the police (representatives of the state and province) look guilty made the Warriors (now representative of all aboriginal people of Canada) look innocent, or at least not the only ones at fault in this standoff. Put another way, what the disorganized surrender of the Warriors managed to highlight was the messiness of the issue of aboriginal rights in Canada. No longer can the governments (provincial and federal) count on passive responses to its failures toward aboriginal people. Even though the Warriors did not manage to regain the land rights regarding the golf course expansion, they did map aboriginal rights onto the conscience of the Canadian people. Even though the moment was fleeting (it took the army and police two hours to regain control), it was nonetheless disruptive and thus offered a final moment of agency for the Warriors. Significantly, the last image shown in this report is the evacuation of soldiers in the helicopter—speaking directly to the recapture of federal control over Canadian context and the loss of Mohawk agency: "by 9:30 pm tonight the army was beginning to pull out at the end of their two and half month siege."[125]

The total cost of the Oka Crisis for both governments (Quebec and Canada) was CAN$50 million. Despite the historic importance of the crisis, most politicians seemed anxious to pretend it never happened. The Quebec government, which had promised a public inquiry into the crisis, cancelled its plans for an inquiry as soon as the siege ended.[126] On April 14, 2008, the government of Canada accepted Kanesatake's specific claim as part of the seigneury of the Lake of the Two Mountains, which includes the land claim for the golf course that started the entire affair. Chief federal negotiator Fred Caron was appointed July 9, 2010, to work with the Mohawk Council of Kanesatake on the implementation of the claim.[127] At the time of writing, this was still ongoing.

CONCLUSION

It is difficult to draw conclusions about an issue that remains unresolved. Moreover, it makes one pause for thought and consider the ethical ramifications of arbitrarily tying up loose ends in an orderly way just to follow academic traditions. Instead, this conclusion resists the temptation to *resolve* the impasse between the Canadian discourse and the Mohawk discourse and will not offer conclusions on the prospect of how to ameliorate the more general issues of aboriginal rights in Canada. However, the academic context in which this case study is written requires a summation of the arguments covered herein. In light of such a dilemma, this conclusion looks at the possibility of recognition, respect and dignity for "Indians" in Canada.

As I have demonstrated, the difficult trajectory of an "Indian" identity in Canada takes place in an exclusionary discourse that adheres to a representational logic that finds it possible to represent the real as fixed. The result of such a discourse for an "Indian" identity is to become an embodied subject limited to the expression "Indian"–aboriginal male body. A further result of becoming an embodied subject is the loss of agency. Because Canadians had the image of a masked Warrior to which they could attribute all their insecurities about sovereignty, peace and security (see Figure 6.6), an "Indian" identity was fixed within the Canadian discourse as symbolizing violence and rebellion, two very un-Canadian attributes. This interpretation stays in the Canadian conscience as a perennial threat rather than as a critique of the Canadian state for failing to address the genuine concerns of the Mohawk people. It is in this way that the Mohawk lost agency, because they lost the support of the Canadian people. Violence remains an unacceptable strategy to resolve conflict. The irony is that the critique of using violence is not applied to the military to the same degree, because of the inherent understanding that troops were just "doing their job."

This case study demonstrates the influence certain discourses exert which allows them to maintain control of context, which has dramatic effects on the possibility for agency. Looking specifically at the Warriors in the Oka Crisis provides a situation in which a visual representation of an "Indian" (Warrior) identity challenges the Canadian context, leaving the Mohawk discourse and the Canadian discourse to fight for control of context and thus shaping the production of meaning. Records of moments of Warrior agency were provided by the media in the form of televised news broadcasts acting as witness to the events. I have shown that the construction of "Indian" in the Canadian discourse, in which the norms of recognition become possible through legislation, failed to recognize the possibility of an empowered "Indian" identity because of the primacy of Canadian sovereignty within the Canadian discourse. For this reason, the Warriors seek recognition for the Mohawk people. They seek recognition, respect and dignity in which being "Indian" means being Mohawk and being Mohawk means being a sovereign nation living on land they have occupied since time immemorial. Before Oka, a majority of Canadian citizens was unaware of aboriginal rights in Canada. Prior to the summer of 1990, Canada's reputation was understood as a country that delivered a better life to those seeking it. The redrafting of the constitution in 1985 (Bill C-31) was designed, among other reasons, to increase the possibility of becoming Canadian in the form of multiculturalism. However, returning "Indian" status to many Mohawks is a misconstrued indulgence. The federal government assumes that having "Indian" status will appease the Mohawk. For the Warriors, it is not desirable to live life as a Mohawk *and* as a Canadian. This clash between the two discourses fuelled the three-month siege at Kanesatake and continues to push a resolution to the land-claim dispute further away.

When the barricades came down and the army pulled out, the possibility of Warrior agency, and with it, Mohawk and "Indian" agency was lost. However, all was not to return to pre-Oka conditions. The visual discourse in Canada had changed. Images of masked Warriors became iconic of aboriginal rights struggles in Canada. Even though the land claim is still unresolved, the visual impact of the standoff has had lasting effects on Canadian context. Consider the Figure 6.7 as an example.

Figure 6.7 appeared on the front cover of *The Hamilton Spectator* on April 21, 2006, and shows a Warrior atop a barricade in Caledonia. Caledonia is the site of a Mohawk reservation located in the Canadian province of Ontario. Given these images, and their likeness to those from Oka (Figure 6.2),

Figure 6.7 A protester stands on top of a Caledonia building site where natives have joined forces to keep housing construction at a halt.

©Ron Albertson/*The Hamilton Spectator* April 21, 2006, A7.

it suggests that images of defiant Warriors have become sedimented in Canada's visual discourse. For Mohawk discourse, this visual sedimentation is bittersweet.

At the end of the Oka Crisis, Canadian discourse recaptured control of Canadian context and removed the possibility of Mohawk agency. The appearance of sedimented Warrior images in more contemporary Mohawk uprisings does not reinstate Mohawk agency but functions instead as another mechanism of Canadian context control. These more current images hark back to a time when Canadian sovereignty was under threat, a time when military presence became part of Canadian context, a time that no Canadian government wants to see repeated. But something more is going on here than just the sedimentation of visual images. Another aspect at work is more damaging to the Mohawk discourse because it functions to remind us how living life as an empowered Mohawk in Canada is still not possible.

The images of Warriors in Oka had a huge impact on the Mohawk people. What these contemporary photographs indicate is that in the Mohawk discourse, these images remind the people of Warrior moments of agency. As a result, these images strengthen the Mohawk discourse within a Mohawk context and perpetuate the use of violence to further land-claim disputes, a tactic of which the federal government is acutely aware. So it seems that although Mohawk agency might have been lost in a practical sense in a Canadian context, it therefore remains in a symbolic sense in both Mohawk and Canadian contexts. Hence, what comes out of this complicated relationship between visual discourse and context is that Figures 6.2, 6.6 and 6.7 are examples of symbolic visual agency. In other words, as the Warriors continue to employ these tactics, and images continue to be generated within the media, the Canadian audience is only reminded of a diffused threat to Canadian sovereignty, because as soon as Oka was no longer prime-time news, Canadians were given the impression that the crisis was over and that Canadian sovereignty prevailed. Moments of visual agency are fleeting when delivered through the media. The viewer is susceptible to context policing and tends to accept that what they see in some way represents reality. For the Mohawk, Oka is the culmination of more than two hundred years of broken promises and subordination. For Canadian politicians, Oka is a stark reminder of how fragile state sovereignty can be.

NOTES

1. CBC (Canadian Broadcasting Company), "Oka," in *Focus North* [Television News Broadcast] (Canada: Canadian Broadcasting Corporation, 1990), 90 08 12, time mark 10: 05: 41.23–10: 06: 07.08.
2. Peter C. Newman, *The Canadian Revolution: From Deference to Defiance 1985–1995* (Toronto: Viking, 1995), 361.
3. CBC, 90 08 12, time mark 10: 07: 20.15–10: 07: 25.09.
4. CBC, 90 08 12, time mark 10: 07: 25.10–10: 07: 34.11.
5. Tu Thanh Ha, "Outside Police Called to Patrol Kanesatake," *The Globe and Mail*, May 6, 2004; and Judith Lachapelle, "Les dissidents mohawks remportent la première manche: dénouement pacifique de la crise à Kanesatake," *La Press*, January 14, 2004, 1.
6. CBC, 90 08 12, time mark 10: 06: 34.05–10: 06: 59.03.
7. CBC, 90 08 12, time mark 10: 06: 59.04–10: 07: 05.03.
8. J. R. Miller, *Lethal Legacy: Current Native Controversies in Canada* (Toronto: McClelland and Stewart Ltd, 2004), 8.
9. Allan D. McMillan and Eldon Yellowhorn, *First Peoples in Canada* (Vancouver: Douglas and McIntyre, 2004), 3.
10. Ibid.
11. Miller, *Lethal Legacy*, 9.
12. McMillan and Yellowhorn, *First Peoples*, 4.
13. Miller, *Lethal Legacy*, 15.
14. Early Canadiana Online, *Canada in the Making: Introduction*, accessed 23 March, www.canadiana.ca/citm/themes/aboriginals_e.html.

15. Ibid.
16. Indian and Northern Affairs Canada, "Fact Sheet: Kanesatake," 2006, accessed July 15 2006, www.ainc-inac.gc.ca/nr/prs/m-a2000/00146_fsa_e. html. Indian and Northern Affairs Canada is now called Aboriginal Affairs and Northern Development. The original page is no longer at this address.
17. Department of Justice Canada, Constitution Act 1982 (Ottawa: Government of Canada, 2014), accessed 23 March 2014, http://laws-lois.justice.gc.ca/eng/ CONST/page-16.html#docCont.
18. Miller, *Lethal Legacy*, 15.
19. Ibid., 18.
20. Ibid., 16.
21. Harry W. Daniels, *Bill C-31: The Abocide Bill*, Congress of Aboriginal Peoples 1998, 2006, accessed August 4, 2006, www.abo-peoples.org/programs/C-31/ Abocide/Abocide-4.html.
22. Aboriginal Affairs and Northern Development, *An Act for the Gradual Enfranchisement of Indians, the Better Management of Indian Affairs, and to Expand the Provisions of the Act 31st Victoria, Chapter 42* (Ottawa: Government of Canada, 2010), accessed March 23, 2014, www.aadnc-aandc.gc.ca/ DAM/DAM-INTER-HQ/STAGING/texte-text/a69c6_1100100010205_eng. pdf.
23. Miller, *Lethal Legacy*, 32.
24. Ibid.
25. Ibid., 33.
26. McMillan and Yellowhorn, *First Peoples*, 80.
27. Miller, *Lethal Legacy*, 33.
28. John Diefenbaker was prime minister of Canada from 1957 to 1963. His Bill of Rights, which was tabled in 1960, was the first attempt to articulate the basic rights of Canadian citizens in law. Because the Bill of Rights was an ordinary federal statute and not a part of the Canadian constitution, it did not codify such rights in an enforceable way, since it could not be used by courts to nullify federal or provincial laws that contradicted it. Thus, its effect on the decisions of the courts, unlike the Canadian Charter of Rights and Freedoms of 1982, was limited.
29. Miller, *Lethal Legacy*, 5.
30. The Maliseet are an aboriginal people who inhabit the Saint John River valley and its tributaries, roughly overlapping the international boundary between New Brunswick and Quebec in Canada and Maine in the United States.
31. Miller, *Lethal Legacy*, 43.
32. Department of Justice Canada, *Constitution Act 1982*.
33. Michael Asch, *Home and Native Land: Aboriginal Rights and the Canadian Constitution* (Vancouver: University of British Columbia Press, 1993), 1.
34. Ibid.
35. Ibid.
36. Aboriginal Affairs and Northern Development, *An Act to Amend and Consolidate the Laws Respecting Indians* (Ottawa: Government of Canada, 2010), accessed March 23 2014, www.aadnc-aandc.gc.ca/eng/1100100010252/1100 100010254.
37. Aboriginal Affairs and Northern Development, *Existing Indian Act Provisions* (Ottawa: Government of Canada, 2010), accessed 23 March 2014, www.aadnc-aandc.gc.ca/eng/1100100032436/1100100032437.
38. Ibid.
39. Ibid. The Indian Act of 1876 was rewritten in 1985. When the Indian Act is referred to in Canadian politics and law after 1985, it denotes the revised

1985 version. For purposes of clarification from here on the Indian Act of 1876 will be referred to as "the old Indian Act," while the Indian Act now means the revised 1985 version.

40. A band is a group of persons recognized for the purpose of the Indian Act because this group holds reserve land, or has funds held for it by the federal government, or has been declared a band by the governor-in-council.
41. McMillan and Yellowhorn, *First Peoples*, 76.
42. Ibid., 98.
43. Mohawk Council of Kahnawake, "History of Kahnawá:ke," 2013, accessed March 23, 2014, www.kahnawake.com/community/history.asp.
44. McMillan and Yellowhorn, *First Peoples*, 97.
45. Ibid., 94.
46. Geoffrey York and Loreen Pindera, *People of the Pines: The Warriors and the Legacy of Oka* (Toronto: Little, Brown & Company [Canada] Limited, 1991), 84.
47. Ibid.
48. Ibid., 85.
49. Ibid.
50. Indian and Northern Affairs Canada, "Fact Sheet."
51. Alanis Obomsawin, "Kahehsatake: 270 Years of Resistance," (Canada: National Film Board of Canada, 1993).
52. York and Pindera, *People of the Pines*, 86.
53. Ibid., 87.
54. The beads of wampum, generally purple (Suckáuhock) and white (Wompam) in color, are traditionally made by rounding small pieces of the shells of quahogs and whelks, then piercing them to create a hole before stringing them. Wampum belts are used as a memory aid in Oral tradition, badge of office, and ceremonial device of indigenous cultures such as the Iroquois. Wampum belts were exchanged when peace treaties were signed. The belts pictorially described the terms of agreement; Obomswain, *Kahahsatake*; and Alanis Obomsawin, *My Name Is Kahentiiosta* (Canada: National Film Board of Canada, 1995).
55. Mohawk Council of Kahnawake, *History*.
56. York and Pindera, *People of the Pines*, 84.
57. Ibid., 87.
58. Ibid., 95.
59. Obomsawin, *Kahehsatake*; and Obomsawin, *My Name Is Kahentiiosta*.
60. York and Pindera, *People of the Pines*, 84.
61. Ibid., 96.
62. Ibid., 102.
63. Ibid., 103.
64. Ibid., 105.
65. Ibid., 106.
66. Ibid.
67. Ibid., 108.
68. Mohawk Council of Kahnawake, *History*.
69. André Picard, "Armed Mohawks, Police in Standoff," *The Globe and Mail*, July 12, 1990.
70. Obomsawin, *Kahehsatake*.
71. Ibid.
72. Mohawk Council of Kahnawake, *History*.
73. York and Pindera, *People of the Pines*, 111.
74. Ibid., 55.
75. Ibid., 258.

76. Tuscaroras and Six Nations, *The Constitution of the Iroquois Nations*, 2007, accessed March 23, 2014, http://tuscaroras.com/pages/history/iroquois_con stitution_2.html.
77. CBC, "Oka"; Alec G. McLeod, *Acts of Defiance* (Canada: National Film Board of Canada, 1992); Obomsawin, *Kahehsatake*; Obomsawin, *Kahentiiosta*; and Alanis Obomsawin, *Rocks at Whiskey Trench*" (Canada: National Film Board of Canada, 2000).
78. York and Pindera, *People of the Pines*, 272.
79. André Picard, "Mood Turning Ugly among Residents of Oka: Insults Hurled at Native Journalist," *The Globe and Mail*, July 16, 1990.
80. CBC, 90 08 12.
81. CBC, 90 08 12.
82. CBC, 90 08 22, time mark 10:10:34.03–10:10:54.29.
83. This is a reference to the fact that the Akwesasne reservation bridges both Canada and the United States.
84. CBC, 90 08 22.
85. CBC, 90 08 22, time mark 10:08:24.20–10:08:32.21.
86. CBC, 90 08 22, time mark 10:08:24.20–10:08:32.21.
87. CBC, 90 08 22, time mark 10:18:35.25–10:19:24.8.
88. CBC, 90 08 22, time mark 10:19:24.19—10:19:24.22.
89. CBC, 90 08 22, time mark 10:08:24.20–10:08:32.21.
90. CBC, 90 08 22, time mark 10:08:52.15.
91. Riots broke out in Châteauguay where local residence began burning effigies of Mohawks in protest of the sustained closure of the Mercier Bridge.
92. CBC, 90 08 22, time mark 10:21:42.38–10:23:01.15.
93. Canada Press, "Chronology of Main Events in Oka dispute," September 3, 1990, A3.
94. Picard, "Armed Mohawks," A1.
95. Interview with CBC video librarian 2005.
96. Ibid.
97. CBC, 90 07 12, time mark 14:48:22.01–14:48:31.16.
98. CBC, 90 07 12, time mark 14:48:34.05–14:48:46.25.
99. Eric Rankin, CBC, 90 07 12, time mark 14:49:45.07–14:49:55.08.
100. CBC, 90 07 12, time mark 14:49:59.14–14:50:19.16.
101. Ibid.
102. CBC, 90 07 12, time mark 14:52:19.08–14:52:32.13.
103. CBC, 90 08 14.
104. CBC, 90 08 14, time mark 10:23:21.26–10:24:19.24.
105. Rudy Platiel, "UN Questions Canada's Image Panel Wants Explanation on Oka," *The Globe and Mail*, August 9, 1990, A7; and Ross Howard, "Oka Standoff Draws Criticism and Concern in Foreign Press: Failure to Resolve Impasse Tarnishes Canada's Image, Media Say," *The Globe and Mail*, July 27, 1990, A4.
106. CBC, 90 08 14, time mark 10:24:31.06–10:23:52.18.
107. CBC, 90 08 14, time mark 10:24:31.06–10:24:49.29.
108. Howard, "Oka Standoff Draws Criticism," A4.
109. Harry Swain, *Oka: A Political Crisis and Its Legacy* (Vancouver: Douglas & McIntyre, 2010).
110. CBC, 90 09 03, time mark 10:26:04.24–10:26:22.09.
111. York and Pindera, *People of the Pines*, 357.
112. Ibid., 374.
113. It is important to note that cellular telephones were a rather new technology in 1990 and were not as widely relied on or available as they are today.
114. CBC, 90 09 03, time mark 10:26:36.00–10:26:49.09.

115. CBC, 90 09 03, time mark 10:27:30.10–10:27:57.29.
116. CBC, 90 09 03, time mark 10:31:50.22–10:32:20.03.
117. CBC, 90 09 03, time mark 10:28:22.12–10:28:26.02.
118. CBC, 90 09 03, time mark 10:29:12.08–10:29:19.09.
119. CBC, 90 09 03, time mark 10:29:12.08–10:29:19.09.
120. Pierre Bourdieu, *On Television* (New York: The New Press, 1998), 21.
121. CBC, 90 09 03, time mark 10:35:11.15–10:35:24.00.
122. CBC, 90 09 03, time mark 10:35:24.00–10:35:37.26.
123. York and Pindera, *People of the Pines*, 370.
124. CBC, 90 09 26 time mark, 10:36:18.03–10:36:41.23.
125. CBC, 90 09 26 time mark, 10:41:20.24–10:41:28.12.
126. Ibid., 405.
127. Aboriginal Affairs and Northern Development, "Fact Sheet—Progress Report—Kanesatake," 2010, accessed March 23, 2014, www.aadnc-aandc.gc.ca/eng/1100100016305/1100100016306.

7 Reflections

What makes the human rights culture so interesting is the way the language of rights allows actors "to make claims and demands which are enforceable."[1] Even though this language may be imperfect and unrepresentative of all humanity, it still functions as a powerful tool in international politics because it carries weight in negotiations. A state's human rights reputation is cultural and political capital. It matters to the international community how states conduct their internal affairs. It matters that states ratify international conventions so that they are seen to be participating in the promotion and the protection of human rights. When states fail to treat their citizens with respect and dignity, there are repercussions. The international community, however inconsistently, does not tolerate human rights abuses. In this framework, the human rights discourse plays a vital role because it provides states with the opportunity to make symbolic gestures, in the form of ratification, which in turn leads to real actions on the ground. This action is rarely initiated by states; it begins with activists appealing to the state to uphold its commitment to the convention it has signed. In this way, the human rights discourse is a way of starting a dialogue that can lead to practical action. This link between language and practical action makes a difference to people's lives. What the case studies have shown is that even when rights language is insufficient, the activism undertaken around the language does change the lives of those suffering abuse.

Amnesty International (AI), reflecting on its 2004 *Stop Violence against Women* campaign, realized that as an organization, it has much more work to do in terms of training staff in gender issues to properly address gender as a theme.[2] However, working alongside other women's groups provided a unique opportunity for learning about its own role in the human rights culture as well as lent substantial support to the work these women's groups were already undertaking. The activism generated in the collaboration between AI and other women's organizations drew significant attention to the issues of violence against women, such that the lives of women were changed. For instance, the first safe house for girls threatened with genital mutilation was opened in Kenya; Kuwaiti women were supported with their long-running campaign to gain the right to vote; South Korean women used as sex slaves by the Japanese Imperial Army during World War II demanded redress; women's rights activists ensured that the Rome Satute of the International Criminal Court recognizes rape and other forms of sexual violence as crimes against humanity.[3] Understanding the nuances of the discourse in fact opens further insight into how and why activism works. A key finding in my research on AI is that given the powerful position it occupies within the field as one of the leading organizations creating the human rights culture; its efforts at representing women in a cultural sense reduced its agency because the strategy of using human rights language to secure women's safety and protection was carried out through stories of victimhood. This is a perfect example of how discursive foundations for activism can often be unsuccessful and yet continue to produce practical meaning because activists are in the business of shaping discourse through their activism.

Nowhere is this point truer than in the case of the Mohawk at Oka. Shortly after the barricades came down, Prime Minister Brian Mulroney held a meeting of ministers involved in the crisis to reflect on the events at Oka. The outcome was a recognition that the Indian Act is systemically problematic and that the "goal should be to create options for aboriginal people, not take them away."[4] This sentiment was reflected in the statement Mulroney made in the House of Commons on September 25, 1990 (the day before the end of the siege): "The *Indian Act* is largely unchanged since the Victorian age. It fosters Indian dependency on the state, frustrates Indian self-sufficiency and undermines Indian self-respect. It diminishes Indians and non-Indians alike."[5]

The Canadian government's relationship with indigenous peoples was never the same after the events at Oka because it could no longer deny its colonial past and had to accept its domestic human rights record of abuse. The Mohawk rebellion at Oka paved the way for a government commitment to acknowledging and responding to indigenous issues within Canada.

For the Mohawk, the standoff at Oka created a powerful public image of an independent Mohawk culture, with a sense of history reaching back to before the development of the Canadian state itself. This identity, dominated by the Warriors, resonated within the Mohawk community as much as it did within non-aboriginal Canadian communities. For the Mohawk, political power comes from asserting their culture. Recognition of their lands and culture is at the heart of the crisis and their relationship with the Canadian state. As a strategy to gain recognition, they use human rights language to expose the Canadian state as hypocrites, cheats and liars. For the Mohawk, the human rights discourse is an effective tool because it allows them cultural recognition by drawing on supranational power to acknowledge their claims of sovereignty. It is all about finding a way to have their culture valued. If they gain international institutional support, it means that their culture has been recognized and that they become more equal partners in the negotiations.

The Mohawk had a heroic defeat. Their strategic surrender, as they exited the woods in a disorderly fashion, caught the army unaware and forced their hand. Army officers were seen beating and restraining the Warriors, exposing the Canadian state as the perpetrator. This tactic shows how visual and symbolic politics can be transformative. The image of masked, armed Warriors is overturned to show the Warriors as victims of state brutality. This counter-discourse remains as Figure 6.7 shows. A Warrior's masculinity is replicated in his own culture, which has both positive and negative results. Because the struggle became fixed as a conflict of sovereignties, the Warrior identity led to feelings of victimization. It is here that we see the problem clearly. The Mohawk marginalize themselves in the political field, which hampers their ability to participate as agents in future negotiations, because the Warriors' tactics are to resort to rebellion. The obstinacy of the Warriors and the tactics of visual agency have resonance, such that politicians and government officials are always aware that failing to conduct open and honest negotiations with the Mohawk will result in rebellion and media attention:

> Intimidation, arms and barricades manifestly work. No leader of white society wants to be remembered as the Butcher of Oka or Caledonia. So long as the Warriors can convince the authorities that the consequences of enforcing the law will be widespread bloodshed, they win—even in the more severe climate of public opinion in the post-9/11 era.[6]

The Mohawk know they have succeeded in changing the indigenous rights debate in Canada. However, their structural power lies only in the threat of violence and in the risk of losing face this poses for politicians. Therefore, any solution must prioritize reconciliation as the impetus for negotiations. Through open and honest negotiations committed to resolving long-standing issues, both the Mohawk and the Canadian government will avoid further violence and will build new relationships that value Mohawk culture and sovereignty. This will take an investment of time and patience on both sides. The only offer the Canadian state can make to the Mohawk is "a positive invitation to belong voluntarily to Canada, without giving up a distinctive identity."[7] The lesson here is that you cannot change the culture by upholding those structures that put them there in the first place. This goes for both the Mohawk and Canadians.

In looking at how social practices produce meaning, I have also been looking at the fate of political agency. I have been looking for "new empirical routes into the problem of *the political*, as it is currently experienced and constructed."[8] Human rights are political, and those exercising human rights are engaged in political acts. Often, the legal and moral dimensions cloud the real innovation going on when human rights work is being done. What matters to me are the people doing the work and the people for whom the work is being done. International politics is frequently discussed in unpopulated ways, as the work of vacuous states. However, as feminists have shown, *we the people* are everywhere. My approach has been to make academic audiences aware of the strategic importance of populating our intellectual fields with people, so that the knowledge we produce, that on occasion influences policy, reflects the diversity of ways we live our lives. When academics engage in these pursuits, then we transform the culture. This agenda involves looking at language and social movements within a cultural perspective. We need to look at how support for human rights broadens beyond certain groups and actors.

More so than academics, activists are vital to the delivery of human rights provisions. Their role is to bring change through their practice and to undertake political activism that will nurture a human rights culture and protect those in danger of abuse.[9] There is rarely a moment when the political struggle lets up enough to give time to pause and reflect on best practice. But in these rare and fleeting moments, reflection is essential. As the cases have shown, it is through reflection that the underlying issues are addressed and that new commitments are made to tackle the difficult problems that require complex and long-term solutions. Through this type of reflective practice, activists are able to transform human rights culture in meaningful ways, ways that empower people through human rights and ways that help adjust the language of human rights so that it better reflects the needs of those who need to use it.

This book is a reflection on my own quest to understand why, in a moral framework that is meant to recognize and value every person on this planet, such gross inequality exists. I have focused on the consequences of being left out and of denying respect and dignity. Thinking through the relationship among gender, agency and practice highlighted the difficulties in exercising human rights. Using feminist discourse analysis was helpful as a tool for uncovering the linguistic contours of the human rights discourse and the challenges these pose for protection. However, simply changing the discourse will not make it easier for people to exercise their human rights. We must also consider practice. People struggle to exercise their human rights because institutionalizing language does not guarantee human rights protection. Human rights practice perpetuates a culture of human rights, creating cultural and political capital, which becomes powerful currency in international politics. Therefore, studies that explore this relationship will be the most valuable.

NOTES

1. Darren O'Byrne, "On the Sociology of Human Rights: Theorising the Language-structure of Rights," *Sociology* 46, no. 5 (2012): 829–43.
2. Tim Walace and Helen Baños Smith, *A Synthesis of the Learning from the Stop Violence against Women Campaign 2004–10* (Amnesty International,

2010), accessed 23 March 2014, www.amnesty.org/sites/impact.amnesty.org/files/PUBLIC/FINAL%20SVAW%20REVIEW%20SYNTHESIS%20act770082010en.pdf.

3. Amnesty International, *It's in our Hands: Stop Violence against Women* (London: Amnesty International Publications, 2004), 2, 6, 66, 70.

4. Harry Swain, *Oka: A Political Crisis and Its Legacy* (Vancouver: Douglas & McIntyre, 2010), 158.

5. Ibid., 159.

6. Ibid., 203.

7. Ibid.

8. Nick Couldry, *Listening beyond the Echoes: Media, Ethics, and Agency in an Uncertain World* (Boulder, CO: Paradigm Publishers, 2006), 71.

9. Hannah Miller, "From 'Rights-Based' to 'Rights-Framed' Approaches: A Social Constructionist View of Human Rights Practice," *International Journal of Human Rights* 14, no. 6 (2010): 915–31.

Bibliography

Aboriginal Affairs and Northern Development. 2010. *An Act for the Gradual Enfranchisement of Indians, the Better Management of Indian Affairs, and to Expand the Provisions of the Act 31st Victoria, Chapter 42*. Ottawa: Government of Canada. Accessed March 23 2014. Available from www.aadnc-aandc. gc.ca/DAM/DAM-INTER-HQ/STAGING/texte-text/a69c6_1100100010205_ eng.pdf.

———. 2010. *An Act to amend and consolidate the laws respecting Indians*. Ottawa: Government of Canada. Accessed March 23, 2014. Available from www.aadnc-aandc.gc.ca/eng/1100100010252/1100100010254.

———. 2010. *Existing Indian Act Provisions*. Ottawa: Government of Canada. Accessed March 23, 2014. Available from www.aadnc-aandc.gc.ca/eng/110010 0032436/1100100032437.

———. 2010. "Fact Sheet—Progress Report—Kanesatake." Accessed March 23, 2014. Available from www.aadnc-aandc.gc.ca/eng/1100100016305/11001000 16306.

Ackerly, Brooke A., Maria Stern, and Jacqui True, eds. 2006. *Feminist Methodologies for International Relations*. Cambridge: Cambridge University Press.

Agathangelou, A. M., and L. H. M. Ling. 2004. "Power, Borders, Security, Wealth: Lessons of violence and desire from September 11th." *International Studies Quarterly* 48 (3): 517–38.

Amnesty International. 1995. *Human Rights Are Women's Rights*. London: Amnesty International Publications.

———. 2001. *Broken Bodies, Shattered Minds: Torture and Ill-Treatment of Women*. London: Amnesty International Publications.

———. 2003. *Combating Torture: A Manual for Action* London: Amnesty International Publications.

———. 2004. *It's in our Hands: Stop Violence against Women*. London: Amnesty International Publications.

———. 2014. "My Body, My Rights." Accessed March 23, 2014. Available from https://campaigns.amnesty.org/campaigns/my-body-my-rights.

Anthias F., N. Yuval-Davis, and H. Cain, eds. 1993. *Racialized Boundaries, Race, Nation, Gender, Colour and the Anti-Racist Struggle*. London: Routledge.

Asch, Michael. 1993. *Home and Native Land: Aboriginal Rights and the Canadian Constitution*. Vancouver: University of British Columbia Press.

Ashworth, Georgina. 2001. "The Silencing of Women." In *Human Rights in Global Politics*, edited by T. Dunne and N. Wheeler, 259–76. Cambridge: Cambridge University Press.

Baer, Susanne. 2004. "Citizenship in Europe and the Construction of Gender by Law in the European Charter of Fundamental Rights." In *Gender and Human Rights*, edited by K. Knop, 83–112. Oxford: Oxford University Press.

Baskerville, Stephen. 2011. "Sex and the Problem of Human Rights." *The Independent Review* 16 (3): 351–79.

Basu, Amrita. 2000. "Globalization of the Local/Localization of the Global: Mapping Transnational Women's Movements." *Meridians: Feminism, Race, Transnationalism* 1 (1): 68–84.

Begin, Patricia, Wendy Moss, and Peter Niemczak. 1990. *The Land Claim Dispute at Oka.* Ottawa: Library of Parliament, Government of Canada.

Blanchard, Eric M. 2003. "Gender, International Relations, and the Development of Feminist Security Theory." *Signs* 28 (4): 1289–313.

Booth, Ken. 1995. "Human Wrongs and International Relations." *International Affairs* 71 (1): 103–26.

———. 2001. "Three Tyrannies." In *Human Rights in Global Politics*, edited by T. Dunne and N. Wheeler, 31–70. Cambridge: Cambridge University Press.

Bourdieu, Pierre. 1977. *Outline of a Theory of Practice*, trans. Richard Nice. Cambridge: Cambridge University Press.

———. 1980. *Questions de sociologie.* Paris: Editions de Minuit.

———. 1984. *Distinction: A Social Critique of the Judgement of Taste.* Cambridge, MA: Harvard University Press.

———. 1991. *Language and Symbolic Power*, edited and introduced by John Thompson, trans. Gino Raymond and Matthew Adamson. Cambridge: Cambridge University Press.

———. 1998. *On Television.* New York: The New Press.

———, and Loïc Wacquant. 1992. *An Invitation to Reflexive Sociology.* Chicago: University of Chicago Press.

Bovarnick, Silvie. 2007. "Universal Human Rights and Non-Western Normative Systems: A Comparative Analysis of Violence against Women in Mexico and Pakistan." *Review of International Studies* 33:59–74.

Bradley, Mark Philip, and Patrice Petro, eds. 2002. *Truth Claims: Representation and Human Rights.* London: Rutgers University Press.

Brautigam, Christine Ainetter. 2002. "International Human Rights Law: The Relevance of Gender." In *The Human Rights of Women: International Instruments and African Experiences*, edited by Wolfgang Benedek, Esther M. Kisaakye, and Gerd Oberleitner, 3–29. London: Zed Books.

Brown, Chris. 2001. "Moral Agency and International Society." *Ethics and International Affairs* 15 (2): 87–98.

———. 2002. *Sovereignty, Rights and Justice: International Political Theory Today.* Cambridge, UK: Polity Press.

Brown, S. 1998. "Feminism, International Theory and International Relations of Gender Inequality." *Millennium* 17 (3): 471–85.

Brugger, Winfried. 1996. "The Image of the Person in the Human Rights Concept." *Human Rights Quarterly* 18 (3): 594–611.

Buchanan, Tom. 2002. "The Truth Will Set You Free: The Making of Amnesty International." *Journal of Contemporary History* 37 (4): 575–97.

Buergenthal, Thomas. 1997. "The Normative and Institutional Evolution of International Human Rights." *Human Rights Quarterly* 19 (4): 703–723.

Bunch, Charlotte. 1995. "Transforming Human Rights from a Feminist Perspective." In *Women's Rights, Human Rights: International Feminist Perspectives*, edited by J. Peters and A. Wolper, 11–17. London: Routledge.

Butalia, Urvashi. 2001. "Women and Communal Conflict: New Challenges for the Women's Movement in India." In *Victims, Perpetrators or Actors? Gender, Armed Conflict and Political Violence*, edited by C.O.N. Moser and F. C. Clark, 99–113. London and New York: Zed Books.

Butler, Judith. 1993. *Bodies that Matter: On the Discursive Limits of Sex.* London: Routledge.

————. 1999. *Gender Trouble: Feminism and the Subversion of Identity*. London: Routledge.

————. 2004. *Undoing Gender*. London: Routledge.

Campbell, David. 2003. "The Ones that Are Wanted: Communication and the Politics of Representation in Photographic Exhibition." *Journal of Modern African Studies* 41 (2): 331–32.

Canada Press. 1990. "Chronology of Main Events in Oka Dispute." *The Globe and Mail*, September 3.

Carver, Terrell. 1996. *Gender Is Not a Synonym for Women*. London: Lynne Rienner Publishers.

————. 2003. "Gender/Feminism/IR." *International Studies Review* 5 (2): 288–90.

————, M. Cochran, and J. Squires. 1998. "Gendering Jones: Feminisms, IRs, Masculinities." *Review of International Studies* 24 (2): 283–97.

CBC (Canadian Broadcasting Company). 1990. "Oka." In *Focus North* [Television News Broadcast]. Canada: Canadian Broadcasting Corporation.

Chandler, David G. 2001. "The Road to Military Humanitarianism: How Human Rights NGOs Shaped a New Humanitarian Agenda." *Human Rights Quarterly* 23 (3): 678–700.

————. 2001. "Universal Ethics and Elite Politics: The Limits of Normative Human Rights Theory." *The International Journal of Human Rights* 4 (5): 72–89.

Charlesworth, Hilary. 1994. "What Are 'Women's International Human Rights'?" In *Human Rights of Women: National and International Perspectives*, edited by R. Cook, 58–84. Philidelphia: University of Pennsylvania.

————. 1995. "Human Rights as Men's Rights." In *Women's Rights Human Rights: International Feminist Perspectives*, edited by J. Peters and A. Wolper, 103–113. London: Routledge.

————, and Christine Chinkin. 2000. *The Boundaries of International Law: A Feminist Analysis*. Manchester, UK: Manchester University Press.

Charvet, John, and Elisa Kaczynska-Nay. 2008. *The Liberal Project and Human Rights: The Theory and Practice of a New World Order*. Cambridge: Cambridge University Press.

Chinkin, Christine. 1998. "International Law and Human Rights." In *Human Rights Fifty Years On: A Reappraisal*, edited by T. Evans, 105–131. Manchester, UK: Manchester University Press.

Ci, Jiwei. 2005. "Taking the Reasons for Human Rights Seriously." *Political Theory* 33 (2): 243–65.

Cixous, Hélène. 1992. "We Who Are Free, Are We Free?" In *Freedom and Interpretation: Oxford Amnesty Lectures 1992*, edited by B. Johnson, 17–44. New York: Harper Collins.

Clark, Ann Marie. 2001. *Diplomacy of Conscience: Amnesty International and Changing Human Rights Norms*. Princeton, NJ: Princeton University Press.

Cockburn, Cynthia. 2001. "The Gendered Dynamics of Armed Conflict and Political Violence." In *Victims, Perpetrators or Actors? Gender, Armed Conflict and Political Violence*, edited by C. Moser and F. Clark, 13–29. London: Zed Books.

Cohn, Carol. 1990. "'Clean Bombs' and Clean Language." In *Women, Militarism and War: Essays in History, Politics and Social Theory*, edited by J. B. Elshtain and S. Tobias, 33–55. Lanham, MD: Rowman and Littlefield Publishers Inc.

————, and Cynthia Enloe. 2003. "A Conversation with Cynthia Enloe: Feminists Look at Masculinity and the Men Who Wage War." *Signs* 28 (4): 1187–207.

Collins, Dana, Sylvanna Falcón, Sharmila Lodhia, and Molly Talcott. 2010. "New Directions in Feminism and Human Rights." *International Feminist Journal of Politics* 12: 3–4, 298–318.

Cook, Rebecca J. 1994. "Women's International Human Rights Law: The Way Forward." In *Human Rights of Women: National and International Perspectives*, edited by R.J. Cook, 3–36. Philadelphia: University of Pennsylvania.

Copelon, Rhonda. 1994. "Intimate Terror: Understanding Domestic Violence as Torture." In *Human Rights of Women: National and International Perspectives*, edited by R. Cook, 116–152. Philadelphia: University of Pennsylvania Press.

Couldry, Nick. 2006. *Listening beyond the Echoes: Media, Ethics, and Agency in an Uncertain World*. Boulder, CO: Paradigm Publishers.

Crimp, Douglas. 1993. "The Photographic Activity of Postmodernism." In *Postmodernism: A Reader*, edited by T. Docherty, 172–79. London: Harvester Wheatsheaf.

Daniels, Harry W. 2006. *Bill C-31: The Abocide Bill*. Congress of Aboriginal Peoples, 1998. Accessed August 4, 2006. Available from www.abo-peoples.org/programs/C-31/Abocide/Abocide-4.html.

Department of Justice Canada. 2014. *Constitution Act 1982*. Ottawa: Government of Canada. Accessed March 23, 2014. Available from http://laws-lois.justice.gc.ca/eng/CONST/page-16.html#docCont.

———. 2006. "Indian Act." Accessed July 15, 2006. Available from http://laws.justice.gc.ca/en/i-5/282382.html.

Donnelly, Jack. 1989. *Universal Human Rights in Theory and Practice*. Ithaca, NY: Cornell University Press.

———. 2001. "The Social Construction of International Human Rights." In *Human Rights in Global Politics*, edited by T. Dunne and N. Wheeler, 71–102. Cambridge: Cambridge University Press.

———. 2003. *Universal Human Rights in Theory and Practice*. 2nd ed. London: Cornell University Press.

Dorf, Julie and Gloria Careaga Pérez. 1995. "Discrimination and the Tolerance of Difference: International Lesbian Human Rights." In *Women's Rights Human Rights: International Feminist Perspectives*, edited by J. Peters and A. Wolper, 324–34. New York: Routledge.

Dowd, Siobhan. 1995. "Women and the Word: The Silencing of the Feminine." In *Women's Rights Human Rights: International Feminist Perspectives*, edited by J. Peters and A. Wolper, 317–23. New York: Routledge.

Dunne, Tim and Nicholas Wheeler. 2001. "Introduction: Human Rights and the Fifty Years' Crisis." In *Human Rights in Global Politics*, edited by T. Dunne and N. Wheeler, 1–28. Cambridge: Cambridge University Press.

Eagleton, Terry. 1992. "Deconstruction and Human Rights." In *Freedom and Interpretation: Oxford Amnesty Lectures 1992*, edited by B. Johnson, 122–45. New York: Harper Collins.

Early Canadiana Online. 2014. "Canada in the Making: Introduction." Accessed March 23, 2014. Available from www.canadiana.ca/citm/themes/aboriginals_e.html.

Edkins, Jenny. 1999. *Poststructuralism & International Relations: Bringing the Political Back In*. Boulder, CO: Lynne Rienner Publishers.

Edkins, Jenny, and Véronique Pin-Fat. 1997. "Jean Bethke Elshtain: Traversing the Terrain in Between." In *The Future of International Relations*, edited by I. B. Neumann and O. Waever, 290–315. London: Routledge.

Eisenstein, Zillah. 2004. *Against Empire: Feminism, Racism and the West*. London: Zed Books.

Elias, Juanita. 2007. "Women Workers and Labour Standards: The Problem of 'Human Rights.'" *Review of International Studies* 33:45–57.

Elliott, Michael A. 2007. 'Human Rights and the Triumph of the Individual in World Culture'. *Cultural Sociology* 1 (3): 343–63.

Elshtain, Jean Bethke. 1981. *Public Man, Private Woman: Women in Social and Political Thought*. Princeton, NJ: Princeton University Press.
———. 1987. *Women and War*. Chicago: University of Chicago Press.
———. 1998. "Women and War: Ten Years On." *Review of International Studies* 24:447–60.
Enloe, Cynthia. 1989. *Bananas, Beaches and Bases: Making Feminist Sense of International Politics*. Berkeley: University of California Press.
———. 1993. *The Morning After: Sexual Politics and the End of the Cold War*. Berkeley: University of California Press.
Evans, Tony. 1998. "Introduction: Power, Hegemony and the Universalization of Human Rights.: In *Human Rights Fifty Years On: A Reappraisal*, edited by T. Evans, 2–23. Manchester, UK: University of Manchester Press.
———, ed. 1998. *Human Rights Fifty Years On*. Manchester, UK: Manchester University Press.
Farrior, Stephanie. 2009. "Human Rights Advocacy on Gender Issues: Challenges and Opportunities." *Journal of Human Rights Practice* 1 (1): 83–100.
Fellmeth, Aaron Xavier. 2000. "Feminism and International Law: Theory, Methodology, and Substantive Reform." *Human Rights Quarterly* 22:658–733.
Fields, Belden A. and Wolf-Dieter Narr. 1992. "Human Rights as a Holistic Concept." *Human Rights Quarterly* 14:1–20.
Foucault, Michel. 1978. *The History of Sexuality: An Introduction*. Harmondsworth, UK: Penguin.
———. 1983. "The Subject in Power." In *Michel Foucault: Beyond Structuralism and Hermeneutics*, 208–228. Chicago: University of Chicago Press.
Franck, Thomas M. 2001. "Are Human Rights Universal?" *Foreign Affairs* 80 (1): 191–204.
Fraser, Arvonne S. 1999. "Becoming Human: The Origins and Development of Women's Human Rights." *Human Rights Quarterly* 21:853–906.
Freeman, Michael. 2002. *Human Rights: An Interdisciplinary Perspective*. Cambridge, UK: Polity Press.
———. 2011. *Human Rights*. 2nd ed. Cambridge, UK: Polity Press.
Fuery, Patrick, and Kelli Fuery. 2003. *Visual Cultures and Critical Theory*. London: Arnold/Hodder Headline Group.
The Globe and Mail. 1990. "Chronology of Main Events in Oka Dispute." *The Globe and Mail*, September 3.
Goldberg, Pamela. 1995. "Where in the World Is There Safety for Me? Women Fleeing Gender-Based Persecution." In *Women's Rights Human Rights: International Feminist Perspectives*, edited by J. Peters and A. Wolper, 345–55. New York: Routledge.
Goodhart, Michael. 2003. "Origins of Universality in the Human Rights Debates: Cultural Essentialism and the Challenge of Globalization." *Human Rights Quarterly* 25 (4): 935–64.
Grant, Rebecca. 1992. "The Quagmire of Gender and International Security." In *Gendered States: Feminist (Re)Visions of International Relations Theory*, edited by V. S. Peterson, 83–97. Boulder, CO: Lynne Rienner.
———, and Kathleen Newland, eds. 1991. *Gender and International Relations*. Milton Keynes, UK: Open University Press.
Guerrina, Roberta, and Marysia Zalewski. 2007. "Negotiating Difference/Negotiating Rights: The Challenges and Opportunities of Women's Human Rights." *Review of International Studies* 33:5–10.
Hajjar, L. 2005. "Toward a Sociology of Human Rights: Critical Globalisation Studies, International Law, and the Future of War." In *Critical Globalization Studies*, edited by R.P. Appelbaum and W.I. Robinson, 207–16. New York: Routledge.

Halley, Janet. 2004. "Take a Break from Feminism?" In *Gender and Human Rights*, edited by K. Knop, 57–82. New York: Oxford University Press.

Harding, Sandra. 1998. *Is Science Multicultural?: Postcolonialism, Feminisms and Epistemologies*. Bloomington: University of Indiana Press.

Hatner-Burton, A. Emilie, and Kiyoteru Tsutsui. 2005. "Human Rights in a Globalising World: The Paradox of Empty Promises." *American Journal of Sociology* 110 (5): 1373–411.

Hesford, Wendy S. 2005. "*Kairos* and the Geopolitical Rhetorics of Global Sex Work and Video Advocacy." In *Just Advocacy? Women's Human Rights, Transnational Feminisms, and the Politics of Representation*, edited by W. S. Hesford and W. Kozol, 146–72. London: Rutgers University Press.

———, and Wendy Kozol. 2005. "Introduction." In *Just Advocacy? Women's Human Rights, Transnational Feminisms, and the Politics of Representation*, edited by W. S. Hesford and W. Kozol, 1–29. London: Rutgers University Press.

Hird, Myra J. 2000. :Gender's Nature: Intersexuality, Transsexualism and the Sex/Gender Binary." *Feminist Theory* 1 (3): 347–64.

Hooper, Charlotte. 1998. "Masculinist Practices and Gender Politics: The Operation of Multiple Masculinities in International Relations." In *The "Man" Question in International Relations*, edited by M. Zalewski and J. Parpart, 28–53. Boulder, CO: Westview.

Hopgood, Stephen. 2006. *Keepers of the Flame: Understanding Amnesty International*. Ithaca, NY: Cornell University.

Howard, Ross. 1990. "Oka Standoff Draws Criticism and Concern in Foreign Press: Failure to Resolve Impasse Tarnishes Canada's Image, Media Say." *The Globe and Mail*, July 27.

Hughes, Cheryl L. 1999. "Reconstructing the Subject of Human Rights." *Philosophy and Social Criticism* 25 (2): 47–60.

Humphrey, John P. 1993. "Why Human Rights?" In *Human Rights Issues and Trends*, edited by A. Lodhi and R. McNeilly. Toronto: Canadian Scholar's Press Inc.

Hunt, Lynn. 2007. *Inventing Human Rights: A History*. New York: W. W. Norton & Company.

Hynes, P., M. Lamb, D. Short, and M. Waites. 2010. "Sociology and Human Rights: Confrontations, Evasions, and New Engagements." *International Journal of Human Rights* 14 (6): 810–30.

Indian and Northern Affairs Canada. 2006. "Historical Background." Accessed July 15, 2006. Available from www.ainc-inac.gc.ca/pr/trts/hti/t6/bkg_e.html.

———. 2006. "Fact Sheet: Kanesatake." Accessed July 15, 2006. Available from www.ainc-inac.gc.ca/nr/prs/m-a2000/00146_fsa_e.html.

Ishay, Micheline R. 2008. *The History of Human Rights: From Ancient Times to the Global Era*. 2nd ed. Berkeley: University of California Press.

Jabri, Vivienne. 1998. "Restyling the Subject of Responsibility in International Relations." *Millennium* 27 (3): 591–611.

———. 2004. "Feminist Ethics and Hegemonic Global Politics." *Alternatives* 29:265–84.

Jacobson, David, and Galya Benarieh Ruffer. 2003. "Courts across Borders: The Implications of Judicial Agency for Human Rights and Democracy." *Human Rights Quarterly* 25:74–92.

Johnstone, Rachael Lorna. 2006. "Feminist Influences on the United Nations Human Rights Treaty Bodies.: *Human Rights Quarterly* 28:148–85.

Kant, Immanuel. 1970. "Perpetual Peace: A Philosophical Sketch." In *Kant: Politica Writings*, edited by H. Reiss, 93–130. Cambridge: Cambridge University Press.

Knights, David, and Deborah Kerfoot. 2004. "Between Representation and Subjectivity: Gender Binaries and the Politics of Organizational Transformations." *Gender, Work and Organization* 11 (4): 430–54.

Knop, Karen. 1994. "Why Rethinking the Sovereign State Is Important for Women's International Human Rights Law." In *Human Rights of Women: National and International Perspectives*, edited by R. Cook, 153–64. Philadelphia: University of Pennsylvania.

Koo, Jeong-Woo, and Francisco O. Ramirez. 2009. "National Incorporation of Global Human Rights: Worldwide Expansion of National Human Rights Institutions." *Social Forces* 87 (3): 1321–353.

Kozol, Wendy. 1994. "Domestication NATO's War in Kosovo(a): (In)Visible Bodies and the Dilemma of Photojournalism.: *Meridians: Feminism, Race, Transnationalism* 4 (2): 1–38.

Kurasawa, Fuyuki. 2007. *The Work of Global Justice: Human Rights as Practice*. Cambridge: Cambridge University Press.

Lacey, Nicola. 2004. "Feminist Legal Theory and the Rights of Women." In *Gender and Human Rights*, edited by K. Knop, 13–55. New York: Oxford University Press.

Lachapelle, Judith. 2004. "Les dissidents mohawks remportent la première manche: dénouement pacifique de la crise à Kanesatake. " *La Press*, January 14, 1.

Langlois, Anthony J. 2002. "Human Rights: The Globalisation and Fragmentation of Moral Discourse." *Review of International Studies* 28 (3): 479–96.

Lewis, Norman. 1998. "Human Rights, Law and Democracy in an Unfree World." In *Human Rights Fifty Years On: A Reappraisal*, edited by T. Evans, 77–104. Manchester, UK: University of Manchester Press.

Lisle, Debbie. 2000. "Consuming Danger: Reimagining the War/Tourism Divide." *Alternatives* 25:91–116.

Lloyd, Moya. 2007. "Women's Rights: Paradoxes and Possibilities." *Review of International Studies* 33 (1): 91–103.

Lorentzen, Lois Ann, and Jennifer Turpin, eds. 1996. "Introduction: The Gendered New World Order." In *The Gendered New World Order: Militarism, Development, and the Environment*, 1–12. New York: Psychology Press.

Lyon, Arabella. 2005. "Misrepresentations of Missing Women in the U.S. Press." In *Just Advocacy? Women's Human Rights, Transnational Feminisms, and the Politics of Representation*, edited by W. S. Hesford and W. Kozol, 173–92. London: Rutgers University Press.

Lyotard, Jean-Francois. 1993. "The Other's Rights." In *On Human Rights: The Oxford Amnesty Lectures 1993*, edited by S. Shute and S. Hurley, 135–48. New York: Harper Collins.

MacKinnon, Catherine, A. 2006. *Are Women Human: And Other International Dialogues*. London: The Belknap Press of Harvard University Press.

Man Ling Lee, Theresa. 2001. "Feminism, Postmodernism and the Politics of Representation." *Women & Politics* 22 (3):35–57.

Marchand, Marianne H., and Jane L. Parpart, eds. 1995. *Feminism/Postmodernism/Development*. London: Routledge.

Martinsons, Barbara. 1996. "The Possibility of Agency for Photographic Subjects." In *Technoscience and Cyberculture*, edited by S. Aronowitz, B. Martinsons, and M. Menser, 231–51. London: Routledge.

Marx, Karl. 1956. *Selected writings in sociology and social philosophy*, edited by T.B. Bottomore and M. Rubel. New York and London: McGraw-Hill.

McLeod, Alec G. 1992. *Acts of Defiance*. Canada: National Film Board of Canada.

McMillan, Allan D., and Eldon Yellowhorn. 2004. *First Peoples in Canada*. Vancouver: Douglas and McIntyre.

McNay, Lois. 2000. *Gender and Agency: Reconfiguring the Subject in Feminist and Social Theory*. Cambridge: Polity Press.

Miller, Hannah. 2010. "From 'Rights-Based' to 'Rights-Framed' Approaches: A Social Constructionist View of Human Rights Practice." *International Journal of Human Rights* 14 (6): 915–31.

Miller, J. R. 2004. *Lethal Legacy: Current Native Controversies in Canada*. Toronto: McClelland and Stewart Ltd.

Morgan, R., and B. S. Turner, eds. 2009. *Interpreting Human Rights: Social Science Perspectives*. London: Routledge.

Moghadam, Valentine M. 1993. *Identity Politics: Cultural Reassertions and Feminism in International Perspectives*. Boulder, CO: Westview Press.

Mohanty, C. T. 1988. "Under Western Eyes: Feminist Scholarship and Colonial Discourses." *Feminist Review* 30:60–88.

Mohawk Council of Kahnawake. 2013. "History of Kahnawá:ke." Accessed March 23, 2014. Available from www.kahnawake.com/community/history.asp.

Molloy, Patricia. 2000. "Theatrical Release: Catharsis and Spectacle in 'Welcome to Sarajevo.'" *Alternatives* 25:75–90.

Moser, Caroline O. N. 2001. "The Gendered Continuum of Violence and Conflict: an Operational Framework." In *Victims, Perpetrators or Actors: Gender, Armed Conflict and Political Violence*, edited by C.O.N. Moser and F. C. Clark, 30–52. London: Zed Books.

Murphy, Craig. 1998. "Six Masculine Roles in International Relations and their Interconnection: A Personal Investigation." In *The "Man" Question in International Relations*, edited by M. Zalewski and J. Parpart, 93–108. Boulder, CO: Westview Press.

Nash, Kate. 2009. *The Cultural Politics of Human Rights: Comparing the US and UK*. Cambridge: Cambridge University Press.

Newman, Peter C. 1995. *The Canadian Revolution: From Deference to Defiance 1985–1995*. Toronto: Viking.

Obomsawin, Alanis. 1993. *Kahehsatake: 270 Years of Resistance*. Canada: National Film Board of Canada.

———. 1995. *My Name is Kahentiiosta*. Canada: National Film Board of Canada.

———. 2000. *Rocks at Whiskey Trench*. Canada: National Film Board of Canada.

O'Byrne, Darren. 2012. "On the Sociology of Human Rights: Theorising the Language-structure of Rights." *Sociology* 46 (5): 829–43.

Osborne, Peter, and Lynne Segal. 1993. "Extracts from Gender as Performance: An Interview with Judith Butler." Accessed June 10, 2007. Available from www.theory.org.uk/but-int1.htm.

Padgen, Anthony. 2003. "Human Rights, Natural Rights, and Europe's Imperial Legacy." *Political Theory* 31 (2): 171–99.

Peerenboom, Randall. 2000. "Human Rights and Asian Values: The Limits of Universalism." *China Review International* 7 (2): 295–319.

Perry, Michael J. 1997. "Are Human Rights Universal? The Relativist Challenge and Related Matters." *Human Rights Quarterly* 19 (3): 461–509.

———. 1998. *The Idea of Human Rights*. Oxford: Oxford University Press.

Peterson, V. Spike. 1990. "Whose Rights? A Critique of the 'Givens' in Human Rights Discourse." *Alternatives* 15:303–44.

———, ed. 1992. *Gendered States: Feminist (Re)Visions of International Relations Theory*. Boulder, CO: Lynne Rienner.

———. 1992. "Security and Sovereign States: What Is at Stake in Taking Feminism Seriously?" In *Gendered States: Feminist (Re)Visions of International Relations Theory*, edited by V. S. Peterson, 31–64. Boulder, CO: Lynne Rienner.

———. 1992. "Trangressing Boundaries: Theories of Knowledge, Gender and International Relations." *Millennium* 21 (2): 183–206.

———. 1995. "Reframing the Politics of Identity: Democracy, Globalization and Gender." *Political Expressions* 1 (1): 1–16.

Peterson, V. Spike, and Laura Parisi. 1998. "Are Women Human? It's not an Academic Question." In *Human Rights Fifty Years On: A Reappraisal*, edited by T. Evans, 132–60. Manchester, UK: Manchester University Press.

———, and Anne Sisson Runyan. 1999. *Global Gender Issues*. Boulder, CO: Westview Press.

———, and Jacqui True. 1998. "New Times and New Conversations." In *The "Man" Question in International Relations*, edited by M. Zalewski and J. Parpart, 14–27. Boulder, CO: Westview Press.

Pettman, Jan Jindy. 1996. *Worlding Women: A Feminist International Politics*. London: Routledge.

Picard, André. 1990. "Armed Mohawks, Police in Standoff." *The Globe and Mail*, July 12.

———. 1990. "Mood Turning Ugly among Residents of Oka: Insults Hurled at Native Journalist." *The Globe and Mail*, July 16.

Pin-Fat, Véronique. 2000. "(Im)Possible Universalism: Reading Human Rights in World Politics." *Review of International Studies* 26:663–74.

———. 2005. "The Metaphysics of the National Interest and the 'Mysticism' of the Nation-state: Reading Hans J. Morgenthau." *Review of International Studies* 31 (2): 217–36.

———. 2010. *Universality, Ethics and International Relations: A Grammatical Reading*. New York: Routledge.

———, and Maria Stern. 2005. "The Scripting of Private Lynch: Biopolitics, Gender and the "Feminization" of the U.S. Military." *Alternatives: Global, Local, Political* 30 (1): 25–53.

Platiel, Rudy. 1990. "Analysis: Growing Indian Militancy Is Linked to their Poorly Understood Attachment to Property, Native's Top Priority Has Always Been Land." *The Globe and Mail*, July 17.

———. 1990. "UN Questions Canada's Image Panel Wants Explanation on Oka." *The Globe and Mail*, August 9.

Qureshi, Shazia. 2013. "The Recognition of Violence against Women as a Violation of Human Rights in the United Nations System." *Research Journal of South Asian Studies* 28 (1): 187–98.

Redhead, Robin. 2007. "Imag(in)ing Women's Agency: Visual Representation in Amnesty International's 2004 Campaign 'Stop Violence against Women.'" *International Feminist Journal of Politics* 9 (2): 218–338.

———, and Nick Turnbull. 2010. "Towards a Study of Human Rights Practitioners." *Human Rights Review* 12 (2): 173–89.

Reilly, Niamh. 2009. *Women's Human Rights: Seeking Gender Justice in a Globalising Age*. Cambridge, UK: Polity Press.

Rendal, Margherita. 1997. *Whose Human Rights*. London: Trentham Books Limited.

Richards, Patricia. 2005. "The Politics of Gender, Human Rights and Being Indigenous in Chile." *Gender and Society* 19 (2): 199–220.

Robinson, Fiona. 1998. "The Limits of a Rights-Based Approach to International Ethics." In *Human Rights Fifty Years On: A Reappraisal*, edited by T. Evans, 58–76. Manchester, UK: University of Manchester Press.

———. 2003. "Human Rights and the Global Politics of Resistance: Feminist Perspectives." *Review of International Studies* 29:161–80.

———. 2003. "NGOs and the Advancement of Economic and Social Rights: Philosophical and Practical Controversies." *International Relations* 17 (1): 70–96.

Romany, Celina. 1994. "State Responsibility Goes Private: A Feminist Critique of the Public/Private Distinction in International Human Rights Law." In *Human*

Rights of Women: National and International Perspectives, edited by R. Cook, 85–115. Philadelphia: University of Pennsylvania Press.

Rorty, Richard. 1993. "Human Rights, Rationality and Sentimentality." In *On Human Rights: The Oxford Amnesty Lectures 1993*, edited by S. Shute and S. Hurley, 111–134. New York: Harper Collins.

Rubio-Marín, Ruth, and Martha I. Morgan. 2004. "Constitutional Domestication of International Gender Norms: Categorizations, Illustrations, and Reflections from the Nearside of the Bridge." In *Gender and Human Rights*, edited by K. Knop, 113–52. New York: Oxford University Press.

Said, Edward W. 1992. "Nationalism, Human Rights, and Interpretation." In *Freedom and Interpretation: Oxford Amnesty Lectures 1992*, edited by B. Johnson, 175–205. New York: Harper Collins.

Sellers, Patricia Viseur. 2004. "Individual(s') Liability for Collective Sexual Violence." In *Gender and Human Rights*, edited by K. Knop, 153–84. New York: Oxford University Press.

Shapiro, Michael J. 1988. *The Politics of Representation: Writing Practices in Bibliography, Photography and Policy Analysis*. Madison: University of Wisconsin Press.

———. 1990. Strategic "Discourse/Discursive Strategy: The Representation of 'Security Policy' in the Video Age." *International Studies Quarterly* 34 (4): 327–40.

Sharoni, Simona. 2001. "Rethinking Women's Struggles in Israel-Palestine and the North of Ireland." In *Victims, Perpetrators or Actors? Gender, Armed Conflict and Political Violence*, edited by C.O.N. Moser and F. C. Clark, 85–98. London and New York: Zed Books.

Short, Damien. 2007. "The Social Construction of Indigenous 'Native Title' Land Rights in Australia." *Current Sociology* 55 (6): 857–76.

Shue, Henry. 1980. *Basic Rights: Subsistence, Affluence, and US Foreign Policy*. Princeton, NJ: Princeton University Press.

Smith, Steve. 1998. "'Unacceptable Conclusions' and the 'Man' Question: Masculinity, Gender and International Relations." In *The "Man" Question in International Relations*, edited by M. Zalewski and J. Parpart, 123–41. Boulder, CO: Westview Press.

Stamatopoulou, Elissavet. 1995. "Women's Rights and the United Nations." In *Women's Rights Human Rights: International Feminist Perspectives*, edited by J. Peters and A. Wolper, 36–48. London: Routledge.

Stammers, Neil. 2009. *Human Rights and Social Movements*. London: Pluto Press.

Steans, Jill. 1998. *Gender and International Relations: An Introduction*. Cambridge: Polity Press.

———. 2007. "Debating Women's Human Rights as a Universal Feminist Project: Defending Women's Human Rights as a Political Tool." *Review of International Studies* 33:11–27.

Stemple, Laura. 2011. "Human Rights, Sex and Gender: Limits in Theory and Practice." *PACE Law Review* 31 (3): 824–36.

Sullivan, Donna. 1995. "The Public/Private Distinction in International Human Rights Law." In *Women's Rights Human Rights: International Feminist Perspectives*, edited by J. Peters and A. Wolper, 126–34. New York: Routledge.

Swain, Harry. 2010. *Oka: A Political Crisis and Its Legacy*. Vancouver: Douglas & McIntyre.

Swartz, David. 1997. *Culture and Power: The Sociology of Pierre Bourdieu*. Chicago: University of Chicago Press.

Sylvester, Christine. 1998. "'Masculinity', 'Femininity' and 'International Relations': Or Who Goes to the 'Moon' with Bonaparte and the Adder?" In *The "Man" Question in International Relations*, edited by M. Zalewski and J. Parpart, 185–98. Boulder, CO: Westview Press.

———. 2002. *Feminist International Relations: An Unfinished Journey*. Cambridge: Polity Press.

———. 2005. "The Art of War/The War Question in (Feminist) IR." *Millennium* 33 (3): 855–78.

Teitel, Ruti G. 2004. "For Humanity." *Journal of Human Rights* 3 (2): 225–37.

Thanh Ha, Tu. 2004. "Outside Police Called to Patrol Kanesatake." *The Globe and Mail*, May 6.

Tickner, Ann J. 1992. *Gender in International Relations*. New York: Columbia University Press.

———. 1995. "Re-visioning Security." In *International Relations Today*, edited by K. Booth and S. Smith, 175–97. Cambridge: Polity Press.

———. 2006. "Feminism Meets International Relations: Some Methodological Issues." In *Feminist Methodologies for International Relations*, edited by B. A. Ackerly, M. Stern, and J. True, 19–41. Cambridge: Cambridge University Press.

Tong, Rosemarie. 1989. *Feminist Thought: A Comprehensive Introduction*. London: Unwin Hyman.

True, Jacqui. 2001. "Feminism." In *Theories of International Relations*, edited by S. Burchill, R. Devetak, A. Linklater, M. Paterson, C. Reus-Smit, and J. True, 231–76. Houndmills, UK: Palgrave.

Tsutsui, Kiyoteru, and Christine Min Wotipka. 2004. "Global Civil Society and the International Human Rights Movement: Citizen Participation in Human Rights International Nongovernemental Organisations." *Social Forces* 83 (2): 587–620.

Turshen, Meredeth. 2001. "The Political Economy of Rape: An Analysis of Systematic Rape and Sexual Abuse of Women during Armed Conflict in Africa." In *Victims, Perpetrators or Actors? Gender, Armed Conflict and Political Violence*, edited by C.O.N. Moser and F. C. Clark, 55–68. London and New York: Zed Books.

Tuscaroras and Six Nations. 2007. "The Constitution of the Iroquois Nations." Accessed March 23. 2014. Available from http://tuscaroras.com/pages/history/iroquois_constitution_2.html.

United Nations. 1948. "The Universal Declaration of Human Rights." Accessed March 23, 2014. Available from www.un.org/en/documents/udhr/.

———. 1945. "Charter of the United Nations: Preamble." Accessed March 23, 2014. Available from www.un.org/en/documents/charter/preamble.shtml.

Vincent, R.J. 1986. *Human Rights and International Relations*. Cambridge: Cambridge University Press.

Walby, Sylvia. 1997. *Gender Transformations*. London: Routledge.

Walace, Tim and Helen Baños Smith. 2010. *A Synthesis of the Learning From the Stop Violence against Women Campaign 2004–10*. London: Amnesty International 2010. Accessed March 23, 2014. Available from www.amnesty.org/sites/impact.amnesty.org/files/PUBLIC/FINAL%20SVAW%20REVIEW%20SYNTHESIS%20act770082010en.pdf.

Wali, Sima. 1995. "Human Rights for Refugee and Displaced Women." In *Women's Rights Human Rights: International Feminist Perspectives*, edited by J. Peters and A. Wolper, 335–44. New York: Routledge.

Weber, Cynthia. 1998. "Performative States." *Millennium* 27 (1): 77–95.

Wente, Margaret. 2006. "The New Warrior Class: Native Academics Are Schooling the Next Generation in the Politics of Resistance." *The Globe and Mail*, July 15.

Wilson, Ara. 2002. "The Transnational Geography of Sexual Rights." In *Truth Claims: Representations and Human Rights*, edited by M. P. Bradley and P. Petro, 251–65. London: Rutgers University Press.

Wittgenstein, Ludwig. 1958. *Philosophical Investigations*. Oxford: Blackwell.

Woodiwiss, A. 2005. *Human Rights*. London: Routledge.

Yeatman, Anna. 2000. "Who Is the Subject of Human Rights?" *American Behavioral Scientist* 43 (9): 1498–513.

———. 2004. "Right, the State and the Conception of the Person." *Citizenship Studies* 8 (4): 403–417.

York, Geoffrey, and Loreen Pindera. 1991. *People of the Pines: The Warriors and the Legacy of Oka*. Toronto: Little, Brown & Company (Canada) Limited.

Youngs, Gillian. 2003. "Private Pain/Public Peace: Women's Rights as Human Rights and Amnesty International's Report on Violence against Women (Women and World Peace)." *Signs* 28 (4): 209–22.

———. 2004. "Feminist International Relations: A Contradiction in Terms? Or: Why Women and Gender Are Essential to Understanding the World 'We' Live In?" *International Affairs* 80 (1): 75–87.

Yuval-Davis, N., and F. Anthias, eds. 1989. *Women-Nation-State*. London: Macmillan.

Zalewski, Marysia. 1994. "The Women/'Women' Question in International Relations." *Millennium* 23 (2): 407–23.

———. 1995. "Well, What Is the Feminist Perspective on Bosnia?" *International Affairs* 71 (2): 339–56.

———. 1998. "Introduction: From the 'Woman' Question to the 'Man' Question in International Relations." In *The "Man" Question in International Relations*, edited by M. Zalewski and J. Parpart, 1–13. Boulder, CO: Westview Press.

———. 2000. *Feminism after Postmodernism: Theorising through Practice*. London and New York: Routledge.

———. 2006. "Distracted Reflections on the Production, Narration, and Refusal of Feminist Knowledge in International Relations." In *Feminist Methodologies for International Relations*, edited by B. A. Ackerly, M. Stern, and J. True, 42–61. Cambridge: Cambridge University Press.

———, and Cynthia Enloe. 1995. "Questions about Identity in International Relations." In *International Relations Theory Today*, edited by K. Booth and S. Smith, 279–305. Cambridge: Polity Press.

Zarkov, Dubravka. 2001. "The Body of the Other Man: Sexual Violence and the Construction of Masculinity, Sexuality and Ethnicity in the Croatian Media." In *Victims, Perpetrators or Actors? Gender, Armed Conflict and Political Violence*, edited by C. Moser and F. Clark, 69–82. London: Zed Books.

Index